THE DONUT:
A CANADIAN HISTORY

In Canada, the donut is often thought of as the unofficial national food. Donuts are sold at every intersection and rest stop, celebrated in song and story as symbols of Canadian identity, and one chain in particular, Tim Hortons, has become a veritable icon with over 2500 shops across the country. But there is more to the donut than these and other expressions of 'snackfood patriotism' would suggest. In this study, Steve Penfold puts the humble donut in its historical context, examining how one deep-fried confectionary became, not only a mass commodity, but an edible symbol of Canadianness.

Penfold examines the history of the donut in light of broader social, economic, and cultural issues, and uses the donut as a window onto key developments in twentieth-century Canada such as the growth of a 'consumer society,' the relationship between big business and community, and the ironic qualities of Canadian national identity. He goes on to explore the social and political conditions that facilitated the rapid rise and steady growth of donut shops across the country.

Based on a wide range of sources, from commercial and government reports to personal interviews, *The Donut* is a comprehensive and fascinating look at one of Canada's most popular products. It offers original insights on consumer culture, mass consumption, and the dynamics of Canadian history.

STEVE PENFOLD is an assistant professor in the Department of History at the University of Toronto.

THE DONUT

A Canadian History

STEVE PENFOLD

UNIVERSITY OF TORONTO PRESS
Toronto   Buffalo   London

ISBN 978-0-8020-9797-2 (cloth)
ISBN 978-0-8020-9545-9 (paper)

Library and Archives Canada Cataloguing in Publication

Penfold, Steven, 1966–
    The donut : a Canadian history / Steve Penfold.

Includes bibliographical references and index.
ISBN 978-0-8020-9797-2 (bound)
ISBN 978-0-8020-9545-9 (pbk.)

1. Doughnuts – Social aspects – Canada.   2. Fast food restaurants – Social
aspects – Canada.   3. Fast food restaurants – Economic aspects – Canada.
4. Franchises (Retail trade) – Canada – History.   5. Consumption (Economics) – Canada – History.   6. Canada – Social conditions – 1945–.   I. Title.

HD9057.C32P45 2008   306.30971'09045   C2007-904776-9

University of Toronto Press acknowledges the financial assistance to its publishing program of the Canada Council for the Arts and the Ontario Arts
Council.

University of Toronto Press acknowledges the financial support for its
publishing activities of the Government of Canada through the
Book Publishing Industry Development Program (BPIDP).

This book has been published with the help of a grant from the Canadian
Federation for the Humanities and Social Sciences, through the Aid to
Scholarly Publications Programme, using funds provided by the Social Sciences
and Humanities Research Council of Canada.

For the historian, there are no banal things.

– Sigfried Giedion, *Mechanization Takes Command: A Contribution to Anonymous History*

Contents

Acknowledgments

I am so thoroughly sick of donuts, I could die. I'm often asked about my favorite donut, but I barely want to think about them. Any random confrontation with a round object makes me physically ill. Pumping up a tire makes me dizzy. I can't even look at a DVD. Don't mention the word 'dip' or 'glaze' anywhere within earshot: it is likely to send me into a deep depression. That I survived this decade-long snack-food ordeal owes much to the advice, kindness, and comments of a number of supportive people whom I can now take the time to thank.

The study started as a PhD thesis in the Department of History at York University. My thesis committee challenged me to take the topic seriously but allowed me to see the humour in it as well. From the time I bumbled into his office with little more than a vague idea of doing labour history and a pressing need to move to Halifax, Craig Heron was a model supervisor. He was supportive, challenging, generous, and patient, and he managed to let me be goofy without letting me run wild. My other committee members were also challenging and kind. Chris Armstrong, a historian of business and politics who missed his calling as a stand-up comedian, was the only person who didn't laugh when I suggested a thesis on the donut, and he subsequently offered incisive criticism of each of the original chapters. Kate McPherson pushed me to think seriously about many key issues, particularly relating to popular culture and Canadian identity, and was always ready to issue marching orders and keep me focused on getting things done. As members of the defence committee, Glen Norcliffe, Marlene Shore, and Keith Walden offered pointed comment at the end.

I was fortunate to pass through York with an absolutely phenomenal group of graduate students, who offered intellectual cooperation and companionship, challenging comments, lively discussion, patient tolerance, and drunken theories, often offered on the long bus ride to and from York's rather unfortunate location. This group is now so thoroughly dispersed across the country that it seems appropriate to enumerate them geographically (by job or residence): Lisa Chilton and James Moran (Charlottetown), Gillian Poulter and Stephen Henderson (Wolfville, Nova Scotia), Magda Fahrni (Montreal), Alexandra Mosquin (Ottawa), Dimitry Anastakis (Peterborough), Camille Soucie, Amanda Crocker, and Joseph Tohill (Toronto), Fiona Miller (Hamilton), Rob Kristofferson (Brantford), Sarah Elvins, Chris Frank, and Adele Perry (Winnipeg), Jeet Heer and Robin Ganev (Regina), James Muir (Edmonton), Sharon Wall (Prince George), and Matthew Evenden (Vancouver).

Teaching colleagues at various institutions deserve thanks for kindnesses large and small. At Seneca College, Jim Moran, Henry Decock, and Mark Moss (sorry about those pizza boxes) gave me work and intellectual friendship. At Nipissing-Muskoka, Jan Lucy tolerated my visceral fear of snow-covered highways. Since I arrived four years ago, everyone at University of Toronto has been so abnormally friendly that I now suspect they want to lure me into a cult. I should explicitly thank Dan Bender, Vicky Dingillo, Jennifer Francisco, Katherine Glaser, Allan Greer, Rick Halpern, Franca Iacovetta, Louise Nugent, Ian Radforth, Arthur Silver, Paul Rutherford, and Michael Wayne. From this list of colleagues, I have drawn critical commentary, useful advice, bemused tolerance, free lunches, answers to stupid questions, parenting tips, bunk beds for my daughters, and the best ribs I have ever tasted. (All things considered, a pretty good haul.) Though never colleagues, Marc Abrahams, Warren Belasco, Chris Dummitt, Wayne and Naomi Elvins, Russ Johnston, Alan Gordon, Jarrett Rudy, and Jordan Stanger-Ross offered comments, research leads, or sent useful clippings from their local newspapers. On more than one occasion, Norman and Sylvia Swartz turned over their basement in Burnaby to the writing process. At the University of Toronto Press, Len Husband has been a stellar (read: patient but not too patient) editor and all-around good chap. Frances Mundy expertly shepherded the book through its production; Matthew Kudelka did an appropriately aggressive copy edit on my convoluted prose. Additional thanks to the Cartography office at the University of Toronto for preparing the maps. Otto Seegers kindly consented to having a bag from his Baker's Donut Shop (Chatham, Ontario, 1966) adapted for the cover of the book.

As this project moved from thesis to book manuscript, I benefited enormously from the comments of three anonymous readers. One reader in particular launched a devastating critique of an earlier draft that was very much in need of this kind of treatment, and while I doubt s/he will be happy with the result, I very much appreciate the way s/he looked past the quirkiness of the topic to point more seriously to the weaknesses of analysis and organization. The two other readers also provided much needed prods, particularly about overall organization, periodization, and geography. Various audiences commented on versions of chapters: the Toronto Labour Studies group, the Toronto Consumer History group, Josée Johnson's graduate class on the Sociology of Food, the Institute for the History and Philosophy of Science and Technology at U of T, the Food and Drink in Consumer Societies conference at the Hagley Museum, the Winnipeg History Workshop, the IgNobel Lectures in Boston, the Montreal History Group's May Day conference, and the annual meeting of the Canadian Historical Association.

Nobody wants to hear about footnotes over dinner, so writing an academic book is a good way to drive everyone around you nuts. Thanks, then, are owed to my family for their patience and support. My brother, Jay, always seemed to know when he shouldn't ask about the project (which, to be frank, was all the time). My mother, Mary, taught me long ago to revel in banter, conversation, and argument, an approach suited to both donut shops and academia. My daughters, Ruby and Mira, were a constant source of much appreciated distraction. Ruby deserves particular thanks for suggesting, as her very first New Year's Resolution, that we both eat fewer donuts. Diane Swartz has been a true partner, confronting all the challenges of career, research, and parenthood with her typical mixture of patience and sarcasm. I owe her big-time, a fact that she does not hesitate to point out.

My father did not live to see either the thesis or the book, but he is the reason they were written. I can still picture him reading the newspaper at the counter of the local donut shop, stylishly decked out in his mangled pajama top, trying to convince the servers to put one more shot of cream in his coffee. 'Would you like some coffee with your cream, Mr Penfold?' they would tease. I miss him, even if the last time I saw him he gave me the finger.

THE DONUT:
A CANADIAN HISTORY

Introduction:
History from the Bottomless Cup

It seems like everybody I meet wants to be an expert on donuts. Everyone has a cousin or father with some insight, some theory, or some rant about the important place of the donut in Canadian life. In many places across Canada the donut is believed to be the unofficial national food, celebrated in song and story as a sort of ironic replacement for the dramatic national symbols found south of the 49th parallel. 'If there's one thing that is distinct, that is ours, that Canadians can claim as theirs,' Canadian-born comedian Eugene Levy told a half-American audience, 'I'd say it's donuts.' Bill Kennedy of North York, Ontario, told the CBC that 'the donut has to be Canada's national food. Now of course I know that they're not created here but they've been perfected here, and it's part of our national identity. To criticize the donut is to criticize Canada.' This idea is common lore in the donut shops that seem to populate every corner of the country. 'Was there [a time] before Tim Hortons?' asks Steve Evenden of Halifax, Nova Scotia. 'They seem to have always been with us. [They're a] kind of a uniquely Canadian thing ... It's one thing that the Americans don't have that we have. Lots of coffee, lots of donuts.' To study the donut shop is simply to be overwhelmed by examples of the donut's iconic status in Canadian life.[1]

It was refreshing, then, to speak to Costas Kiriakopoulos, a genuine expert who spent a lifetime in the donut and coffee business in Canada. In 1966, Kiriakopoulos's father, who had worked in food service since arriving in Canada from his native Greece ten years earlier, was looking for a small business. On the advice of Chris Pappas, a friend who happened to be the first Country Style Donuts' franchisee, the Kiriakopoulos family bought the second Country Style outlet, located at Weston

Road and Lawrence Avenue in northwestern Toronto.[2] It was a good location, perched just off the commercial strip that had once been the village of Weston. Long before the 1960s, Weston had passed beyond anything resembling the peaceful village stage of urban development. However reluctant the old village was to admit it – not long before the Kiriakopoulos family arrived on the scene, Weston Road was still called Main Street – the area had long ago been swept into the burgeoning suburban growth of Toronto. Around here, *things moved*: cars, workers, and products moved in and out in a buzz of activity.

The most striking movement, at least to local merchants, was not in and out, but past and through. The few small parking lots swelled with shoppers, to be sure, but many more were heading out to the shopping malls that had sprung up near major highways. Workers streamed along Weston Road and Lawrence Avenue on their way to and from growing industrial areas across the new, sprawling Toronto. Few of these commuters, it seemed, were keen to shop in Weston. Indeed, much to the chagrin of the traditional merchants in the area – who pressed local officials for more parking lots, more promotions, more ways to get customers to stop – Weston was by 1966 a lot like hundreds of other strips around Toronto's suburbs at the time: a place that people passed on their way to somewhere else.

The transitory nature of local traffic didn't much matter to the Kiriakopoulos family, however, as they had bought into a passing-by kind of business. Their shop was in a settled area of the city, with lots of potential donut eaters nearby, but few customers were inclined to hang around. 'At that time, I would say it was 75 per cent take out,' Kiriakopoulos recalled. 'People seemed like they had no time.' Besides, the outlet itself was hardly built to encourage lingering: it was small – less than 1,200 square feet – and there were only about a dozen stools, which did not bother the customers, who mostly stopped to catch a quick caffeine and sugar fix before work. 'We had buses on Weston Road and Lawrence Avenue,' Kiriakopoulos recalled, 'and all the buses at that time leaving from that area to go to the ... airport ... They were taking all the workers to the area and [the] factories.'

At the time, Country Style was a chain of about ten outlets – a solid number for 1966, but hardly a big player in Canada's franchise race, falling well behind fast food pioneers like Kentucky Fried Chicken (188 outlets) and A&W (158 outlets), which were spread right across Canada. But already, the three-year-old donut chain had a big imagination. Though based in Toronto, its founder, entrepreneur and pilot Alan

Lowe, had started the company with the intention of spreading out. There were already Country Style outlets, built to standard design, 400 kilometres north in Sudbury and 200 kilometres west in London. For the Kiriakopoulos family, the chain promised the affordability and security of a well-defined production and management system. 'At the time there was no way that somebody [could] open your own [shop],' he told me. 'You didn't know how to start it, how to put this concept together. I guess money was an issue, and knowledge.' Like other donut chains, Country Style provided that knowledge through an in-store training system. For Kiriakopoulos, however, the learning did not end when the family took over the outlet. He put in long hours, doing almost every job in the shop at one time or another. 'I was a young man at the time,' he recalled, 'and I worked very hard and I learned the business inside-out, twenty-four hours, seven days.'

Kiriakopoulos's entrepreneurial ambition kept him in motion. The family did not linger long in the donut business, selling out in 1970, having spent four years churning out donuts and training incoming franchisees for the chain. For almost a decade, Kiriakopoulos sold commercial and industrial real estate around Greater Toronto. In 1979, still a real estate agent, he spotted a piece of commercial property in Bramalea, the massive web of subdivisions that had been grafted onto the staid old community of Brampton in the late 1950s and 1960s. The location looked perfect for a donut shop, and Kiriakopoulos knew he could use his business experience to establish the beachhead of a new donut chain, which he eventually called O'Donuts. 'The idea when I started was to build a chain, to build more stores ... Learning from Country Style, [I knew] the way the whole thing was set up ... and I [had] the knowledge of the real estate locations, for financing, [so I] organized things and I opened the first one in Bramalea.'

At the time, starting a new chain of donut shops was not exactly looked upon as a brilliant outlet for entrepreneurial ambition. Indeed, to some observers, the comparatively sparse donut geography of the late 1970s already looked a little crowded. 'When I opened my first store,' Kiriakopoulos laughed, 'everybody told me that I was a little bit out of my mind, opening a donut chain, because there were so many around.' Tim Hortons was already establishing its hegemony in the donut business, growing in the late 1970s by almost twenty outlets per year, more than the other big franchisors combined, all of which continued the moderate growth that had characterized the industry since its arrival in Canada in the early 1960s. At this point, many independents were opening up around the Golden Horseshoe as well, building on a concept that had proven successful in the case of the chains. But Kiriakopoulos's hunch was sound, and his timing was perfect, and he got in at the beginning of a wave of smaller franchisors with names like Donut Castle, Donut World, Donut Delite, and Donut Diner (among others), all of which were building chains of ten to twenty outlets in the crevices left unfilled by the larger companies.

This burst of small donut franchisors meant that, by the mid-1980s, things were getting much more crowded along the coffee-soaked commercial strips of southern Ontario. Kiriakopoulos could see that the old model of the donut shop – find a high-traffic site, slap up a small building, and start pouring coffee – was passing into oblivion. While everybody was adding products like soup and sandwiches, the big players like Tim Hortons and Country Style were redefining the economics of location. 'The change was that there was no more you can do with fifteen or sixteen hundred square feet of space,' he said. 'We saw Tim Hortons going to bigger locations, like two-and-a-half thousand square feet. I think that Tim Hortons foresaw that they needed the space, because they became ... a coffee shop, [with] sandwiches, a full blown coffee shop.' O'Donuts had good locations, but Kiriakopoulos decided it was a good time to move on, and he sold his eighteen outlets to Country Style just before the expansion of the big chains started to seriously pinch the many smaller operations.

By this time, Kiriakopoulos had spotted a new trend. Since the early 1980s, upscale coffee shops like Second Cup and Timothy's had been outgrowing their cramped locations in shopping malls and moving to freestanding, storefront locations on busy pedestrian streets. Kiriakopoulos spent a few years researching the concept while working in Country Style's real estate department. In 1991 he opened his first gourmet coffee outlet in a regional mall in St Catharines. It did well, and Java Joe's grew to more than fifteen locations.

Kiriakopolous's career in donuts has paralleled the evolution of the industry over the past forty years. He was not in Canada in the 1930s and 1940s when a group of entrepreneurs took the donut out of kitchens and small bakeries and began to mass produce it in large quantities using automatic processes, but his life has intersected with the three more recent waves of the donut business in Canada: the advent of the first donut chains in the 1960s; the burst of second-tier companies after 1975; and the difficulties these smaller operations faced by the late 1980s as they tried to compete with larger, better-financed operations like Tim Hortons. His career has also paralleled the path of the retail coffee industry, which has moved out of car-based, downscale operations serving limited product lines into fancier, upscale shops selling atmosphere and lattés.

Yet there is more to Kiriakopoulos's career than the history of a particular commercial form: his business strategies connected him to a number of broad social, economic, and geographic developments. His initial foray into Country Style, for example, was based not simply on an objective analysis of its economic potential, but on connections of kin and ethnicity. The decision to join a franchised chain was more than an expression of small business mythology; it also tied his family to a broader network of small entrepreneurs who were operating Country Style outlets in other communities. His family's outlet on the fringe of prewar development tapped a series of movements through postwar urban space: of industries to the suburbs, of workers who followed factories outward, of gas-powered automobiles that traversed this sprawling metropolitan area. Weston was just old enough that these outward movements were beginning to pass the village by – the following decade would be a story of economic decline – but in 1966, the Country Style outlet was still well positioned to ride the postwar economic boom. Though donut shops were relatively new in the area, local workers were already familiar with similar institutions of 'petty consumption' like lunch counters and coffee shops, so it made sense for them to make the Country Style a regular stop, grabbing coffee to go on their way to work and dozens of donuts for their families on the way home. Even at this profoundly local level, the story of the donut shop reveals larger themes. When consumer and entrepreneur exchanged money for goods across a three-foot counter, they were connecting themselves to economic structures that stretched well beyond Lawrence Avenue. Those donuts and coffees tied Kiriakopoulos and his customers to commodity chains with extensive reach, running from coffee plantations in Latin America and wheat farms in western Canada through a network of processors, wholesalers, and distributors to consumers across southern Ontario. The donut, then, was more than just a tasty treat: it connected Kiriakopoulos to social networks, to changes in urban space, to larger chains of production and distribution, and to complex configurations of consumption in the postwar era. It blended, in other words, the production of a mass commodity with the organization of social life.

This book examines the history of the donut and the donut shop by telling the stories of people like Costas Kiriakopoulos. Even in an intellectual age obsessed with analysing 'ordinary people,' this may seem a trivial intellectual pursuit. But the Canadian donut industry is interesting simply for its size and scope: by 1999, there were about six thousand donut shops in Canada, representing one-tenth of the nation's commercial restaurants, selling more than $2 billion in products annually, employing upwards of 100,000 people, and serving diverse and disparate Canadian communities.[3] Beyond its mere numbers, however, the donut is brimming with analytic possibilities. Looking at Costas Kiriakopoulos's story alone suggests that the donut shop can be a window onto some of the central developments in twentieth-century Canada: the growth of a 'consumer society,' the character of car culture, the resilience of small business mythology in a corporate age, and the relationship between mass institutions and local neighbourhood life. Throughout these issues runs a central question: What is the link between commodities (economic goods that can be bought and sold) and culture (the values, ideas, and practices that give meaning to everyday life)?

This central problem is partly inspired by the burgeoning literature in cultural studies. Articles on Nike shoes and McDonald's hamburgers have entered the academic mainstream as part of a considerable theoretical and analytic effort to examine the relationship between the production of consumer products and their reception and use. Scholars in several disciplines have debated whether life in mass culture is fashioned by structure and domination or by subversion and contestation.[4] In one sense, this conflict simply parallels the long-standing debate between structure and agency that has characterized much of the past several decades of progressive scholarship (and has fundamentally shaped my own thinking).[5] But despite these parallels, I consciously avoid any explicit examination of the nature of resistance and subversion among consumers. In my view, cultural studies scholars and their critics have magnified all of the worst tendencies of the structure/agency debate without paying much attention to its considerable strengths. One side has romanticized what it sees as the more authentic forms of popular culture that have been transformed (for some, obliterated) by mass marketers. The other has elevated simple individual acts – shopping for shoes, wearing hockey sweaters, buying CDs – to creative acts of self-fashioning and transcendent 'agency.' More disturbing has been the tendency of both sides to exaggerate the political import of publishing scholarly articles – an approach reflected in a tone of intellectual machismo and denunciation. Thankfully, scholars are now moving beyond these polarized and rhetorically overheated debates, concentrating instead on more concrete examinations of the on-the-ground relationship between economic forces and social experience at particular historical moments.[6]

The basic economic fact is that the donut was invented as a mass commodity over the course of the twentieth century, first by mass production innovations and then by mass retailers (and their imitators), who built standard stores in communities across the country. Kiriakopoulos reminds us that these economic developments were deployed in particular communities, joining business strategies to networks of friendship and kin, to processes of ethnic migration and association, to movements through new configurations of city space. The rise of the donut from minor product to mass commodity and cultural icon was the result of many perceptual leaps: entrepreneurs and consumers forged connections between business strategies and community networks, between economic forms and social myths, and between older cultural categories and new consumer spaces. These connections were drawn in ways that were profoundly historical. They drew meaning not just from their relationship to contemporary cultural forms – whether across the street or across the country – but also from continuities with the past and changes over time.

To follow the history of the donut, I build on a growing international historiography on consumption, a literature that links the studies of business, politics, geography, and identity and that has thrived in many different national fields. Whether the subject is movies, television, canned goods, or restaurants, historians have examined a series of innovations in production, distribution, retailing, marketing, and all their attendant cultural meanings and effects.[7] Though some scholars have found the emergence of consumer identity as early as the eighteenth century, much of this literature has focused on the period between the 1880s and the 1930s, when a *mass* consumer society is said to have emerged and triumphed in North American social life.[8] Mass culture is a particular expression of consumer culture, characterized by commodities that can be reproduced across time and space (chain stores, standardized products, vast distribution networks) and sold by businesses and consumed by consumers that, at some level, defy boundaries (taste, class, ethnicity, and geography).[9] While these economic and cultural changes took shape in the early twentieth century, they blossomed after the Second World War, and a few historians have followed the story into this period.[10] Canadian historians are typically behind in volume of literature, but some recent studies have made suggestive beginnings on the emergence of mass culture in the early twentieth century and its consolidation and acceleration after the Second World War.[11]

In some ways, the history of the donut and the donut shop fit into the mainstream of Canada's consumer society in the twentieth century, and tracing out these connections is an important theme of the book. Like many scholars of consumer culture, I spend considerable time examining various attempts to forge controllable and efficient production regimes, to disperse commercial forms across space, to deflect existing ways of seeing commodities towards more modern, industrial products, to create and broadcast brand names that encapsulate both economic value and cultural meaning, and to spin spectacular narratives around practical products. We could find all of these dynamics in some form in other industries as well, especially in the historiographic staples of consumer society: department stores, automobiles, fashion, processed foods, and so on.

It would be foolish to imagine, however, that the donut is somehow representative of all consumption. Terms like 'consumer society' and 'consumer culture' are more convenient shorthands for a range of economic and cultural changes than they are precise or entirely accurate descriptions of social life. As much as these concepts encapsulate some broad, meaningful trends in twentieth-century North America (the shift from a production to a consumption ethos, the purported triumph of spending over thrift, the injunction to endless novelty, and the grafting of 'consumer' onto other forms of identity[12]), there is always the danger of moving from convenient shorthand to problematic distraction. A 'consumer society' is in fact an aggregate of many commodity chains, social narratives, and cultural trajectories, sometimes interacting and reinforcing one another, but at other times working at cross purposes or simply proceeding on their own course. Though a product of consumer culture, the donut can hardly be made to represent some generic narrative of mass commodities, since it had particular characteristics that affected its historical development.

We might start simply with the product itself. A donut tastes best when eaten soon after it is produced – a mundane fact that had enormous consequences for the product's history. Like many other commodities, the donut became more and more the object of mass production processes over the course of the twentieth century. At the same time, the question of staling meant that it was best consumed fairly close to where it was produced – a fact that pulled it decisively towards local regimes of production. Many scholars have pointed to the link between the rise of mass production processes and the emerging culture of mass consumption. Yet Philip Scranton has countered that a surprising number of mass consumer staples were in fact produced in 'batch' and 'flexible' production regimes.[13] For its part, the donut stands somewhere in between these two developments: over the twentieth century, two regimes of mass production competed with each other and with more primitive and small-scale methods.

The issue is further complicated by the fact that the donut is not really one product, but two. Cake donuts are the smaller of the two, and (today) are often marketed under names like 'Old Fashioned Plain' and 'Old Fashioned Glazed.' Yeast donuts are lighter in colour and texture, having been 'proofed' (or raised) in a 'proofer' (a temperature and humidity controlled box) for about forty minutes. In donut shops today, they are often identified by the word 'raised,' as in 'Raised Chocolate.' As we'll see, these differences go beyond taste and consumer preference: each type of donut raises quite different production problems, and the product's complex trajectory through twentieth-century industrial culture was partly the result of efforts to deal with the characteristics of each.

Beyond these material considerations, the donut has had an ambivalent meaning within the broader contours of Canadian mass consumption. As a food, the donut is an ephemeral and discretionary purchase, often eaten as a snack or treat rather than a meal, as an item of taste and pleasure rather than need and nutrition. In a small way, then, we might consider the donut a perfect expression of North America's emerging consumer society, in which a consumption ethic has replaced a production ethos, pleasure has trumped thrift, and desire has replaced need.[14] Indeed, when donut shops arrived in the 1960s, they constructed a commercial speech that spoke to these new values in an age of relative prosperity and security. At the same time, however, the donut was an item of 'petty consumption,' a small and cheap product within the means of a wide range of classes and income levels, even in poorer economic times. As we'll see, when postwar prosperity came to an end in the 1970s and early 1980s, the donut shop thrived, not in defiance of the poor economy but *because* of it.[15]

The donut also fit into a particular thread of consumer culture. In trying to understand the meaning of consumption, scholars – especially in cultural studies – have often been drawn to its most spectacular and transgressive aspects. The donut leads us to many such narratives, sometimes in amusing ways, but it also directs us to everyday routines. Indeed, the donut has derived much of its social power and cultural meaning from mundane questions of convenience. Donut shops, for example, have always been unpretentious and utilitarian places (unlike, say, department stores, which have often aimed for spectacular designs). Indeed, many of the stories we will analyse are quite ordinary and pedestrian, and while it is true that the mythic and spectacular can be found in the mundane and everyday, it is equally the case that the everyday contains much that is simply everyday. In the spirit of the intellectual age, we might call this perspective the 'meta-mundane.'[16]

These basic features – ephemerality, discretion, cheapness, convenience, and routine – hardly remove the donut from the broad trajectory of consumer culture, but they do help clarify its particular place in that culture. The product's history has also been shaped by the historical moment. The core of this study is the period from about the end of the Second World War to the turn of the twenty-first century. If historians have demonstrated that mass commodities were somewhat novel in the early twentieth century, much of my study examines a later, 'second' generation of consumer culture, when many of the basic institutions and values of mass consumption were recognizable, even if not widely shared. As we'll see, as donut shops began to spread across space in the postwar years, entrepreneurs and consumers were confronting commodities, institutions, forms of sociability, and cues to cultural meaning that were in some ways new, but in many others seemed quite familiar.

This 'postwar' chronological focus follows the donut through two distinct economic periods: the boom from the mid-1940s to the mid-1970s, and the period of 'economic challenge' that followed.[17] But neither the growing historiography about postwar Canada nor the historical trajectory of the donut adhere rigidly to this fundamental economic distinction. Cultural historians often inherit 'eras' from grand narratives of politics, diplomacy, or economics ('the interwar years,' the 'Great Depression,' the 'postwar' era, etc.). Four decades of the 'new' social history have taught us that these 'big events' usually impinge on ordinary people in powerful ways; yet at the same time they don't always provide convenient or useful standards for marking fundamental transitions in daily life. From this perspective, the history of the donut reflects three recent trends in postwar historiography. First, historians are increasingly pointing to the continuities between prewar and postwar developments. Discussing tourism in British Columbia, for example,

Mike Dawson connects Depression-era marketing plans to the more familiar postwar boom, arguing that many of the key institutions and ideas of postwar consumption were actually defined in the 1920s and 1930s. The invention of the donut as a modern, mass commodity, which I discuss in chapter 1, reinforces the analytic value of this observation.[18] Second, historians are now taking a more serious look at the periodization of the postwar era itself, noting that the shorthands that define the period – prosperity, conformity, Americanization, and so on – tend to break down on closer inspection. For their part, donut shops emerged amidst postwar prosperity, but came relatively late in its development, part of a configuration of mass marketing that emerged around 1955, one characterized by such staples of present-day car culture as shopping malls, chain fast food, and mass-produced suburbs.[19] Third, the donut complicates the period of economic challenge that began in the mid-1970s. Even when the foundations of postwar prosperity fell away, donut chains did not slow down; if anything, the donut shop entered its golden age after 1975.

If the donut raises difficult issues of periodization, it also challenges our sense of analytic scale. Any 'Canadian' history has to confront real issues of regional fragmentation – in many chapters, much of my evidence (though certainly not all) is drawn from southern Ontario, largely because donut shops were most common there until the 1980s. I do, however, try to see this central Canadian evidence in terms of the regional nature of Canadian popular culture, rather than as standing in for larger Canadian developments. 'National' questions are more central later in the book, where I trace the spread of donut shops across more extensive geographies. But even then, region continues to be a crucial theme. From a broader perspective, moreover, accounting for the history of the donut in 'Canada' requires a lens that is global and continental as well as regional and local. In economic and cultural terms, southern Ontario is both centre and margin: it is at once the 'heartland' of Canada and the 'hinterland' of the northeast and midwest of the United States. Indeed, the Canadian history of the donut was powerfully defined by the product's place in a continental network of food service ideas, institutions, and personnel. At a greater scale, this history brings together commodity chains with global reach: coffee, spices, sugar, and so on.

With these issues of time and scale in mind, each chapter examines the donut's interaction with one or a few key developments in twentieth-century history. Chapter 1 examines the emergence of the donut as a mass commodity. Between the 1930s and the 1960s, a group of capitalists applied mass production ideas to the manufacture of donuts, and worked to define marketing strategies that would convince both entrepreneurs and consumers of the value of their more modern product. Chapter 2 examines the emergence of the donut shop in the 1960s as an expression of a new configuration of consumer culture after the war, especially by recreating the social space of the neighbourhood diner for car-driving customers. Since this second generation of mass marketers adopted the franchise model to build their chains of donut drive-ins, Chapter 3 traces the development of donut franchising, focusing on the constellation of institutions, ideas, and practices that gave shape and meaning to this business form. The final two chapters extend the discussion past the mid-1970s, when the donut entered a new phase in terms of both business and culture. The major chains, most notably Tim Hortons, redefined the donut shop and saturated the foodscape. Chapter 5 argues that both these trends – the transformation and expansion of the donut shop – provided the foundation for the emergence of the donut as an 'ironic icon' of local and national identity.

To examine these questions, the book builds on the experiences of people like Costas Kiriakopoulos, telling their stories through written and oral sources. Sadly, there is no archive of the donut, no research institute devoted to fried snack foods that can be visited and mined. Thus, my historical research has had to combine surveys of trade publications, local newspapers, government records and reports, and business materials in private collections. I also conducted more than sixty-five oral histories with a wide range of people: company executives, franchisees, independent owners, workers, customers, city officials, and others.[20]

None of these sources offers a perfect window onto the past. Business and government records have particular collection strategies; trade publications are often more concerned with economic potential than cultural meaning; local newspapers are alternately boosterish or sensationalist (and sometimes both at once). Relying on personal testimonies provides an intimate but problematic picture of history. Interviews are, in a very real sense, acts of imagination. Oral historians have paid increasing attention to the place of the interviewer and the subject in producing history. These concerns go beyond simple questions of reliability and accuracy – they relate to the way memory itself is the product of complicated social processes, and remind us that oral testimonies are complex texts that need to read carefully for narrative structures, self-presentations, and myths.[21] While attentive to these questions, most historians resist their ultimate logic (which is to make social historians into literary critics), and instead adopt a pragmatic approach to the use of oral evidence, treating it as a complex text even while using it to understand the historical process, however complicated a notion that might be. In the case of a subject like donut shops, these analytic questions and practical problems are especially pointed. On the one hand, the history of donut shops could not be written without oral sources. On the other hand, donut shops are partly built on a culture of banter, conversation, and exaggeration, which makes oral testimonies uncertain analytic ground.

The culture of banter in donut shops speaks to the link between a commercial institution and a social space. This book is a business history of a product and the institutions that produced and sold it, a social history of the people who shaped them, and a cultural exploration of their meaning in everyday life. I view it as following in the tradition of social and cultural history, a sort of history from the bottomless cup, using written and oral sources to understand the experience of people like Costas Kiriakopoulos in the context of economic developments, their cultural meaning, and the relationship between the two. I spend some time analysing business forms and developments, but readers hoping to find a blow-by-blow account of the entrepreneurs who created donut shops should look elsewhere.[22] Readers will also notice that the book is not about Tim Hortons, but the donut and donut shops more broadly. That few people in the early twenty-first century distinguish between the product, the place, and the brand name reflects the economic and cultural hegemony of the company as well as its remarkable success in penetrating the intellectual world of Canadians, but it does not reflect either my interest or the historical record. The hegemony of Tim Hortons, in both economic and cultural terms, is really a story of the 1990s, and I leave it to the later chapters of the book.

Adopting a more general lens, then, the book examines the way one commodity intersected with broad social forces and sweeping cultural developments. The donut reminds us that banal things can have considerable analytic power. In this small product – in the technologies that produced it, the places that sold it, and the consumers who ate it – several economic, social, cultural, and political narratives converge.

Ideas of mass production, business practice, geography, consumption, convenience, and identity profoundly shaped the product's history. In the end, however, the donut's banality exerted the greatest influence. As a cheap, discretionary product sold in simple, utilitarian shops, the donut fit into a tradition of 'petty consumption,' one built largely on everyday consumer decisions about mundane rather than spectacular business institutions. From banality, a grander history flowed.

1 Faith, Efficiency, and the Modern Donut: Inventing a Mass Commodity, 1920–1960

By the time Ernest Atalick returned to Port Colborne, Ontario, after the Second World War, the family bakery was deeply in debt. 'They were selling the bread so cheap because of the competition,' he recalled between sips of coffee at his home outside St Catharines. 'They were selling it for six cents a loaf, because the baker around the corner was selling it for that ... But they were losing money.'[1] Only six years into their dream of owning a small business, the red ink was deeply disturbing to the Atalick family, who had no intention of going back to the world of waged labour. 'Just to have a business, no matter what kind, you know, they got programmed that way,' he said of his parents. Much of the Atalick family economy was directed towards keeping the tiny business afloat. His father had arrived in Canada from Yugoslavia in 1924, settled in Port Colborne, and landed a job at the local nickel plant. The rest of the family, including Ernest, came three years later. By 1939 they had scraped together enough money to buy a small bakery in town. They hired one employee, an English baker who had the trade skills they needed, but most of the work was done by the Atalick family. Even with the efforts of Ernest and his mother, father, and uncle, making ends meet was a constant struggle. 'That bread was all hand worked,' said Atalick. 'It was very, very hard work, and you were getting no place. As a matter of fact, we had a bigger building, [and] we used to keep boarders – because they'd work in the nickel plant there – and that would help to pay for the expenses in the bakery.' By the end of the war, competition from other bakeries, the continuation of wartime rationing, and the small local market had all conspired to push the family into debt.

The breaking point seemed to come when Ernest returned from his stint in the army to find the business owing for eleven loads of flour, a total of 440 bags. The English baker suggested they could bring in some extra cash by selling donuts, and he offered to teach the family the process. At the time, donuts were something of a time-consuming treat. They were not a common product in local bakeries, and most people ate donuts made from scratch by mothers or wives in a labour-intensive process: mixing and cutting the dough by hand, frying them while bent over a hot kettle, and sprinkling them with sugar or cinnamon. Yet donuts were cheap to produce, and when the Atalicks started churning out one line of glazed yeast donuts in 1945, they sold like wildfire. 'I would take them into different stores in Port Colborne,' Ernest remembered, 'and sometimes by the time they would pay me, the donuts would be sold.' The family paid off the eleven loads of flour and began specializing in producing yeast donuts for local restaurants and grocery stores.

In 1946, they spotted a bakery for sale in St Catharines and leaped at the chance to move their burgeoning donut operation to a larger market. From the Homestead Bakery on St Patrick Street, they turned out hundreds of donuts a day, wholesaling them to restaurants and school cafeterias and retailing them from an outlet on St Paul Street, the commercial main street of the city. Soon they were installing machines, adding varieties, and upping their daily production. Periodic visits to Freddie's Donuts, an operation in Buffalo that Ernest remembered as the 'Cadillac of donuts,' inspired the Atalicks to improve the production process, first getting a local welding firm to rig up a mechanized cutter, later installing an automatic roller, and finally acquiring 'a fancy new fryer that automatically flipped the donuts.' Along the way, the company left the old commercial area of the city for a more spacious $25,000 factory out near the Queen Elizabeth Way, the four-lane highway that divided the 'garden city' in two. Their big break came in 1956, when Dominion grocery stores started buying Homestead's Donuts. Three years later, twelve employees were producing about 1,200 dozen a day.[2] Four trucks shipped the Atalicks' donuts across the Niagara Peninsula and as far away as Kitchener. They had just wanted to pay off their debt, but the story of Homestead Donuts ended up being one of single-product specialization, increasing volumes, developing mechanization, and wide wholesale distribution. 'If it wasn't for that English baker,' Atalick laughed, 'we'd still owe for those eleven loads of flour.'

The particulars of their tale are unique, but the Atalicks were just a local version of a much larger story – the transformation of the donut into a mass commodity. Beginning in the 1920s, long before donut shops became a key feature of the Canadian foodscape, a group of North American capitalists transformed the donut by applying the ideas of the Second Industrial Revolution, aiming for the continuous-flow processes that were typical of mass production factories. Significantly, these mass producers set out not only to produce large volumes of donuts, but also to transform the production techniques of smaller bakers by marketing their innovations in method, machinery, and materials. Across Canada, this vision reached down the bakery hierarchy. Indeed, by the standards of the 1950s, Homestead remained a relatively modest operation. 'We're only in the kindergarten class as yet. There are plenty of bigger bakeries, but we are growing rapidly,' Ernest told *Canadian Baker* in May 1959.[3] Locally, this process was often driven by individual entrepreneurs, petty producers, and family businesses, but they were picking up on broader innovations in production that were continental and even global in scope. The story of the Atalicks, then, was intertwined with economic and cultural themes much larger than the lowly donut. In a quirky and mundane way, the Atalicks' career in the donut business testifies to the North American 'ethos of mass production,'[4] and their new donut to the twentieth-century faith in modern technology.

'Our Present Wonderful Atomic Age'

When they turned to donut specialization in the 1940s, the Atalicks were not alone. In the decade after the Second World War, many bakeries across Canada were starting to specialize in donuts: Margaret's Fine Foods, the Doughnut House, and Primrose Bakery in Toronto; Glaz-O-Nut, Max's Donuts, and Honey Cream Donuts in Vancouver; Val's Donuts in Edmonton; Purity Bakery in Montreal; Deluxe Donut Company in Fort William, and Lakeside Honi-Dipt Do-Nuts in Hamilton ... the list goes on. These companies were growing by leaps and bounds in the 1950s. Margaret's started as a delicatessen in east-end Toronto, but shifted to donuts in 1951 and was producing seven thousand a day only six years later. Honey Cream of Vancouver boosted its volume 1,000 per cent between 1943 and 1960. The Doughnut House in Toronto started in 1950, and just over a decade later had reached a daily production of 36,000.[5]

The donut specializers faced competition from the large bakeries, which were producing donuts as part of their varied product lines. For companies like Vachon of Montreal, Morrison-Lamothe of Ottawa, and Eastern Bakeries of Saint John, the donut was a relatively minor product, one item among many bakery and confectionery items produced in large volumes and distributed over great distances. By 1947, Eastern Bakeries was producing about 100 dozen donuts per hour at its new Moncton plant – a decent figure for the time, but only a minor part of its production at six plants across New Brunswick and Nova Scotia. At Morrison-Lamothe's 100,000-square-foot plant in Ottawa, 400 employees were producing 2,000 dozen donuts per day in 1954, but the company's production in other products was much more impressive: 3,000 loaves of bread and 700 dozen hot dog buns *per hour*. Vachon was producing an impressive number of donuts, but 75 per cent of its sales were in its dime specialty cakes, like the 'Jos. Louis,' which it distributed to grocery stores, supermarkets, factories, vending machines, and high school cafeterias. Vachon, like these other companies, had built an extensive distribution network for its varied products, although the staling properties of the donut (which was best if sold within a few days, even when packed in cellophane) shortened delivery distances considerably. Vachon had a donut plant in Toronto for a time, but closed it in the mid-1960s and returned to shipping donuts to Toronto from its Montreal operations. Vachon also delivered from its twelve distribution centres across New England and eastern Canada.[6]

Lurking behind many of the innovations in donut production was the Doughnut Corporation of America (DCA), a company founded by the Gutenberg of fried snack foods, Adolph Levitt. Levitt had come to New York in 1916 to start a chain of retail window bakeries. At the end of the First World War, soldiers recently returned from America's coffee break in the trenches (where they had been mass-fed donuts by the Salvation Army) inundated Levitt's operation with requests for the fatty treat. To keep up with demand, Levitt put his inventive spirit (and a lucky meeting with an engineer) to work on constructing an automatic donut-making machine, the first real mass production process for donuts. He pushed the contraption into the window of his bakeries, and the machine became as popular for its process as for its product. Levitt eventually teamed up with Maxwell House Coffee to open a chain of eighteen Mayflower donut stores across the United States; he also set up DCA to sell the machines to other operators. In 1921 he sold 128 compact machines (which produced about eighty dozen per hour) to grocery stores, five and dimes, bakeries, and restaurants.[7]

Soon, the company was expanding to serve a continental market. Initially, DCA shipped some individual machines across the Canadian border – a vendor at Hanlan's Point Pavilion on Toronto Island, for example, used one in the early 1920s.[8] Marketing efforts in Canada became more systematic during the Depression, however. In 1935, Levitt sent longtime employee T.E. Andrews to Toronto to establish a Canadian division, dubbed the Canadian Doughnut Company (CDC).[9] Initially, CDC was simply a distribution company, importing machines and mixes from DCA's American operations and shipping them out from its office at the Terminal Warehouse Building (now on Queen's Quay) in Toronto, but the company quickly set up modern production facilities. In 1936, Andrews took over four floors of the building to install $50,000 worth of processing equipment to churn out premade donut mixes for Canadian bakers. Two years later, CDC opened a large production facility in Trenton, Ontario, complete with machine shop, egg-drying facilities, and cereal plant.[10] The Trenton plant stayed on the cutting edge, installing an automated bulk handling system in 1956, in which raw materials moved along conveyors and tubes by air pressure from unloading to processing. The system was a classic example of continuous flow automation: 'The complete unloading process and handling of the flour within the plant from storage bins to mixers and blenders ... is entirely automatic and requires the attention of one man only to start the system in operation. The automatic system is so complete that when a bin is filled ... the flour is automatically shut off.' The company's donut plants in Toronto and Montreal were equally impressive. The Montreal plant, opened in 1948, was said to be the 'largest donut production plant in the British Empire' (although it is not clear that this was an especially dramatic claim) and used automatic equipment for almost every step of the manufacturing process.[11]

CDC and its American parent shared one of the quintessential capitalist dreams of the twentieth century: to transform production in small batches into specialized, mechanized, and standardized processes. Since the late nineteenth century, manufacturers in many industries had been working to maximize 'throughput' by applying electric power, improving raw materials, increasing mechanization, and adopting new management techniques to speed up and coordinate the flow of goods.[12] In manufacturing, Henry Ford became the most famous advocate of this transformation, but he merely applied existing continuous flow processes to a more complex product. Between 1908 and 1914, Ford remade his company's production process, subdividing work into smaller jobs, codifying craft knowledge into engineering rules, and (most significantly) rearranging machines and workers along a moving assembly line – an arrangement that subordinated the worker's sense of pace to the timing of the machine. Ford's innovations did more than catapult his company to the top of the car business. Though his methods never represented the dominant form of production in North America, they were 'symbol-making technologies' that helped inspire and reinforce an 'ethos of mass production' – a kind of cultural faith in technological advancement – that spanned industries and sometimes defied the actual level of mechanization in specific companies.[13] Even before Ford, however, industries handling smaller products – and even more notably, those handing liquids, paper, and light powders – had been applying continuous flow methods to refining and producing a variety of goods. In refining, the sugar and oil industries led the way; in foods, meatpacking, beverages, and canning had been the innovators.[14]

By the 1940s, some producers had pushed the vision of continuous flow production past its earlier conception towards a rudimentary form of automation. During the 1930s and 1940s, companies in industries like petroleum and chemical processing – with plants that processed liquid materials – set up continuous flow processes that could be monitored by a single worker in a central location, often far removed from the actual production line. This was not the complex form of automation we associate with the auto plants of the 1960s, with robots performing intricate assembly tasks. The point here was simply to establish continuous movement of the product through the production process without human intervention – a goal pursued by large companies in many industries after the Second World War. The results were uneven, but as with Ford's earlier innovations, the dream of automated production created a general sensation.[15]

By the First World War, some large Canadian bakers were adopting early continuous flow methods, applying electricity to run mechanized kneading bins, conveyor belts to move the bread at precise intervals, automatic cutting and wrapping, and other innovations.[16] The travelling oven made it possible for bread to be moved automatically in and out of the oven by machine rather than by workers. Bakeries continued to push production technology and volumes after the war. In 1924, Ideal Bread in Toronto bragged about operating five travelling ovens with an hourly capacity of 15,000 loaves.[17] Full automation would not come to baking until the 1950s, when technology replaced the need for a human worker to prepare the dough and feed it into the machines. Yet already by the dawn of the Great Depression, through mergers and innovations in production, the four largest bakeries in Canada had grown so productive that their capacity to produce far outstripped the demand for their product; they began then to divert more and more of their resources to marketing, rather than producing, bread and other products. Indeed, bread production was so efficient (and its marketing so convoluted) in the interwar years that for large bakeries, the cost of selling a loaf far surpassed the costs of production.[18] Modern packaging, aggressive salesmanship, and clever advertising became inseparable from progressive business practices. In some minds, though, all of this violated the modern moral economy of bread.[19]

Innovations came later to donut production than to bread making, mainly because donuts involved smaller volumes and a more specialized product (the donut was never the staff of life, after all). Until Levitt set up CDC in 1935, baking innovations in Canada had been confined to the highest-volume products. Bakers who wanted to increase their production of more specialized products like donuts had three options: hire more workers, use larger kettles, or both. When the Salvation Army decided to feed donuts to soldiers in the trenches of the First World War, for example, it increased the normal output by filling garbage barrels with oil; this was a change in the size of the fryer rather than the technology of production.[20]

In contrast, DCA altered the production system itself, especially the quality of machinery. Looking back at Levitt's innovations in 1948, *Canadian Food Industries* noted that in 1919 'a qualified baker could cut and fry something like 250 dozen daily,' while Levitt's first machine was designed to automatically produce 80 dozen per hour – an output his company had doubled by 1928.[21] Over the next few decades, DCA's engineers continued to construct larger, faster, and more technically sophisticated systems, which included new technologies (like the semi-automatic equipment for yeast donuts in 1949), standardized production processes (enabling producers to 'control fat absorption to within a tenth of an ounce in a dozen doughnuts'), and much higher outputs (increasing from 80 to 600 dozen per hour in three decades). For DCA executives, these developments placed the company in the mainstream of scientific and engineering advancement. Increased outputs in the postwar years, said Bert Nevins, marked 'the difference between the Age of Ford and our present wonderful Atomic Age.'[22]

While engineers tinkered with machinery, DCA chemists improved materials. With its arrival in Canada in 1935, CDC introduced Canadi-

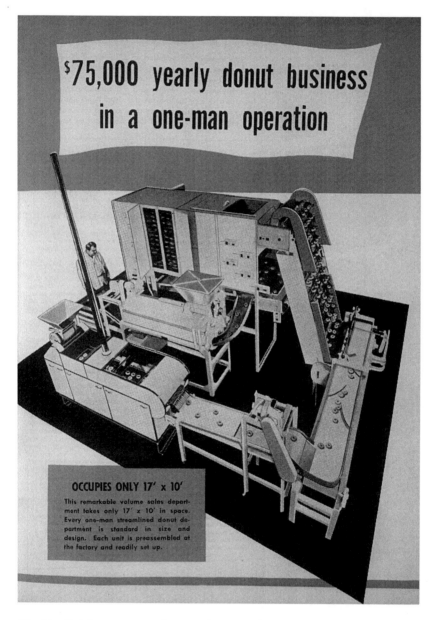

The 'Fordist' donut, 1946. The Canadian Doughnut Company applied the assembly line concept to donuts, then worked to convince other bakers to adopt the technology. (*Canadian Baker*, February 1946, 23)

ans to the wonders of scientifically formulated premade mixes, which standardized the quality of the dough and eliminated one of the more tricky operations in donut production – the need to portion and mix the ingredients. Scientific research and formulation continued. In America, DCA's research efforts led to wartime innovations like the 'Nutro Donut,' although it never managed to convince the U.S. government of the health advantages of the product's enriched ingredients. After the war, the company's scientific research expanded, and by 1949 it had opened a five-storey lab in New York. 'The top floor where ingredients are tested might be the work room of a scientist engaged in some sort of atomic experiments,' the *New York Times* enthused. 'There are complex mechanisms that measure the water absorption of flour, dough elasticity, the softness of the doughnut, its sugar content.'[23] CDC drew from its American parent's scientific research and also did some of its own. CDC laboratories employed chemists to analyse the chemistry of flour and the dynamics of frying. In 1942 the *Globe and Mail* marvelled at how the company's egg-drying facility in Trenton was 'kept under laboratory control at all times,' including testing for 'moisture content, bacteria count, palatability, and other qualities.' Six years later, the *Globe* described the company's 'clean, shiny laboratory' atop its Trenton factory, where two employees tested ingredients, measured for proteins and bacteria, and fried sixty dozen donuts a day to check the quality and uniformity of the mix. After the war, the company rolled out a new yeast donut mix, branched out to cake and muffin mixes, and experimented with frozen donuts.[24]

Though DCA and CDC were the loudest and strongest proponents of the modern, industrial, scientific donut, other companies joined the fray. Procter & Gamble, the maker of Crisco shortening, conducted studies of frying action, including 'the experimental frying of more than 20,000 dozens of doughnuts in eighteen different fats,' and produced two pamphlets to help bakers standardize their donut production. The pamphlets were testaments to the growing professionalization of food research. Scientists – depicted in clean white lab coats (despite the messiness of donut making) and as working in sleek, modern laboratories – coloured frying fats with oil-soluble dyes to analyse the effects of mixing time, ingredients, frying temperature, and other factors. True to the rhetoric and symbols of the scientific method, they graphed the 'cooling curve' (the internal temperature of a donut in relation to time) and the rate of 'staling,' emphasizing throughout the controlled, scientific nature of their experiments.[25]

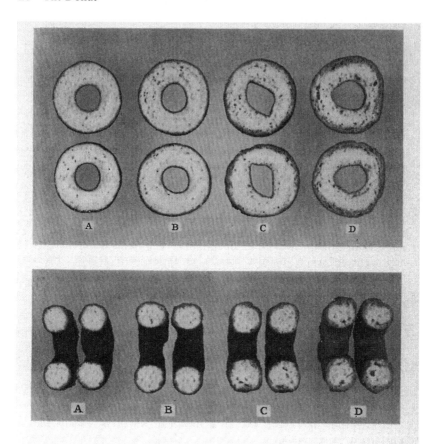

Figure 5—Influence of temperature on absorption of frying fat. These photographs show cross- and end-sections of doughnuts fried at: A—410°, B—390°, C—375°, and D—350° F. The lower temperatures did not seal the surfaces of doughnuts C and D quickly enough to prevent the soaking-in of excess fat, as shown by the dark layers under the crust.

An artifact of the scientific donut. In 1932, Procter & Gamble dyed frying oil to plot the effects of temperature on fat absorption. (Bakery Research Department, Procter & Gamble, 'Dollars to Doughnuts,' Crisco Bakery Service Series No. 2, Cincinnati, 1932, 33)

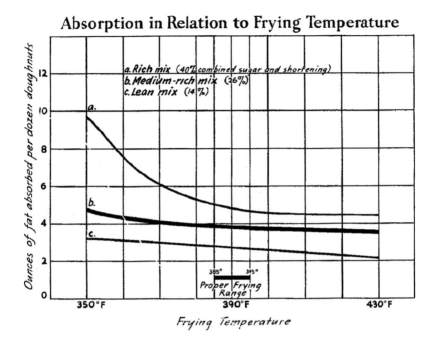

An artifact of the scientific donut. Though few bakers would have found this graph useful, it reinforced the scientific nature of Crisco's frying experiments. (Bakery Research Department, Procter & Gamble, 'Dollars to Doughnuts,' Crisco Bakery Service Series No. 2, Cincinnati, 1932, 35)

Others worked on machinery of various sizes and complexity, especially after the Second World War. Jo-Lo, Belshaw, Moline, and other firms designed and marketed big and small donut machines as part of their broader lines of foodservice and bakery equipment. Jo-Lo also distributed donut mixes. Another way to transform donut production was by selling compact automatic machines to bakers, restaurateurs, and small retailers. This had been Levitt's original approach: in 1921, he had sold 128 compact machines (which produced about eighty dozen per hour) to grocery stores, five and dimes, bakeries, and restaurants. Over time, Levitt faced increasing competition from other companies selling similar machines. In Canada, throughout the 1950s, two branches of Hol'n One Donuts sold small machines and donut mixes across British Columbia and Ontario.[26]

Selling modern production at Jo-Lo, 1946. (*Canadian Baker*, January 1946, 11)

Nothing annoyed donut professionals more than the haphazard nature of handicraft and domestic production. 'It is unlikely that two bakers, each using the same formula, will produce the same results,' Crisco's research department complained, enumerating problems ranging from poor ingredients to careless mixing.[27] At the time, few bakers devoted much time, space, or energy to ongoing donut production; often, they churned them out (almost, it seemed to donut scientists, at a whim) in cramped corners of shops devoted to staples like breads and cakes. Home cooking was not much better: it might evoke memories of maternal love and labour, but it did not meet the standards of modern diets and tastes. 'There is hardly a Canadian man or woman who does not carry fond memories of the donuts "Mother used to make,"' Arthur Mills of CDC admitted. 'If we could be transported back to our pantry at home, we would possibly find a jar of donuts, warm from the stove, misshapen and grease soaked. They were hardly a healthful, scientific food product suitable for our modern market; nevertheless a tasty treat for a hungry boy.'[28] Even a cursory survey of cookbooks from the early twentieth century indicates a startling variety in recipes and procedures, despite the relative simplicity of the product. One cookbook alone included seventeen different donut recipes; others made it clear that the donut was not a thing of science but of verse, as in this rhyming recipe from Mrs E.J. Powell:

One cup of sugar, brown or white,
Now add an egg, and beat it light,
A little salt, with spice to taste
Baking powder too, must now be placed,
Three teaspoonfuls bought of Gillet,
I find as good as any yet,
One cup of milk now stir together,
They will prove as light as any feather;
Just enough flour to roll them out,
But you must mind what you're about,
And keep your lard at proper heat –
You'll find these doughnuts hard to beat.[29]

In fact, there was much that was modern about this homemade donut. Even this poetic recipe stood at end of continental and global commodity chains of sugar, wheat, shortening, and spices, and used ingredients that were creatures of modern distribution and marketing machines.

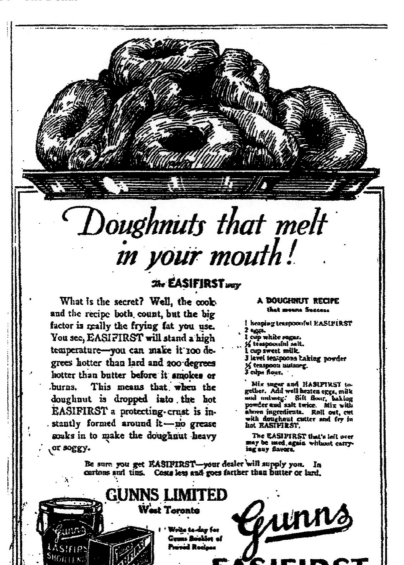

(*Toronto Daily Star*, 15 March 1920, 10)

Large food processors worked hard in the early twentieth century to establish brand identities for products and to convince women that brand-name ingredients produced better results.[30] 'Doughnuts that melt in your mouth! What is the Secret?' asked one such ad, from Gunn's Shortening. 'Well, the cook and the recipe both count, but the big factor is really the frying fat you use ... When the doughnut is dropped into the hot EASIFIRST a protecting crust is instantly formed around it – no grease soaks in to make the doughnut heavy or soggy.'[31] Flour companies grafted nostalgic and maternal language onto this modern marketing agenda. 'You can taste them in memory – those mother-made doughnuts that crowned the old School Lunch,' declared one advertisement for Five Roses Flour. 'Crisp rings of crackling gold, yielding and porous to the eager bite, nutlike, wholesome, satisfying.' For all its maternal rhetoric and home kitchen setting, the ad itself demonstrated that the donut was becoming an expression of newer economic developments. Five Roses Flour was the brand name of the Lake of the Woods Milling Company, which was based in Winnipeg and Montreal but distributed its products (including 500,000 cookbooks) across Canada. That a company based in Quebec and Manitoba would advertise in New Brunswick was testimony to the donut's links to networks of distribution somewhat larger than the home kitchen.[32]

Still, at the point of production, the home-baked or small bakery donut remained a remarkably primitive product, one that DCA and other companies hoped to transform using 'modern methods of production.' 'The automatic machine, the scientific mixture, a perfect frying fat ... here were the tools,' Arthur Mills declared. Of course, though the rhetoric and the tools of donut industrialists were modern and scientific, the main purpose of all the research work for new machines and better raw materials was to sell more products. Some scientific purists – who engaged in a surprisingly heated debate about bake-test methodologies during the interwar period – would have questioned the scientific authenticity of such experimenting, which focused less on pure chemistry than on improving a particular product.[33] But the scientific gaze of DCA and Crisco was outward into the bakery industry rather than inward to the cerealist community. Indeed, donut boosters like Arthur Mills unapologetically embraced science in the service of capitalism. 'As faith in this new donut grew,' Mills summed up in 1942, 'profits increased.' Procter & Gamble wanted to sell more shortening, and not surprisingly, its graph of 'Moisture Content in Relation to Storage Time' demonstrated the superiority of Crisco over oils or compounds: 'Doughnuts fried in Crisco ... retain their freshness longer because they lose their moisture more slowly ... Crisco sets up on the doughnut, forming a film which holds the moisture.'[34] Nor was Adolph Levitt a scientific ideologue: the more efficient the production method, the more DCA donut mix would be needed.

Yet DCA's modern tools were not applied primarily to making and marketing actual donuts. Indeed, the company's main agenda – and that of many of its competitors – was not so much to produce a better product as to help smaller operators like the Atalicks to modernize and improve their operations. From a product standpoint, this made sense. In many ways, Levitt's company stood in the mainstream of progressive twentieth-century industrial culture, applying a scientific agenda to the central tenets of capitalist efficiency: economies of scale, continuous flow, bypassing skilled workers, and reducing labour costs. Yet economies of scale could take donut efficiency only so far: since a donut tasted best within a day or so of production and was virtually inedible after two or three days, it had to be consumed relatively close to where it was produced. These material considerations, especially when combined with the prospect of relatively small volumes compared to staples like bread, strongly suggested (but did not require) a decentralized network of plants that could nonetheless take advantage of DCA innovations.[35] DCA, then, needed to balance the drive towards modernity with local regimes of production and distribution. To do so, it envisioned a form of petty mass production, where small- or medium-sized operators like the Atalicks could be persuaded to modernize their production and distribute their donuts in local, metropolitan, or at most regional markets.

Crowning the Doughnut Queen

Here, the rhetoric and technology of modern production met the hype of salesmanship and marketing. Both CDC and Jo-Lo expended considerable resources convincing widely dispersed operators of the value of improving production by installing machines and buying premade mix. Both companies built impressive networks of sales representatives across Canada, who actively courted local entrepreneurs. 'DCA suggested that as my volume was increasing that I should consider higher production equipment which they had available,' remembered Wayne Spencer of Val's Donuts in Edmonton. 'They shared the expense to make a trip to Chicago and Akron, Ohio, to check large volume producers ... I signed a lease, of course, [and] used tons and tons of donut mix over the years.'[36] Spencer could also benefit from CDC's training program, ongoing service, and troubleshooting assistance in the event of problems. DCA also promised these local entrepreneurs increased consumer acceptance, arguing that in the new consumer age, modern baking practices had the best chance of replacing home production. 'When sugar rationing ends,' CDC asked Canadian bakers in one postwar ad, 'will Canadian housewives resume home baking? As far as cake donuts are concerned, the answer is no!'[37]

Promising increased consumer acceptance obviously required DCA to address consumers, especially housewives. Bakers and prospective entrepreneurs like the Atalicks and the Spencers may have been initially impressed by the rhetoric of science and efficiency, but their businesses wouldn't last long without a market for their increasing volumes. Bakers had been hoping to displace home production for years, although they often complained of the reluctance of consumers to buy non-staple items like cakes and pies.[38] To market the new industrial donut, DCA targeted consumers both directly and indirectly. The company did advertising and promotion of its own, particularly in newspapers, on radio, and on billboards (renting an impressive 1,037 in the summer of 1949).[39] The company also engaged in public relations efforts, including National Doughnut Month (inaugurated in the United States in October 1928) and National Doughnut Week (founded April 1935). DCA also created the National Dunking Association, an organization of card-carrying donut eaters that included Broadway actors, Hollywood stars, and famous sports figures, though these celebrity dunkers were usually American and the idea seems to have been less aggressively promoted in Canada. In the postwar period, these annual efforts included crowning a Doughnut Queen.[40] And the company often donated donuts to youth groups, high school charity drives, and veterans' hospitals. For many of these public relations efforts, CDC linked itself with other large companies or trade groups: it joined the National Dairy Council and Dairy Farmers of Canada to promote donuts and milk in 1953; and it joined with Coca-Cola to promote donuts and Coke three years later, and with competitor Jo-Lo in several years after the war.[41]

CDC marketing efforts also aimed to improve the advertising and promotional efforts of bakers, supermarkets, and eateries. The firm (and eventually other donut companies, including Jo-Lo) distributed premade promotional materials to bakers and grocery stores, organized public relations stunts, and performed marketing studies to help retailers

To promote donut consumption, DCA crowned a Donut Queen every October. (*Canadian Baker*, October 1953, 42)

promote donut consumption. The company also developed (and heavily promoted) the Twin Baker Trademark, and encouraged its use in donut promotions by supermarkets and bakers, as a sign of consistent quality and reliable product.[42] Focusing on local promotional needs and point-of-purchase marketing was especially important for an impulse purchase like donuts. It also fit well with the regional and local nature of consumer tastes, allowing local retailers to gear their products to, for example, Quebec's notorious sweet tooth or Ontario's taste for nutmeg. 'CDC, recognizing that every baker's product and market is different, works with the baker to help him get the right donut ... that will yield the greatest volume in his market.'[43]

In pursuing these strategies, CDC constructed a 'commercial speech' that aimed less to create new meanings for the donut than to redirect existing ones towards the company's modern, industrial version.[44] By the time CDC came on the scene, Canadians had been eating donuts for at least a century, whether as part of daily routines, family time, parties, or seasonal festivals and celebrations. In its efforts to encourage greater overall consumption and to persuade Canadians to eat commercially bought donuts, CDC played on the product's long-standing meanings and associations. The donut, for example, had long been a staple of holidays and festivals. Literary accounts and surviving diaries from as far back as the nineteenth century speak of the donut as a mainstay of Christmas and Thanksgiving feasts. In a typical description, the National Council of Women's discussion of 'French Canadian Customs' highlighted the donut's place in maternal labour and family celebrations: 'The recurring fête days cause great sensations in rural districts. In the large kitchen, where swarm the whole family, feasts and prospective joys are prepared. While on the stove, encumbered with simmering pots, the odorous doughnut is fried under the superintendence of the mother, others knead pie crust into innumerable tarts, season the stews or pluck the fowls.'[45] The company's promotional efforts updated these festival associations, tying them to the modern holiday calendar: ads featured Santa Claus eating donuts, and lengthy pamphlets gave detailed instructions on how to run Halloween, birthday, and Christmas parties that included donuts as fun and food.[46]

Tying the product to the modern festival calendar also continued the donut's long-standing maternal associations. As in other consumer sectors, the baking industry often imagined its typical market exchange in gendered terms, usually between Mr Baker and Mrs Housewife, Mrs Consumer, Mrs So-and-So, or Mrs Smith.[47] Not surprisingly, then,

DCA encouraged mothers to integrate donut consumption into holiday parties. (*Canadian Baker*, October 1948, 17)

much of DCA's commercial speech addressed women as housewives and mothers. While some ads and public relations efforts were ostensibly neutral, many spoke directly to women – they suggested recipes to spruce up store-bought donuts, and donut games for parties and rainy days, and they advised that happy children resulted from serving store-bought donuts. Of course, these ads and booklets never suggested techniques for making donuts or for improving home-made procedures; they stayed focused on fun ways to make maternal labour easier through consumption. This was a good argument, since donut making was a hot, smelly task and prone to many problems. In newspapers, homemakers' columns were littered with complaints and troubleshooting advice.[48] Home donut making was not highly skilled, but it was tricky. Oil had to be at a precise temperature, mixes were hard to assemble and never satisfying, and the job was hot and dangerous. Newspaper reports testified to the way that pools of hot oil caught fire or spilled onto cooks and family members with disturbing regularity. 'Mrs. Mike Burak of Winnipeg today was considering the advisability of purchasing doughnuts hereafter from the corner bakery,' a Canadian Press story reported in 1937. 'Doughnut-making cost her a burned hand and an insurance company $750 when fat from the pan set fire to her home.'[49]

At the retail level, DCA and other companies made the donut machines themselves part of their commercial speech. From the beginning, Levitt had recognized the promotional value of automatic technology, attracting large crowds by pushing his donut contraptions up to the window of his New York bakeries.[50] In Toronto, Downyflake Donuts took a similar approach, serving a standard coffee shop menu of simple meals but using the donut-making display to attract the attention of passers-by. Some grocery and department stores took a similar approach.[51] The promotional appeal of the small machines probably combined the promise of fresh, hot donuts with the attraction of technology and the distortion of scale. In the twentieth century, except for special displays at exhibitions and fairs, real mass production was typically not a public spectacle (better, in fact, to hide it away); yet there was something astonishing about this form of miniature donut automation, and its popularity at amusement parks and along commercial streets testified to its sublime appeal.[52]

Notwithstanding these tiny technological spectacles, much of DCA's marketing aimed at daily routines in fairly mundane ways. In-store posters promoted simple consumer actions like buying donuts and coffee for breakfast, or they encouraged buying throughout the day (a donut went 'with a snack [or] with any meal,' the company noted).[53] Such regular consumption was unlikely, however, so long as the donut was considered unhealthy and hard to digest. For many years, drug companies marketed stomach remedies with reference to the lowly snack. 'Doughnuts should not be eaten,' declared Owl Drug Stores, nonetheless suggesting a bit of 'Adeliska' to relieve the resulting intestinal distress. Other critics focused on the donut's fattening qualities and its relative lack of nutritious ingredients. DCA responded to these concerns with scientific and expert rhetoric. The modern donut, it argued, promised to solve both problems: standardized ingredients and processes made for a more digestible donut, and the company went so far as to publicize (through women's pages and local ads) Dr J. Howard Crum's 'Donut Reducing Diet,' consisting of two donuts and a glass of milk for breakfast and lunch.[54] DCA went even further, arguing that the modern donut, with its chemically sound ingredients, scientific enrichment, and standardized process, was actually nutritious and healthy. 'The modern donut is made of wheat flour (in many cases enriched), soya flour, sugar, vegetable shortening, egg yolk and dry milk solids. These ingredients contribute many of the basic food elements needed by the body,' the company asserted in a wartime pamphlet called *The Nourish-Meter*, reproducing a 'Nutritional Balance Chart' to extol the healthful qualities of the donut.[55]

As *The Nourish-Meter* example suggests, health was a particular problem in wartime, as it intersected with the patriotic project of winning the war. CDC and its American parent worked hard to convince both governments and consumers that eating donuts was good for one's health. In 1942, DCA developed what it called a 'Nutro donut,' which was said to 'supply naturally' several essential vitamins and minerals. CDC submitted an analysis of the donut's digestibility to L.B. Pett, Director of Nutrition Services in Ottawa, and widely publicized his conclusion that 'Tested Quality Doughnuts are a valuable food, since one doughnut supplies twice as many calories, nearly three times as much calcium, phosphorus, and iron, and nearly twice as much of vitamins A, B, and Riboflavin, as one slice of ordinary white bread ... It also appears that under the standardized method of manufacture only a small amount of fat is absorbed in frying.' The company also boldly declared that the product fit into the broader war project. 'Donuts fit right into the government program which urges homemakers to turn to baked products and cereal foods in order to release less plentiful foods to the war effort,' the company claimed in 1943.[56]

In a broader way, CDC joined its American parent (and many iconic American brands) in constructing a commercial speech that linked donuts to the war effort. For example, it delivered machines and supplies to military canteens (modernizing the Salvation Army's 'doughnut girl' concept from the First World War), and it made prominent use of soldiers in public relations materials. The company's efforts were never as comprehensive as those of Coca-Cola, which developed a complex infrastructure of production and distribution that in many ways paralleled and merged with the American military apparatus, but DCA/CDC's wartime strategies explored similar thematic ground.[57]

'A Series of Compromises'

According to CDC's published statistics, the donut enjoyed a renaissance during the war, although whether this was the result of marketing themes or wartime social and political developments is unclear. The company claimed that the Canadian donut market had grown from eight million dozen in 1940 to twenty million dozen by 1945, but even it recognized that wartime shortages of alternative bakery items, the decline in home baking caused by women's war work, and the increased caloric needs caused by longer and harder work had helped donut sales tremendously. These social developments were often reinforced by government rationing policies. When the Wartime Prices and Trade Board established regulations to discourage between-meal coffee and tea consumption, restaurants in Vancouver responded by instituting 'no coffee alone' policies and by treating a coffee and donut as a meal. Donut (and, to a degree, pie) sales increased.[58]

Underneath the optimistic messages about increasing wartime volumes, then, lay the ambivalence of Canada's 'reconstruction culture.'[59] Wartime growth in the demand for donuts had the potential to reverse itself in the postwar years, as the unique conditions of rationing and disrupted families ended. DCA joined planners, politicians, and the public in hoping for a revved up postwar economy – a hope tinged with a certain anxiety. 'The Challenge of Tomorrow,' the company declared in February 1945, would be 'to provide peak employment for our fighting men when they return. It is a challenge that can only be met by peak production and an ever-increasing volume of sales.' From the broad standpoint of the Canadian economy, the claim was misleading: CDC's automatic donut equipment promised to *reduce* labour needs, not to create peak employment – a fact that was perhaps

Figure 1.1   Donut consumption per capita by province, 1951–1961

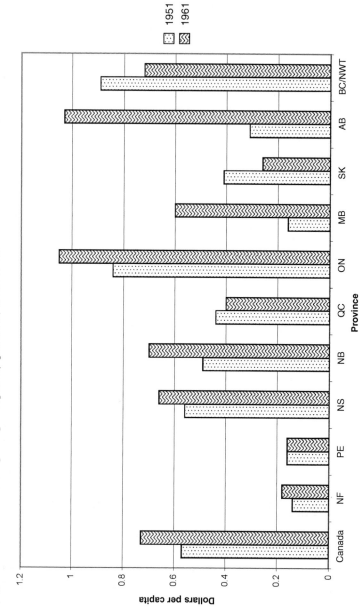

Sources: Donut volumes from DBS, Cat. 32-203, Bakeries, 1961, table 6; Populations from Canada Year Book, 1966, 177.

more obvious a decade later, when the promise of automation seemed less glowing.[60] But this kind of rhetoric fit with the broader ambivalence of wartime thinking about the future: Canadians could hope for new days of prosperity and still worry about postwar challenges. Regardless, as early as 1946, ads directed at bakers sounded more optimistic, linking the company's wartime strategies to future volume and growth. 'Over 1,000,000 Canadians engaged in wartime activities have been sampling donuts regularly during the last five years,' CDC reminded bakers early that year. 'A gigantic donut market is available to you.'[61]

In the end, as in other sectors of the economy, there was good reason for optimism in the postwar donut business. Though donut purchasing continued to be frustratingly impulsive from the point of view of the industry, consumption climbed dramatically. In the decade after 1951, Canadian donut sales (measured in dollar volume) increased 28 per cent above the combined effect of inflation and population growth, suggesting that the typical consumer was buying many more donuts than ever before (although buying actually declined in a few provinces; see figure 1.1).[62] Moreover, production not only increased to keep up, but more and more donut producers bought in, literally and figuratively, to DCA's modern project. In 1947 a *Canadian Baker* correspondent marvelled at the automated production of Eastern Bakeries' new plant in Moncton: 'Dough is placed in a container at the top of the doughnut machine and regulated air pressure cuts the dough and forms the doughnut. Then it enters the frying fat where it is evenly fried on both sides. It then leaves the fryer and drops on the conveyer belt, which takes it to the drier and cooler. An endless belt takes them through the cooler until they are the right temperature to handle. They are deposited on the packaging table where they are wrapped immediately.'[63] A decade later, Wayne Spencer of Val's Donuts made 'it a point to remind his customers that Val's equipment is completely automatic. Donuts are never touched by human hands.'

Throughout the 1950s, trade magazines happily contrasted the new automated production plants with the primitive methods of past decades. In 1950, Val's Donuts had been a 'one-man show,' turning out 20 dozen; only eight years later, it was producing 4,000 dozen daily. Under the tutelage of the Gagnon brothers, Honey Cream of Vancouver went from 'hand cut donuts fried in small cooking kettles' to an 'automation volume of 900 dozen an hour' with donuts 'handled automatically from cutters to packaging.'[64] In 1967, Sid Brazier of Margaret's looked back on the development of the company since its beginnings as an east Toronto delicatessen in the 1940s: 'We started with equipment which was "less than nothing" ... with a pot to fry maybe two dozen donuts at a time and they were turned [over during frying] at that time with a stick as many of the small bakers are presently doing. But we have kept up with the machine age ... If we were producing donuts today the way we produced them 15 years ago, we would need a hundred hour day at the very least ... to keep up with our present demands.'[65]

Their motives may have been practical and economic, but DCA and other companies turned innovation into a commodity and transformed the production methods of smaller operators. A few companies spent time tinkering on their own. At Honey Cream in Vancouver, donuts moved automatically along a 350-foot conveyor system, passing through machines built by co-owner Ed Gagnon to his own designs. But most donut specializers in this period lacked the knowledge and resources to design and improve their own production processes. Most companies 'kept up with the machine age' by simply purchasing or leasing machines from DCA. 'Ninety percent of the equipment in our plant with the exception of our conveyors is DCA,' Ron Brazier of Margaret's told Bakers Journal in 1967. In setting up its Toronto donut plant, Vachon followed a similar strategy of borrowing innovation, in this case from Jo-Lo.[66] Donut producers were just as enthusiastic about advances in ingredients. In 1974, Bakers Journal estimated that 90 per cent of donuts produced in Canada were being made from a premade mix. Two years later, it put the figure at 95 per cent.[67]

Yet barriers to modernization remained. The donut is a deceptively simple product and raises many technical problems for a continuous flow operation. It was easy enough to break down production into its five key steps – preparing the dough (measuring ingredients, mixing, fermenting), forming the donut (rolling and cutting or extruding), proofing (yeast donuts only), frying (feeding the fryer, flipping the donut to fry both sides, removing from oil), and finishing (drying, cooling, and glazing or icing). It was much harder to actually automate each step. Mixes made preparation fairly simple (although yeast mixes remained a tricky problem until 1947), but the process remained in the hands of human bakers, who prepared the dough and fed it into the first machine. Farther down the line, forming the cake donut mechanically was not an engineering problem, but machines for yeast products remained a significant production challenge even into the 1960s. In the mid-1950s, Glaz-o-Nut in Vancouver experimented with a mechanized extruder for yeast donuts, but found that the machine had drawbacks in terms of appearance and quality: '[A] lot of these [machines] didn't work. Like ... what they called an extruded donut machine – an extruder ... The dough would go through this machine and it would be extruded out through air pressure, and it looked like a cow flop with a hole in it if it came out, and of course I don't think the gluten was as well developed as it would have been in a hand process.'[68]

Even devotees of mechanization had to acknowledge that the old hand-cutting methods had advantages. 'There is a difference in flavor [between the hand cut and machine cut],' James Hook of Lever Brothers admitted to the Bakery Production Men's Club of Ontario in 1953, 'and the doughnut is crispier because of less moisture in the dough.' Yet despite these sorts of limitations, Hook remained committed to machine production: 'To go back to hand labour for the sake of a greater degree of crispiness is certainly a retrograde step and it is challenging to donut flour blenders to build these desirable characteristics into their product.'[69] Research along these lines had begun even before Hook made these comments. As early as 1949, DCA had developed a machine that simulated hand-cut donuts,[70] but the results continued to be uneven throughout the postwar period. As we'll see, when donut shops arrived on the scene in the early 1960s, fresh, hand-cut donuts were a key selling point.

Other design problems were quirkier. One of the most difficult problems was the hole in the middle of the yeast donut (cake donuts were extruded in round form). Aloyzia Atalick remembers picking them out by hand. 'Your fingers would go really quick [to] pick out the centres. You get used to it, so then you can go fast. At first you don't, just like any job.' The process was eventually mechanized. 'A New Donut Hole Picker has been developed by Moline Inc., Duluth, to bring maximum automation to yeast raised donut production,' reported *Bakers' Journal* in 1960. 'Designed to operate in conjunction with the hexagon donut cutter, it has been perfected to pick up the centre pieces of the cut donut, thus offering tremendous savings in labor costs.'[71]

Even where DCA and the other companies could crack the technical (do)nut, the small scope of many operations limited the adoption of automatic machinery. Around this time, the average bakery was getting larger, in terms of both output and number of employees. After 1938, the number of bakeries fell consistently while the figures for employees continued to rise. More bakeries entered the market in the 1950s, but overall, their average size continued to grow (see figures 1.2 and 1.3). Yet while trade magazines happily celebrated these developments by

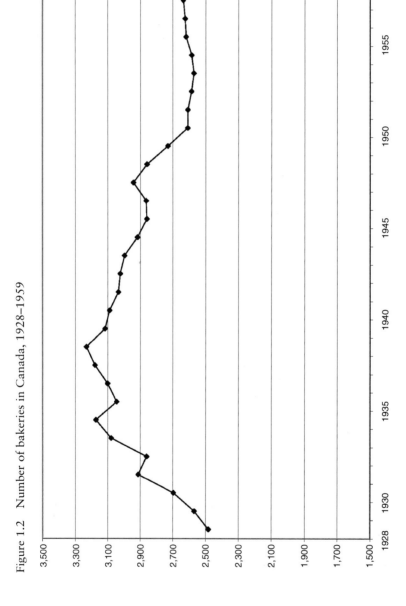

Figure 1.2   Number of bakeries in Canada, 1928–1959

Source: DBS, Bakeries, Cat. 32-203, 1961, table 1.

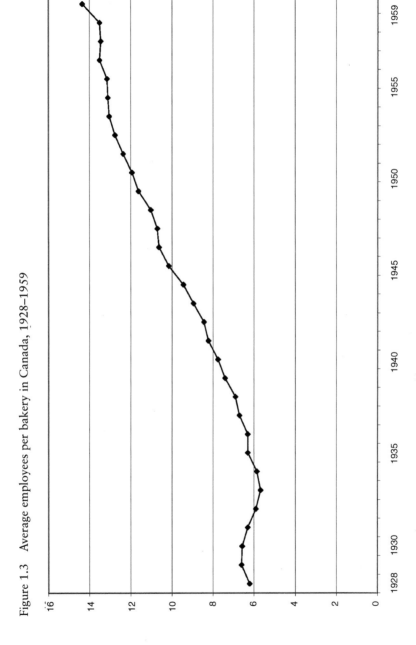

Figure 1.3   Average employees per bakery in Canada, 1928–1959

Source: DBS, Bakeries, Cat. 32-203, 1961, table 1.

Table 1.1 Typical costs for labour-saving doughnut equipment, 1955

Mixer	$1,800 and up
Scales	$25–$1,200
Proofer	$2000–$4000
Cutter	$125–$7,000
Fryer	$300–$9,000
Turner	$600–$700
Glazer	$600–$4,000
Stacker	$1,300–$1,800
Conveyers	Variable
Icing machine	$500–$800
Wrapping machine	Variable

Source: *Canadian Baker*, May 1955, 25.

pointing to the size and modernity of the most advanced firms, baking continued to show a profile that historians have termed 'combined and uneven development,' with large, sophisticated operations existing alongside a variety of smaller and more primitive ones.[72] Even as bakeries became larger on average, the vast majority (almost 70 per cent) of operations continued to be individually owned or family-run, of the sort that produced small batches of a variety of products. Even in 1958, after more than a decade of postwar growth, almost 90 per cent of Canadian bakeries employed fewer than fifteen workers; more than half employed fewer than five.[73]

More striking than total growth was its distribution. Much of the initial postwar growth did not involve large bakeries getting larger, but small ones becoming medium-sized. From 1952 to 1958, for example, the total number of bakeries in Canada increased by fifty-two (from 2,585 to 2,637), but most of the growth was clustered in the middle range of the bakery hierarchy. There were still relatively few large bakeries (those employing more than one hundred actually declined by one), and small bakeries hardly proliferated (growing by only six). The bulk of the growth came in the middle rungs of the bakery hierarchy, among those that employed between five and fifty workers. Though they made up only 43 per cent of bakeries in 1952, middle-range bakeries accounted for 75 per cent of the growth by the end of the decade (if we included bakeries with fifty to ninety-nine employees, the figures would be 43 per cent and 90 per cent). Most donut specializers inhabited this part of the hierarchy. Homestead had grown to about twelve employees by 1959; Honey Cream to twenty employees a year later; and even the

Table 1.2   Canadian bakeries by revenue groups, 1955

Revenue	Number	%
Under $10,000	431	16.5
$10,000–24,999	872	33.3
$25,000–49,999	616	23.5
$50,000–99,999	333	12.7
$100,000–199,999	156	6.0
$200,000–499,999	100	3.8
$500,000–999,999	54	2.1
Above $1,000,000	56	2.1
Total	2,618	100

Source: DBS, 32-203, *Bakeries*, 1955, table 4b.

comparatively large Doughnut House in Toronto employed only thirty-six.[74]

The broader point may be that the modernization of baking in the early postwar period was most often tied to the partial adoption of standardized, mechanized, continuous flow methods by small bakeries that wanted to get a little larger. Certainly, by the 1960s, this is how industry observers described postwar developments. 'There has been a trend in the industry particularly in the middle-size bakeries and smaller ones to meet with the growing demand for doughnuts by installing new equipment,' *Bakers Journal* reported in 1967.[75] But whatever its wider implications, the size of the standard operation had important consequences for the donut business. Mechanization, especially for yeast production, was often quite expensive (automatic proofers particularly so), and large volumes were necessary to justify the expense. The complete package of automatic machinery was certainly out of reach for most Canadian bakers, whose annual sales in the mid-1950s hovered around $25,000 or less (see tables 1.1 and 1.2). Most operations, then, took a pragmatic rather than a scientific approach, automating if possible, mechanizing where practical, and relying on workers for the rest. Machine companies pitched cheaper, less sophisticated equipment, but most production involved mixing human labour into a partially mechanized process. 'Bakers' helpers,' typically young men, might be used to move products between machines, while female workers staffed the packaging and wrapping process, which was often the last procedure to be automated. 'With the exception of a few very large bakers,' *Canadian Baker* noted, 'most donut plants are a series of compromises.'[76]

'In the Kindergarten Class'

At some point in my interview with Ernest and Aloyzia Atalick, their daughter (also named Aloyzia), who had arrived to videotape the interview for family posterity, stepped out from behind her camera to describe a section of the Homestead production line. 'It went down one wall,' she said, sweeping her hands forward and then turning them squarely to the left, 'came around, and went back the other way.' It was a particularly interesting moment in one of my most enjoyable interviews. The Atalicks are an amusing and generous family. They must have served me a dozen pieces of pie while they told entertaining tales of life in the Niagara Peninsula in the 1940s, described the serendipity of economic success in donut wholesaling in the 1950s, and reviewed their ill-fated plunge into the peat moss business in the 1960s. But despite the volume of chocolate cream pie and interesting stories, the image that stuck in my mind was Aloyzia's hands pushing outward and cutting left, mimicking the movement of donuts through Homestead's rollers and cutters.

I could not count the number of times I encountered the same motion during interviews: hands carving linear motions outward from the body, always to illustrate or give shape to some point about the donut business. If I were of a more postmodern bent, I might have spotted the connection earlier, seeing a chance to explore the way ideas inscribe themselves into the very bodies of their subjects, shaping human movement to the linear imagination of modernity. My agenda was somewhat more mundane, but the point remains. In the donut business, capitalists created and captured linear motion. The donut was first invented as a mass commodity by a group of industrial wholesalers, who dreamed not of maternal icons and nostalgic feasts but of the movement of standardized products along continuous flow production lines. In this sense, although the donut was never more than a minor consumer product in those years, it expressed the twentieth-century ethos of mass production, the cultural belief that through scientific research and engineering skill, products could be transformed into standardized, specialized, and modern commodities.

Yet outside the streamlined confines of DCA in Trenton, this kind of continuous flow modernity seemed ad hoc and partial, and innovation seemed to come from several directions, even among the larger operations. Most companies probably adopted the method of the Atalicks, increasing their volumes by mixing designing with buying, tinkering with borrowing. Automation was a kind of mantra, repeated over and over again in trade magazines, a rhetoric that spoke to the promise of technological progress and to the ethos of mass production. But few operations could achieve it in practice. Fewer still adopted the language of science. This is not surprising, since most modernizing projects meet practical limitations of imagination, economics, environment, and distance.[77]

Yet while donut modernity faced real limitations, it did have noticeable effects. Ernest Atalick was no scientist, and by the standards of the 1950s he owned only a medium-sized bakery, inhabiting (in his words) the 'kindergarten class.' Still, he studied other operations like Freddie's with a careful eye, adopting and adapting procedures to improve and streamline his own production. However partial his efforts, he still marvelled at the 'fancy new fryer that automatically flipped the donuts.' Many others saw the promise of new production methods as well, whether it meant rigging or leasing large conveyors and cutters, or just creating a consumer spectacle by rolling a small machine to the window. The invention of the donut as a mass commodity owed not just to large operations like DCA, but to the willingness of smaller, local entrepreneurs to embrace the vision of the modern, industrial donut, even while their decisions were shaped by the economic structure of the industry. By the time the Atalicks left the donut business in 1961, the basic structure of these developments had been set. Big bakeries and emerging donut specializers enthusiastically embraced this modern project, and many continued impressive growth into the 1960s and 1970s.[78]

But if donut specializers like the Atalicks were willing to embrace innovation in production, they never fully understood the promise of direct retailing. Many built impressive distribution networks on their own or through jobbers, but by the 1960s, their marketing strategies seemed curiously old-fashioned. No donut specialist saw much future in retail operations, preferring to leave that end of the business to other organizations that appeared in the first burst of mass consumption in Canada: variety stores, snack bars, and chain stores.[79] Indeed, the wholesalers hardly dealt with the consumer at all. Glaz-O-Nut had a small retail store on Robson Street in Vancouver, but it was a minor part of the operation, one that covered the rent and overhead on the plant but contributed little in the way of profits. In Toronto, Margaret's sold seconds at its East York plant (much to the delight of neighbourhood children), and in the mid-1960s, the company set up a donut shop in one corner of its factory. Later, it toyed with the idea of expanding this retail operation, even hiring a Mister Donut franchisee as a secret consultant on the project. Eventually, the plans were scrapped. 'We were manufacturers, we weren't retailers,' Tom Brazier mused years later, summing up the typical approach of the wholesale operators. 'We dabbled in expanding our retail stores, and hindsight would indicate that it would have been a good thing to focus on rather than dabble in.'[80]

2 'Our New Palace of Donut Pleasure': The Donut Shop and Consumer Culture, 1961–1976

In January 1966, Country Style Donuts invited consumers to its 'new palace of donut pleasure' in Oakville, Ontario, an affluent suburb thirty miles west of Toronto, by placing a half-page advertisement in the local newspaper. At this time, Country Style was an upstart chain with a handful of outlets in Ontario, and the company was no advertising innovator. In both idea and image, the ad was busy, addressing an astonishingly wide variety of potential donut eaters by delivering a two hundred-word pastiche of messages both practical and spectacular. At base, the ad simply announced the core features of a 1960s donut shop. It celebrated, for example, the tremendous variety and outstanding quality of the outlet's offerings, bragging loudly of 'over 56 varieties' (plus fancies) and repeatedly marshalling adjectives like 'mouthwatering' (twice) and 'fresh' (eight times). It suggested buying donuts for special occasions (like church socials) and for everyday routines (inviting regular customers to join the 'Coffee and Counter Club'). Short customer testimonials (presumably apocryphal) highlighted the many virtues of a Country Style shop declaring 'everything is so fresh and clean,' 'there's lots of parking space,' 'the best coffee I've ever tasted,' and 'so many varieties to choose from.' The last one summed the message up: 'Oakville needs something like this.'[1]

If advertising is a form of 'capitalist realism' – a set of aesthetic sensibilities that glorify 'the pleasures and freedoms of consumer choice' and 'articulate some of the operative values of ... capitalism' – then Country Style's invitation to potential customers speaks to much broader ideas and developments.[2] The advertisement was obviously placed for a specific, and local, commercial purpose – to attract consumers to a new business in the area – but it did more than enumerate the many exciting features of one particular donut shop. In a rudimentary way, it articulated many of the core ingredients of postwar consumer culture, bringing together automobile convenience, consistent quality across space, and a tremendous variety of tastes. Moreover, by suggesting that 'Oakville needs' a 'new palace of donut pleasure,' the ad (unintentionally) broke down the distinction between utility and desire, one of the deep tensions in North America's consumer culture. By 1970, residents of nearby Brock Street, engaged in ongoing battles for their neighbourhood peace and quiet, would disagree strongly that the area 'needed' the outlet. At the beginning, though, Country Style promised to merge the mundane pattens of everyday life with new forms of convenience and consumption.

This chapter examines the early years of the donut shop in Canada, focusing on how it structured the consumer experience by offering a combination of convenience, pleasure, and sociability and tried to ameliorate – only half consciously – many of the cleavages and tensions of postwar consumer culture. I start by examining the advent of donut shops in Canada as part of the development of a new geography of convenience that emerged after 1955. Next, I discuss how the donut shop's core products – donuts and coffee – fit the values of postwar consumer culture. Finally, I examine the donut shop's early customer base, its role as a social space, and conflicts over youthful misbehaviour, which raised difficulties for owners and neighbourhoods alike. Throughout, I argue that the donut shop offered a consumer experience that, while in part new, was at the same time built on continuities with earlier forms of popular culture. As such, it exposed some of the tensions inherent in consumer culture; it also expressed the complex social dynamics that arose as various groups – businesses, but also families, youth, police, and government officials – struggled to make (and make sense of) the postwar geography of consumption.

'Markets Today Have a New Dimension'

When Country Style arrived in Oakville, the donut shop idea was not common in Canada, though neither was it entirely new. Before the 1960s, donut retailing had many levels: small bakers, variety stores, street vendors, grocery stores, and others. But except for donut outlets like Downyflake Donuts and Faymakers in Toronto and a few others scattered across big-city Canada, few entrepreneurs were drawn to the idea or the name 'donut shop.' With the advent of shopping malls in the

1950s, a few donut specialty shops began to appear in growing suburban areas. Charles Downyflake Donuts, for example, opened in the Hamilton Shopping Centre in 1956 as an extension of a local coffee-shop business, using a DCA machine to grab the attention of mall patrons. The name was eventually changed to Sally's Donuts, and the outlet passed through several owners.[3]

The genealogy of modern Canadian donut culture begins in 1961 when two American chains, Mister Donut and Dunkin' Donuts, opened outlets in Ontario and Quebec. Both expressed the continental links that shaped Canadian economic development in the twentieth century. Bill Rosenberg started Dunkin' Donuts in Quincy, Massachusetts (near Boston) in 1950. The former shipyard worker built Industrial Luncheon Service into a hundred-unit coffee truck business after the Second World War. He soon realized that donuts accounted for 40 per cent of his sales and profits, so he decided to open a retail donut shop, which he called Open Kettle. In 1955, Rosenberg changed the name to Dunkin' Donuts and began to sell franchises. The idea caught on, and the chain had grown to 350 outlets by 1969. In Canada, Dunkin' opened its first shop in Montreal in 1961, and followed up with a handful of outlets in Montreal and Ottawa over the next decade. Dunkin's major rival, Mister Donut, was founded in 1955 by Rosenberg's accountant. When it arrived in Canada in late 1961 and early 1962 with outlets in Kitchener and Scarborough (a suburb of Toronto), the chain's headquarters was in Westwood, Massachusetts. In 1966, however, it opened a branch office in suburban Toronto.[4]

Tim Hortons and Country Style, Canada's 'indigenous' companies, began in 1962 and 1963, and initially borrowed heavily from existing American chains. Jim Charade came to the donut business as salesman and donut plant manager for Vachon, the iconic Quebec snack food company. Unable to persuade Vachon to open retail donut shops in Ontario, Charade toured Mister Donut's Massachusetts headquarters in the hope of acquiring a franchise north of the border. On his way back to Canada, he decided he could do it himself, and opened his first donut shop, called Your Donuts, on Lawrence Avenue in Scarborough. After meeting hockey star Tim Horton a year later, Charade began to think that celebrity might be an effective marketing tool. The two men formed a partnership, renamed the donut shop Tim Horton Donuts and opened a handful of Tim Horton hamburger restaurants around greater Toronto. The hamburger outlets soon failed, and the donut business expanded slowly, finally opening its first franchise on Ottawa Street in

Hamilton in 1964. Tim Hortons' main Canadian competitor, Country Style Donuts, began when its Canadian founder, Alan Lowe, spotted a small American chain that he figured he could franchise for the Canadian market. Over the next decade, a few independent shops joined these early franchisors, although independents seem to have been comparatively rare until the 1970s.[5]

Donut chains aimed to feed (and to feed off) Canada's burgeoning automobile culture. Motor vehicle registrations in Canada more than doubled between 1945 and 1952, and had doubled again by 1964, far outpacing population growth.[6] Car ownership continued to vary widely by region, type of municipality (urban, surburban, or rural), and income, but the automobile's triumph in everyday life was undeniable. What was particularly notable about car ownership after the war was how deeply it penetrated the populace. Rates of ownership relative to population recorded rapid and steady increases: in 1953, no province averaged one car per household; by 1966, only Newfoundland and Quebec did not. Car ownership was especially common in metropolitan southern Ontario, where donut chains initially thrived.[7]

The raw data only hint at how dramatically the car transformed everyday life. While it had certainly altered city life before the war, it had mainly reshuffled existing urban spaces that had already been stretched out by earlier transportation technologies. Moreover, unlike in the United States, where car ownership continued to grow even during the Great Depression, Canadian figures showed little overall growth until after the Second World War.[8] At that point, however, the car burst out of the existing urban fabric and began remaking the landscape, creating what historian Kenneth Jackson called a 'drive-in society.'[9] Farmers' fields were transformed overnight into webs of subdivisions, at first haphazardly and then with increasing efficiency by the late 1950s. Provincial governments ploughed unprecedented funds into highway building, and municipalities widened roads and built new ones, all to manage the relentless flow of traffic.[10] Economic developments reinforced these trends. Industry had been decentralizing since the late nineteenth century, but the internal combustion engine accelerated the process considerably. A survey conducted by the Canadian Association of Real Estate Boards found that 22 of 32 Canadian cities reported industrial decentralization by 1954 and that 23 had experienced some degree of commercial sprawl. In southern Ontario, huge industrial areas sliced through suburban municipalities like Etobicoke and Scarborough and stretched even farther outwards along the Queen Elizabeth Way and

Highway 401. As workplaces spread out, so did workers. 'Today, it is not unusual for workers to live from between twenty-five and forty miles from their place of work,' the *Financial Post* noted in 1962.[11]

The car was much more than a convenient way to get to work. In Hamilton, Ontario, for example, traffic planners discovered in 1961 that the 'typical' family averaged more than six car trips a day, hinting at a transformation of social patterns that went beyond the daily commute.[12] Most exciting to retailers, of course, was the stretching out of shopping patterns. 'Since before the last World War, our market potentials are no longer ... confined within city and town limits,' L.R. Atwater told the Toronto chapter of the American Marketing Association. 'Markets today have a new dimension, which is changing every day to increase the potential range of every retail business: a dynamic dimension of movement which erases the static lines of civil divisions that used to be our units of measurement. The new dimension is travel time by automobile.' For Atwater, speaking in 1955, the main feature of this new style of commerce was the ability of traditional downtowns to reach out to their fringes, drawing in retail dollars from suburban and exurban areas still underserviced by commercial institutions.[13] But as the 1960s approached, the new dynamics of automobile commerce changed: consumers continued to stretch out their shopping, but increasingly bypassed traditional commercial areas for newer institutions. The shopping mall grew to rival the downtown retail district, keeping more dollars and more consumers in fringe areas, and haphazard auto-oriented commercial strips mushroomed on the outskirts of existing communities as retailers targeted booming residential populations.[14]

Donut chains positioned themselves at the heart of this burgeoning automobile culture. Dunkin' Donuts chose sites on streets where at least 15,000 cars passed by each day at no more than forty miles per hour, figuring that anyone going faster would be unlikely to stop.[15] On its arrival in Canada from the United States in 1961, Mister Donut built freestanding outlets along busy suburban arterials or, less often, at the ends of strip malls on high-traffic roads. Aiming for such locations meant sharing space with other types of drive-in commerce. An A&W hamburger stand, a Midas Muffler outlet, two gas stations and a strip mall flanked the Mister Donut on Eglinton Avenue East in Scarborough.[16] Canadian chains pursued broadly similar strategies. One of Country Style's busiest shops (opened 1965) was located along a drive-in strip on Wellington Road in London, straight across from a large hos-

Aerial view of Scarborough, Ontario, 1949, looking east from Eglinton Avenue and Victoria Park Avenue. By this time, some scattered industrial and residential development had mixed into the area's rural landscape. (City of Toronto Archives, series 35, file 1, Victoria Park and Eglinton, 1949. Reprinted with permission of Northway-Photomap Inc)

pital, on the way to or from Highway 401 (the new cross-province expressway), and on a main commuting route in and out of town. In Scarborough, the outlet at Kennedy Road and Progress (opened 1967) had all the features of a successful donut shop: on a high-traffic strip, just off Highway 401, and at an access point to a large industrial park.[17] Tim Hortons' third outlet (1965) was at University and Weber in Waterloo, a commercial area that had begun developing in 1958, after Weber Street was extended into Kitchener, making it a key north-south route for the Twin Cities.[18] The practice of locating on drive-in strips was not always based on exact traffic counts or precise measures of potential business. Many independent operators chose locations based on their own knowledge of the local community and their intuitive sense of

Aerial view of Scarborough, Ontario, 1973, looking east from Eglinton Avenue and Victoria Park Avenue. By 1973, Scarborough had all the ingredients of donut culture: industrial plants, residential subdivisions, widened roads, and large parking lots. (City of Toronto Archives, series 35, file 1, Victoria Park and Eglinton, 1973. Reprinted with permission of Northway-Photomap Inc)

changing geography, or by informally inspecting traffic flows near a potential location. Even into the mid-1970s, Tim Hortons found many of its locations by flying over a community for a bird's eye view of busy streets.[19]

Besides establishing freestanding outlets on suburban strips, some donut companies opened outlets in new, enclosed shopping malls. Mister Donut's outlet in St Catharines – the first chain donut shop in the city – found a welcome home in the Pen Centre, a regional mall built on the site of an old peach orchard. In 1971, Tim Hortons located its twenty-fourth outlet in Sherway Gardens, a mammoth regional shopping mall 10 kilometres west of downtown Toronto. These indoor

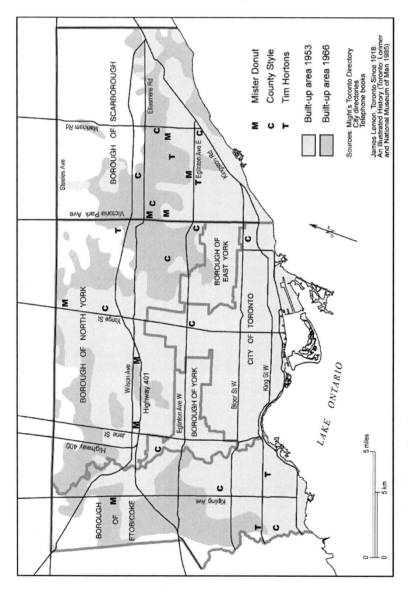

Map 2.1   Chain donut shop locations, Toronto, 1970

THE DONUT HOUSE
- 856 Park Royal -

We are happy and proud to be a new member of the fast growing Park Royal Shopping Centre.
You have no doubt been watching the activity on the corner and been wondering what's going on.
Well, the last nail has been pounded and we are now ready to open our Donut House,
specializing in many varieties of fresh doughnuts made hourly right before your eyes.

**Watch for us in our window
. . . we'll be watching for you**

We Are Open June 28

Hol'n One Donut Co. B.C. Ltd

Advertisement for the opening of the first Hol'n One Donut House, West Vancouver, 1959. (Seller Family Scrapbook, courtesy of Larry Seller)

outlets were comparatively rare in Ontario; for the most part the chains targeted commercial strips and small plazas, where they opened free-standing outlets or storefront shops.[20]

In contrast, out in British Columbia, the Seller family focused on shopping centres. Beginning in 1959, Hol'n One Donuts became the only pre-1960 donut specializer to aggressively open donut shops, finding locations in the largest shopping malls around the Lower Mainland. The family had backed into the idea, however. In the beginning,

Hol'n One had only one small retail shop – 'only a little two-bit thing,' in the words of Nina Seller – in the front of its headquarters on Fraser Street, close to the old core of Vancouver. The Sellers started their first Donut House on the suggestion of real estate scouts from Park Royal Shopping Centre, just across the Lion's Gate Bridge in West Vancouver. 'These three gentlemen came in ... and I gave them their donuts,' she recalled. 'They kept coming back for two or three weeks ...They were from Park Royal and they were out looking for new types of businesses that were out of the ordinary ... They took us over there and this is how we opened our first shop.' Though the new plaza shop was 'out of the ordinary' for Vancouver, it was not entirely new: the Sellers modelled it on a similar effort in Seattle. Over the next decade, the family opened a dozen more Hol'n One Donut Houses, locating almost exclusively in the largest outdoor and indoor malls around Metropolitan Vancouver: Park Royal in 1959, Burnaby's Brentwood Mall in 1961, Richmond Square in 1965, and others, all locations at the core of the area's postwar suburban boom.[21]

Large shopping malls were a key feature of postwar drive-in landscapes, but unlike donut chains in central Canada, Hol'N One Donut Houses were not designed to serve mobile consumers directly. The Sellers opened only two freestanding outlets on suburban commercial strips (both of them outside of Metropolitan Vancouver). Instead of maximizing convenience for drivers, they preferred to open plaza locations that would attract shoppers and mall employees on break from work or shopping. 'We just wanted good locations in the mall where lots of people walked by the front door,' Larry Seller recalled. 'Before we opened Park Royal,' added Nina Seller, 'I would go over there and sit in front of this empty store and count the people that went by to see if there was enough traffic to warrant something like that. We had a very good location because we were across from Woodward's.'[22]

There were many ways to exploit suburbanizing populations. Some donut shops located in small towns that were part of larger metropolitan networks, reflecting the spreading out of both population and patterns of consumption. When the Dominion Bureau of Statistics (DBS) started calculating metropolitan populations in 1951, Ontario's seven largest metropolitan areas already accounted for almost half the province's population, and the figure grew slowly but steadily throughout the next two decades. As they were drawn into the metropolitan network, towns like Dundas and Richmond Hill became attractive to mass retailers despite their small populations. Dundas, for example, had a population of 17,000 when Tim Hortons located there in 1973, but the town was part of the larger Hamilton market and had been trading consumers with the western section of Hamilton for more than a decade. The same point could be made about Mister Donut's Richmond Hill location, which opened in the late 1960s. Although the town had only 20,000 people, it was a suburban community on a main commuting route to Toronto. Moreover, it was growing rapidly: by 1971, its population would exceed 32,000.[23]

Initially, the upstart Ontario chains mapped out yet another strategy for exploiting suburbanizing populations: they located some of their early outlets along established commercial strips on the fringes of prewar development. In 1962, Country Style Donuts opened its first outlet on Yonge Street just south of Eglinton Avenue, an area that had been developed well before the First World War. The chain would continue to focus on traditional retail strips in the Toronto area. Country Style's outlet number two was at Lawrence Avenue and Weston Road, just off the former main street of Weston, which had been founded as a separate village on the Humber River in the nineteenth century before being linked to Toronto by streetcars and commuter rail in the early twentieth. The area became a site for industrial development after the First World War and was finally swept into the first burst of suburban sprawl in the late 1940s. The locations of outlets three and four had similar development histories.[24]

Tim Hortons' early growth was similar. Early growth in its core market around Hamilton emphasized commercial areas such as Ottawa Street, Concession Road, and Westdale, all areas of significant prewar commercial and residential development. The eastward expansion of Hamilton had already reached Ottawa Street by 1910, and the strip was developing as a significant commercial area in years before the First World War. By the 1950s, Ottawa Street had become one of Hamilton's major shopping areas, most famous for its furniture and fabric outlets, which drew customers from around the Metropolitan Hamilton area. Concession Street had been the traditional commercial section of Hamilton Mountain as far back as the 1930s and was entering its 'golden age' in the decades after the Second World War.[25]

While they could trace their origins to earlier pedestrian and streetcar commerce, these traditional commercial strips had been adapting to serve the car long before the advent of donut drive-ins. For example, the site of the Country Style outlet at Danforth and Victoria Park in east Toronto had been a gas station since the 1930s. In Hamilton, the

Ottawa Street business district had been drawing auto commerce since the 1920s. The transformation of these commercial areas accelerated after the war. Ottawa Street was dependent enough on cars by the late 1950s that the city made provisions for off-street parking. In 1955, the site of the old Hamilton Jockey Club racetrack was transformed into the Greater Hamilton Shopping Centre, with parking for 5,000 cars.[26]

Many of these early donut shops were located along well-travelled commuting routes between older fringe areas and the new, postwar suburbs. When Jim Charade chose the site for his first franchise, Ottawa Street ran parallel to Kenilworth, the most direct link between the city's eastern industrial area and the exploding postwar suburbs on Hamilton Mountain. The main Dofasco gate loomed at the north end of Ottawa Street, and Charade was hoping that bleary-eyed shift workers would make the short detour for a coffee and donut.[27] Country Style's Weston location sat in an area that had been well developed for many years, but west across the Humber River, Lawrence Avenue was lined with mass subdivisions of the postwar era. More significantly, though, Lawrence was a bus route linking a number of built-up areas to the new industrial corridor out by the airport.[28]

Donut shops, then, were locating quite deliberately along the geographic mainstream of postwar automobile commerce, with its fast food outlets, shopping malls, and strip plazas. But car culture was not just a metropolitan phenomenon. In the 1960s, the ideal donut community had a minimum population of 50,000, but the figure was never absolute. Early in Tim Hortons' development, co-owner Ron Joyce decided that big-city markets were more complicated than those in smaller cities. Though Tim Hortons did open outlets in major metropolitan areas – its core market was Hamilton, after all, and the chain had three shops in Toronto by 1970[29] – it was also expanding into small cities of 30,000 to 60,000 people: places like Belleville (1968), which had about 35,000, and Welland (1969), which had just over 50,000, just large enough for major donut chains. And Tim Hortons located in places with even smaller populations. Fort Erie's population was 28,000 when the chain opened there in 1973, and Chatham and St Thomas each had about 40,000 people when it arrived in 1975.[30]

In smaller cities, drive-in culture was less developed. When the chain arrived in Welland in 1969, it joined a smattering of other drive-in enterprises along a relatively new commercial strip. Niagara Street was developing into an auto-oriented strip after 1960 (with the process accelerating after 1965), and Tim Hortons was one of the first chain fast food outlets to open there, Dairy Queen having opened two years earlier, and Red Barn Hamburgers at about the same time as Hortons. Yet it was hardly the stereotypical suburban strip. Niagara Street ran from the city's central business district, but the drive-in section was only about two thousand feet long, and once a consumer passed it, the street quickly trailed off into a patchwork of farmers' fields and a few scattered houses. The city itself had experienced only limited decentralization.[31]

The Tim Hortons in Welland, like its big-city counterparts, tapped into the extensive movements of auto-bound customers. But these customers were not the stereotypical suburb-to-city commuters. Niagara Street was a main route to the larger city of St Catharines to the north, which fit a small-city pattern of driving and consumption. Outside large metropolitan centres, the development of drive-in culture seemed less a question of suburbanites choosing between local shopping plazas and traditional downtowns than of commuters' and consumers' willingness to follow better and wider highways to nearby cities and towns, and to commute from rural villages to nearby urban centres. By 1973, marketing students at Niagara College would discover that one-third of Welland residents 'most often' shopped for non-food items by driving twenty miles north to St Catharines instead of making much shorter trips to local businesses. This was no cause for celebration for most St Catharines merchants, however, since 95 per cent of those out-of-towners visited suburban shopping malls like the Pen Centre. Small-city consumers followed similar patterns elsewhere. In 1962 the *Financial Post* reported that 50 per cent of cars leaving discount plazas in London, Ontario, turned south toward St Thomas, twenty miles away. Six months later, the mayor of nearby Woodstock, Ontario, expressed less concern about the growth of local malls than the magnetic attraction of London's shopping areas, which were more than thirty miles away but easy to reach on the newly opened 401 superhighway.[32]

The Geography of Convenience

Car culture, then, had many expressions. Whether a donut shop appeared on a suburban strip in a burgeoning metropolis or on the fringes of a smaller city, automobile convenience remained the key criterion for success. These donut outlets were small, typically between

1,200 and 1,400 square feet, including the production area. Their interior seating was relatively limited – often only twelve stools at the counter and a few tables. Building designs facilitated fast-in, fast-out traffic rather than comfortable surroundings: the take-out area and display cases were directly in front of the door, while the tables and eat-in counter were placed off to the side. But if buildings were small, the parking lots were not, since even a good location was useless without adequate parking. Parking could be a particular problem on traditional strips, no matter how much they had adapted to serve the automobile. John Fitzsimmons, a regular at the first Tim Hortons first franchise on Hamilton's Ottawa Street in the 1960s, remembered that the parking lot at the outlet was so small that cars often lined up into the street, especially during shift change at the Dofasco plant.[33]

Losing cars to line-ups in the street signalled a broader problem. Donuts were an impulse purchase – marketing studies backed up the common-sense view that most customers were attracted by the location rather than advertising or brand name[34] – so visibility and access from the street were crucial ingredients for a successful outlet. Donut shop design was a classic example of what Chester Liebs called 'architecture for speed reading.'[35] Pylon signs were designed for maximum efficiency in attracting motoring customers. They were tall and brightly lit and displayed a minimum number of words. Many of them spun, or were surrounded by flashing lights. Finally, the signs were placed out at the roadway rather than close to the shop.[36] Big, bright signs were useless, however, if the outlet itself was obscured. Alongside raw data from traffic counts, then, the Dunkin' Donuts real estate team considered the visibility of the outlet from either direction at a good distance down the road, since customers needed time to see the shop and slow down. In strip plazas, a location near the entrance was an absolute necessity. The Mister Donut at Kipling Plaza in suburban Toronto was sited right next to the parking lot entrance. At nearby Jane and Wilson, the same chain built a freestanding outlet at the edge of a strip plaza parking lot, positioned to capture drivers off Jane Street as well as shoppers as they came and went.[37]

Donut chains were merely one part of a new trend in the geography of convenience. Between the 1920s and the mid-1950s, roadside food service emerged haphazardly in Canada. Individual entrepreneurs dominated the trade, joined after the Second World War by a few small chains that spanned local markets.[38] Beginning around the mid to late 1950s, however, existing American chains and new Canadian equivalents began to establish a real presence in Canada, altering the geo-

Table 2.1   Fast food/drive-in chains established in Canada, 1953–1965

Chain	Year	Product	First Canadian outlet
Dairy Queen	1953	Ice cream	Estevan, SK
A&W	1956	Root beer/fast food	Winnipeg
Tastee Freez	1958	Ice cream	N/A
Kentucky Fried Chicken	1959	Fried chicken	Saskatoon
Dog 'N Suds	1959	Root beer/hot dogs	Saskatoon
Chicken Delight	1959	Chicken	Winnipeg
Johnny Johnson's*	1959	Hamburgers	Scarborough, ON
Harvey's*	1959	Hamburgers	Richmond Hill, ON
Royal Burger*	1959	Hamburgers	Ottawa
Burger Chef	1961	Hamburgers	Ontario
Henry's	1961	Hamburgers	Ontario
Frostop	1961	Root beer/fast food	Manitoba
Dunkin' Donuts	1961	Donuts	Montreal
Mister Donut	1962	Donuts	North York, ON
Tim Horton Drive-In*	1962	Hamburgers	Scarborough, ON
Tim Horton Donuts*	1963	Donuts	Scarborough, ON
Aunt Jemima Kitchens	1962	Pancakes	Scarborough, ON
Red Barn Systems	1963	Hamburgers	Scarborough, ON
Country Style Donuts*	1963	Donuts	Toronto
Dairy Belle	1964	Ice cream	N/A

Note: 'Chain' refers to a business that grew to multiple outlets beyond a single metropolitan market.
*Canadian chains.
Sources: *Canadian Hotel and Restaurant*; *Restaurants and Institutions*; *Financial Post*, various years.

graphic dynamics of roadside commerce (see table 2.1). Companies like Red Barn Hamburgers, A&W Root Beer, Country Style Donuts, and Mister Donut reached out beyond a single city almost as soon as they began Canadian operations. American donut chains already had impressive reach in the United States, comprising dozens of outlets by the time they expanded into Canada in 1961, and they quickly formed nationwide aspirations north of the border. 'We aim to make Mister Donut a coast to coast franchise chain with units reaching from the Maritimes through Vancouver,' Canadian supervisor Joe Lugossy commented in 1965.[39] Smaller Canadian chains quickly reached out across space as well. In 1966, Country Style was only three years old, but it already had outlets in Toronto, London, and Sudbury.[40]

Donut shops played a minor role in the explosion of chain drive-ins. Although they were in the mainstream of the industry, the growth of the

Table 2.2   Regional distribution of selected fast food and donut chains in Canada, 1970

Company	BC	Pra.	ON	QC	Atl.	Total
Kentucky Fried Chicken	25	72	147	30	31	307
A&W	45	77	76	27	12	237
Dairy Queen (eastern Canada)*	–	–	132	77	22	221
Dairy Queen (western Canada)*	46	47	–	–	–	93
Harvey's Hamburgers	–	1	40	33	2	76
Red Barn Hamburgers	–	–	41	–	–	41
Dog 'N Suds**	12	17	1	–	5	35
McDonald's (2 companies)†	12	7	10	–	–	29
Mister Donut	–	1	18	8	–	27
Country Style Donuts	–	–	21	–	–	21
Tim Horton Donuts	–	–	16	–	–	16

Note: 'Chain' was defined as a company that opened outlets in more than one metropolitan area.
*At this time, Dairy Queen outlets in Canada were operated by two separate companies, one covering central and eastern Canada and one covering the Prairies and British Columbia.
**Franchised units only. An additional eight units were company owned.
†In 1970, McDonald's was still split into two companies in Canada: one in Ontario and one in the West.
Source: *Canadian Hotel and Restaurant*, 15 March 1970, 43–4.

Table 2.3   Estimated share of fast food dollar volume by food type, 1970

Food	Percent
Chicken	32.0
Hamburgers	29.0
Ice Cream	23.5
Donuts	4.5
Pizza	3.5
Hot Dogs	3.0
Other*	4.5

*Other includes fish and chips (2%), pancakes (1.5%), and roast beef (1%).
Source: *Canadian Hotel and Restaurant*, 15 March 1970, 43–4.

Canadian donut business lagged behind developments in other types of fast food until the late 1970s, in terms of both number of outlets and dollar volume (see tables 2.2 and 2.3). Nationally, donuts stood at the top of the second tier of fast food, far behind chicken, hamburgers, and ice cream. Modest sales were reflected in limited size and scope. Donut chains all hovered around twenty outlets in 1970, while the leaders in the drive-in business operated dozens and even hundreds of outlets. Until McDonald's grew to dominance in the 1970s, Dairy Queen (314 outlets in 1970) and A&W (237 outlets) were the undisputed rulers of Canadian fast food, each spanning the nation. At the time, the donut chains were smaller than the modest, regional hamburger companies like Red Barn (41 outlets, mainly in Ontario) and Harvey's (76 outlets, mainly in Ontario and Quebec).[41] Information gathered by one trade magazine in 1971 reinforces these statistics, indicating that donut shops had established a presence in several urban markets but were underdeveloped relative to other types of fast food. In Hamilton, hamburger chains had penetrated the local market at a rate almost three times that of donut shops, with chicken outlets falling in between. The difference was even more dramatic in London, where burgers outpaced donuts by a margin of four to one.[42]

The figures also indicated that at this point, donut shops were still a regional development: no outlets were counted east of Montreal, and only a few west of Windsor.[43] But pull off Highway 401, which ran like a spine through the centre of the heavily industrialized Windsor-Montreal corridor, and you have been hard pressed to find a major town or city without a donut shop. A similar enumeration could have been conducted along the Golden Horseshoe's main highway, the Queen Elizabeth Way.[44] Though national statistics indicated that donuts were a minor fast food, it is fair to say that donut drive-ins had established a 'solid market' in southern Ontario and Montreal, with a very few additional outlets in the near north. This regional pattern probably reflected a number of demographic, economic, and historical factors: the concentration of urban populations in the area, the relative prosperity of the region, its proximity to the most important of the original American donut markets in the northeast and midwest, and a more mundane fact – the early donut entrepreneurs lived in the Golden Horseshoe and built their businesses out from there.[45]

Within that area, the dynamics of growth in donuts and fast food often meant that one lone donut shop sat amid several other fast food outlets. In Scarborough in 1973, the local newspaper counted an astonishing 116 take-out restaurants along the borough's four main thoroughfares, including 34 hamburger stands, 22 pizza parlours ... but only 7 donut shops. In Windsor, Country Style nabbed a great location on Tecumseh Road right across from a large Chrysler plant, yet it faced no donut competition until 1978. In Oakville, the chain had the local donut market to itself until 1969, when Tim Hortons opened across town;

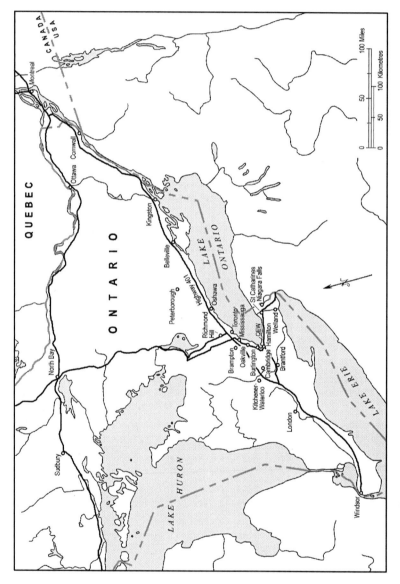

Map 2.2   Cities with chain donut outlets, Central Canada, 1970

after that, amid a proliferation of fast food outlets, no new donut shops entered the area until the 1980s.[46] Hamburger stands, fried chicken outlets, and ice cream companies competed hard for customers along the same drive-in strips, but if a donut shop could be first to an area, it often held a monopoly for a decade or more.

The Political Economy of Convenience

The geography of convenience along streets like Eglinton Avenue and Tecumseh Boulevard did not evolve through some inevitable process – it was *made* through conscious acts and choices. Entrepreneurial and business strategies relating to location, signage, access, and parking helped construct the geography of convenience, and the donut shop's place in it. These decisions, though, were reinforced by the actions and inactions of other groups and institutions.

In their practical daily decisions, for example, consumers helped reinforce the strategies of entrepreneurs. Albert DeBaeremaker was a construction worker in the 1960s, working many sites around Scarborough, Ontario. He remembered the way the Country Style at Progress and Kennedy – just south of Highway 401, right beside a large industrial park – served the car better than existing restaurants. 'In Scarborough, where you had a small restaurant, there was generally no parking,' he recalled. '[There was] maybe parking for one or two cars, [but at] a donut shop you could generally park 10 or 20 cars no problem ...The ones I went to generally had sufficient parking, because they were mainly built as a donut shop ...They were the only one in the area there where anyone could go close by and get a coffee.'[47] Owners learned these lessons quickly, if sometimes painfully. In 1966, Vladimir Ududec located his King Donut shop in a former Chinese food restaurant just down the street from the 'Four Corners' in Oshawa, the main intersection of the city. The location turned out to be a poor one, with only one parking spot in the back. When Mister Donut arrived in town a few years later, it located up the street, along the burgeoning drive-in strip east of the old central business district. Ududec tried to make the business work in Oshawa, but gave up after a couple of years and moved the family to Niagara Falls, where he found a perfect location, this time with 'a grocery store sized parking lot,' on Lundy's Lane, the main tourist route into the city.[48]

Choosing convenience reflected a kind of consumer agency, although not the form we have been trained to expect. When cultural studies scholars began to emphasize 'agency' as a theme in the 1980s, they argued that speaking to, for, and about consumers would reveal more interesting mass culture scripts, showing the reappropriation of commodities and the ironic play and transgression that shaped meaning in consumer societies. Their agenda was partly successful. While some academics now hope to swing the pendulum back towards the power of cultural producers, even scholars who are critical of cultural studies take pains to avoid dismissing consumer intelligence.[49] An additional problem was that cultural studies scholars tended to find agency in the behaviours they found most interesting, reporting the more transgressive and romantic examples and largely ignoring the mundane and routine ones.

But quite often, taking consumers seriously reveals much more pedestrian concerns: consumers might remember their first visit to a donut shop as dramatic, but their ongoing pattern was tied to convenience and routine. In 1969, Al Stortz of Welland, Ontario, owned an autobody shop on Niagara Street with his brothers. When Tim Horton himself came to Welland for the grand opening of outlet number twelve just up the street, Stortz went over, excited more by the great defenceman than by his donuts. 'I got his autograph, which I still have to this day,' Stortz told me, brandishing a letter from the Tim Hortons corporate headquarters to prove the point. He eventually became a regular – an ongoing pattern of consumption tied less to celebrity than to convenience and familiarity. He built few enduring friendships inside the shop but took salesmen there to talk business and became a familiar figure to the workers there. 'I was a regular at that shop back then,' Stortz remembered. 'I never knew the names of the girls, but they got to the point where they'd say "Hi Al" and have my coffee waiting when I came in.' A surprising number of early customers I spoke to remembered precise details about locations and parking lots but couldn't offer even the first name of another customer or staff member. 'This [shop] that used to be on Kennedy Road near Progress,' recalled Debaeremaker, 'they had transports parking on Progress – the side street there – and transport drivers used to whip in, and their parking lot was so full you could hardly get in. The guy in the gas station [next door] blocked people from going in, because a lot were sneaking over to the gas station, and then he couldn't get any of his customers parked when he was repairing the cars.'[50] The culture of donut shops was built on the quotidian and the mundane.

But to recognize that consumer choices helped shape the geography of convenience is not the same as saying that consumers produced it.

Construction at Lawrence Avenue and Markham Road, Scarborough, Ontario, 1961. The growth of automobile commerce was spurred by government spending. In Scarborough, the government of Metropolitan Toronto widened roads and opened the way for cars. Within a year of the construction shown here, the house and barn in the middle would be replaced by a Mister Donut. (City of Toronto Archives, series 3, file 286)

Consumer choices were structured by other forces and institutions. A native of east Toronto, DeBaeremaker moved to Scarborough for cheap housing: as a construction worker, buying a house was a challenge, and he felt he could get the best deal by heading to the fringes. Once there, his consumer preferences became structured by a landscape that he did not make nor entirely choose, and his daily decisions about travelling and stopping were reinforced by public policies that opened roads to drivers and that allowed and even encouraged drive-in commercial development. In the case of Scarborough, the innovative Metropolitan Toronto level of government, created by the province in 1953 and headed by Frederick 'Big Daddy' Gardiner, devoted much of its time and resources to widening, straightening, and improving roads – an agenda that went well beyond the stereotypical examples of urban highways like the Spadina Expressway. Indeed, Metro's modernizing of an entire network of arterial routes and thoroughfares under Gardiner's administration probably had a more far-reaching effect, although it attracted less attention because of the incremental nature of the process.[51]

Gardiner was not alone. Across Canada, provinces and municipalities were spending millions of dollars on both new roads and highways and on widening existing ones, often based on newly minted 'traffic plans' that assumed the automobile was the norm. The consulting firm Damas and Smith alone reshaped the geography of several cities and towns in southern Ontario, using the obstensibly objective tools of traffic counts and destination surveys to set the agenda for change. Based on this approach, consultants normally produced impressively detailed maps of drivers' desires, with arrows and travel lines projected over the existing road grid (symbolically relegated to the background), less often asking questions about how to build communities to make other transportation options viable or to privilege, say, aesthetic considerations over the movement of automobiles.[52]

Commercial zoning policies reinforced these trends. Before the Second World War, roadside commerce often took advantage of the relative lack of commercial regulations in many municipalities, or simply bypassed these rules by locating just over the municipal boundary, where entrepeneurs faced lower (rural) tax regimes and fewer regulations.[53] But even when municipalities took greater control over development and zoning after the war, their decisions often smoothed the way for cars instead of controlling them. Scarborough placed few controls on commercial growth until well after the war; then, when borough zoning regulations became more systematic, they set minimum parking standards, defined rules for proper access, and downplayed calls by some residents for controls on signage and roadside advertising. By the 1970s, many municipal officials and some residents agreed that the borough's commercial policies had helped produce a landscape dominated by fast food, car dealerships, and parking lots. Yet there had been nothing conspiratorial about these decisions. Borough officials had often merely heeded what they believed was a widespread public consensus about the benefits of convenience in car culture. Indeed, when officials began to question this form of development, they discovered that public apathy was often the biggest barrier to change.[54] 'The commercial structure of Scarboro is one of the most visually assertive aspects of the Borough,' noted one planning study in 1976. '[T]he commercial fabric ... appears as a sprawling mass of car lots, fast food eateries, grocery facilities, and department stores ... Parking lots, garish colours, plastic facades, shout and cajole at the passers by. It is only within the inner confines of a few residential neighborhoods that one can seemingly escape the tentacles of this "commercial carnival."' Planners recognized that their evocative language was not likely to produce dramatic results: 'The majority of residents appear to be fairly neutral regarding the appearance of facilities such as ... car lots, take-outs, and service stations.'[55] The tentacles weren't just reaching out. For many of the people in the 'inner confines' of those residential neighbourhoods, the 'commercial carnival' had its attractions.

'Give Ma a Treat!'

Donut shops arrived along auto-oriented commercial strips at a time of change in the consumption of their two core products, coffee and donuts. Traditionally, Canadians had been a nation of tea drinkers, perhaps because of British cultural influence. Even so, coffee's popularity increased steadily over the first half of the twentieth century (see figure 2.1), finally surpassing that of tea after the war. Per capita consumption of coffee increased by over 40 per cent between 1953 and 1962, while tea drinking actually declined by 25 per cent.[56] By the end of that period, coffee had matched tea as a popular beverage, both in raw numbers and as cultural metaphor. The widespread standardization of between-meal breaks in workplaces, designated by the distinctly American term 'coffee break' rather than the more British 'tea time,' perfectly captured the spirit of this new consumer preference. The distinction was more than semantic. By 1956, three-quarters of Canadian workers enjoyed coffee-break privileges and coffee made up half the beverages they consumed, five times as much as tea.[57] 'The coffee break is the greatest single cause for both the relative swing away from coffee in the home and for the increased consumption across the country,' one trade magazine reported of this development. 'More and more employers, realizing the value of the break period, have included them in the working schedule.'[58] Four years later, the Pan-American Coffee Bureau recorded more coffee drinkers than tea drinkers in Canada, and while per capita coffee consumption levelled off during the 1960s, tea continued its long-term decline.[59]

Donut shops appeared, therefore, just as coffee was overtaking tea as the standard hot beverage for many Canadians. Tim Hortons' donut

Figure 2.1 Per capita coffee imports into Canada

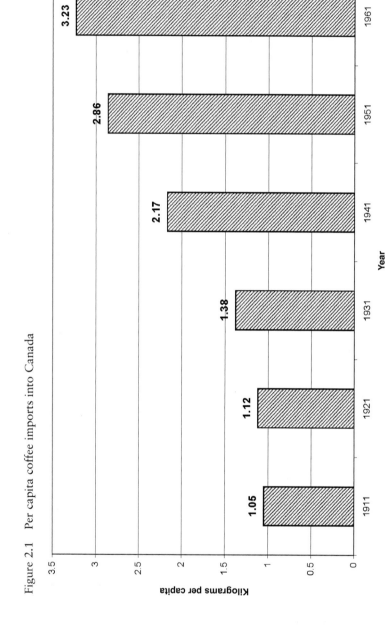

Sources: Import data from W. Clarence-Smith and S. Topik, eds., *The Global Coffee Economy in Africa, Asia, and Latin America, 1500–1989* (Cambridge: Cambridge University Press, 2003), table A19, p. 444.

boxes urged customers to 'take your next coffee break at Tim Hortons,' and even if the Ottawa Street outlet in Hamilton was too far from large factories like Dofasco to attract workers during the day, it became a regular haunt for the merchants and retail workers along the commercial strip. No matter how busy the store got, someone from Canadian Tire managed to make a trip across the street to pick up drinks and donuts for all the workers. At Park Royal Shopping Centre in West Vancouver, Woodward's employees streamed across the open plaza to the Hol'N One Donut House during break time. Many more stopped by on the way home.[60] For the most part, those workers, and other donut shop customers, were ordering coffee rather than tea.[61] It helped that donut shop coffee was fairly good. In the era of Starbucks and Second Cup, many Canadians have been trained to view donut shop coffee as second-rate, but by the standards of the 1960s, its quality was relatively high. For years, industry observers lodged complaint after complaint about poor-quality coffee at Canadian restaurants. By standardizing buying and enforcing brewing times and procedures, donut chains did more to ensure a decent cup than many traditional restaurateurs. For their efforts, two Country Style outlets in Toronto received the Pan-American Coffee Bureau's Golden Cup Award, 2 of only 152 awarded across North America.[62]

Of course, good coffee depended on more than local brewing practice. As the name suggested, the Pan-American Coffee Bureau was an international organization, founded in 1937 and charged by the major producing countries with the task of promoting coffee consumption across North America. In real terms, these countries' economies were at stake: after the mid-nineteenth century, Latin America's economic culture became more and more defined by this valuable export commodity. In the twentieth century, both states and corporate interests became more involved in efforts to stabilize supply, quality, and prices: nations forged international control agreements, scientists defined systems of grading, and corporate interests established brand names by standardizing blends and advertising heavily. By the time coffee reached Scarborough in the mid-1960s, it expressed a global political economy that hardly worked to the advantage of ordinary people in producing countries. At the outlet level, of course, the social relations of coffee were expressed in more local and quotidian terms. In interviews, consumers normally rendered the key distinction as 'grabbing a coffee' or 'going for coffee' – one implying speed and convenience, the other leisure and intimacy – reflecting coffee's dual meaning as a modern stimulant and an excuse for sociability. Through a broader lens, however, both these uses spoke to the 'forgetfulness' of twentieth century consumption – consumers were many layers and vast distances removed from the social relations of production.[63]

Today, it is only a slight exaggeration to say that donut shops are, in essence, efficient caffeine-delivery systems: donuts, bagels, muffins, and other offerings largely serve as marketing tools to sell coffee. But in the early days, although coffee was the most profitable item, selling donuts was still a core part of the business. Chains like Tim Hortons and Country Style came into a thriving donut market, riding the postwar crest of increasing sales first cultivated by industrial producers like Margaret's.[64] In addition to mere volume, donut shops had the advantages of freshness and variety. Indeed, if coffee signals the localization of vast networks of distribution, the donut (though also an expression of global political economy, in that it assembles sugar, spices, and flour from afar) shows another powerful tendency in twentieth-century consumption: the multiplication of superficial choice. For the most part, donut whole-salers specialized in large volumes of limited lines – Val's in Edmonton, for example, sold only glazed cake donuts, while Margaret's produced just four varieties. Donut drive-ins, however, offered what seemed to consumers an astonishing array of choice, with toppings, dips, nuts, fill-ings, jams, powders, and sprinkles added and combined to transform a few basic shells into dozens of varieties.

Indeed, donut drive-ins seemed a perfect metaphor for the two con-tradictory impulses of consumer culture: they multiplied the variety and choice of goods even while homogenizing taste and fashion. From houses to cars to toasters, postwar mass producers offered a basic com-modity with an increasing number of options and colours to give the appearance of maximum choice and varied design.[65] However mundane the particular example, the Country Style sign in front of each store – 'Country Style Donuts, 56 Varieties, Superb Coffee' – announced three key pillars of mass consumption: brand name, near limitless variety, and the promise of consistent quality. That underneath fifty-six icings and glazes lay the same DCA or Jo-Lo mix used at Val's or Margaret's seemed less important to consumers than the almost revolutionary choice of flavours. For Tim Lambert of St Catharines, who grew up on Homestead Bakery's honey-dipped donuts, the spinning donut case at the Mister Donut at the Pen Centre was a minor consumer spectacle, highlighting the tremendous variety and choice available.[66]

The novelty of donut shops came through time and again in interviews with entrepreneurs and customers. The problem, of course, was that novelty was always a risky endeavour, even in a culture obsessed with pursuing it. However varied the appeal to taste, the idea of specializing in donuts did not impress many observers as the brightest entrepreneurial idea. Lynda Lalonde remembered that her friends thought she was crazy going into the donut business in 1969: 'We had ... very little support from anyone ... People thought we were ludicrous, absolutely nuts. I mean, how could you make money off a coffee and a donut?' Brian Wallace recalled thinking the same thing when a friend suggested they visit the Tim Horton Donut Drive-In on Ottawa Street in Hamilton. Wallace agreed, figuring he would get a hamburger, and was surprised and bemused to discover that the drive-in had only donuts and coffee. Wallace remembered going back to his navy post in Halifax and telling all his friends that Horton would surely lose his money on such a silly idea.[67]

Increasing volumes, the wonder of novelty, and the spectacle of limitless variety were values at the core of consumer culture. As early as the 1920s, the mission of sellers and producers across the North American consumer goods landscape had been to increase the appearance of variety within a standardized framework, aiming to stimulate the senses, to free up desire, and to create a new 'consumption ethic' that would break down the distinction between wants and needs. General Motors, with its embrace of colour, style, status, and product line segmentation (offering a variety of cars at different price points for different kinds of customers) was an early pioneer of this strategy, but many companies, from towel makers to stationary suppliers, followed suit. During the postwar boom, more companies joined the fray. Faced with households filled with all the 'required' standard appliances, for example, makers of fridges and stoves embraced model variety as a strategy for maintaining sales, realizing that fewer households would be acquiring a first fridge, but hoping that more affluent families would buy up to better models.[68]

While these sorts of marketing decisions helped redefine the distinction between needs and desires and reinforced the values of consumer culture, at least products like cars and refrigerators had some long-term utility; in many ways they could be seen as labour-saving investments in transportation or domestic technology (as some observers glimpsed, somewhat dimly, at the time).[69] But what could be more consumerist than spending your money on a completely ephemeral treat with little dietary value, a luxury food that came in a wondrous variety of colours that added little real distinctiveness,[70] and that provided good taste and pleasure but rarely replaced a meal? At the time, the donut shop's fast food cousins – fried chicken outlets, hamburger stands, and pizza parlours – were constructing a commercial speech that pitched restaurant food as fun, but also aimed to convince middle-class families to substitute eating out for maternal labour. Long before feminists broke into the mainstream with their critique of the double day, restaurateurs realized that mothers (whether 'working' or not) wanted nights off from cooking, so they appealed to families with slogans like (in the case of one Toronto drive-in) 'Give Ma a Treat! Save Her Cooking a Meal This Week-End.'[71] Whether successful or not, eating out did begin to creep up in the 1960s and 1970s, especially among the metropolitan middle classes, although it never reached the lofty heights predicted by hopeful comparisons to the American market.[72]

The contrast with the donut is instructive. In parts of North America, the donut was often considered a breakfast food.[73] The pattern is difficult to reconstruct in Canada, but surviving evidence suggests that early donut shops promoted coffee-break buying but mainly served snacks and treats to an afternoon clientele. 'American donut shops have their biggest sales in the morning,' Ron Joyce of Tim Hortons commented in 1971, 'while we make most of our sales late in the day. However, morning sales here are increasing.' For its part, Mister Donut discovered that a large majority of its customers ate donuts as a between-meal snack.[74] Donut shops didn't sell meals until the 1980s – before this, even when they did expand their menus, they typically added other treats like ice cream rather than heartier foods like soup or sandwiches, and they constructed the donut business as one selling fun and pleasure.

Many promotional activities aimed to create a carnival atmosphere in the shops. Mister Donut advised its franchisees to mount such public relations stunts as 'Donut a Go Go' (complete with an 'attractive teenager' to impress the crowds), donut-eating contests to draw children and reward maximum consumption, and tie-ins with holidays, movies, and television shows. To spruce up its core product, the chain developed a heart-shaped donut. None of these suggested much utility in buying donuts.[75] Indeed, eating a donut was a classic consumerist activity, since it involved spending on a product with little intrinsic value.

But the question of consumer behaviour was never so simple. It may have been that desire had triumphed over need, and spending over thrift, but many donut eaters were in no position to throw their money around. For many families, eating out at a restaurant continued to be a special

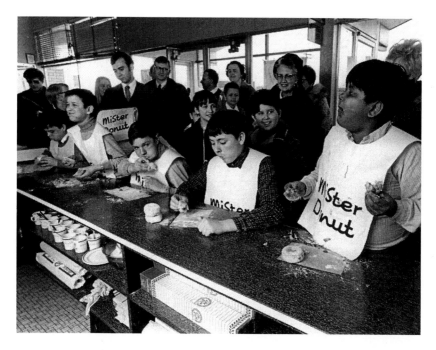

Donut eating contest at Mister Donut, Downsview, Ontario, 1969. To attract families and children, Mister Donut constructed a commercial speech that focused on fun. (York University Archives, Telegram Collection)

occasion, but since the donut was cheap (at about 10 or 15 cents in the mid-1960s, compared to 40 or more cents for a fast food meal), a trip to the donut shop could be routine. The daughter of a truck driver and veterinarian's assistant, Jenny Bryce remembered eating out being an extremely rare and formal occasion – at the nice restaurants 'up along Parkdale Avenue' in Hamilton – but donut shops were not so out of reach.[76] In this sense, the petty consumption of the donut shop reflected the practical balancing of income and pleasure within working-class family economies in a consumer age.

Moreover, even treats had a certain utility, allowing customers to exchange small purchases for time. Surviving on volume, donut shops needed to discourage excessive lingering. Counters and stools and hardback chairs subtly encouraged turnover, and by 1970, 'No Loitering' signs had formalized the encouragement to eat and go, but the question of time remained complex. In Don Mills, youth worker Jesse Dean discovered servers and customers at the Donut Hole practising a kind of moral economy of lingering: 'The regulars had a system worked out,' he reported. 'One cold drink was good for an hour of seating privilege. Then, the waitress would ask them to leave. Five minutes later, the youths returned and there was a repetition of the game one hour later. One of the most interesting things was the way the waitresses and youths managed to get along, always on a friendly basis, even when the youths had been expelled a number of times the same day.'[77] Of course, the power of consumer culture was that it offered both pleasure and utility in spending and buying. Going to a donut shop offered more than products to buy – it offered a social space to experience, one that drew together several broad social developments in postwar North America.

'Neither Very Rich Nor Poor'

For an ideal Mister Donut neighbourhood, Director of Franchising Robert Danziger told the *Financial Post* in 1966, find a site 'in a middle-income community with plenty of people aged between 19 and 35 – the peak doughnut eating age.'[78] Danzinger's comment was an interesting combination of the mythic and the mundane. Mundane because it could have described the ideal location for virtually any mass consumer business in the postwar period: it didn't take a marketing genius to see who had money in their pockets waiting to be spent on everything from new cars to new appliances to pot roasts and hamburgers. Real incomes almost doubled in the thirty years after the Second World War, and while access to this new prosperity continued to be defined by the vagaries of Canada's resource-based economy, by urban–rural divides, by regional underdevelopment, and by social factors such as gender, ethnicity, and class, the nation's prosperity was nonetheless real, and the middle-income category was growing by leaps and bounds.[79] Mythic because selling to this 'middle income community' took on an almost religious quality in the postwar period. 'More and more, retailers are selling to a mass market where the buyers are neither very rich nor poor,' retail analyst Morgan Reid noted enthusiastically as early as 1953.[80] For mass marketers, the growth of the middle rungs of the income ladder promised new heights of prosperity and profit; to some sociologists and journalists, it signaled the arrival of a new middle class: the section of the populace – from the households of skilled workers to those of white-collar professionals – that was 'neither very rich nor poor,' that owned cars and houses, that shopped at supermarkets and plazas, and that lived in nuclear families.[81] Other commentators, then and since, were more suspicious of claims to class unity, and with good reason. Labour conflict continued; social mobility remained an elusive goal for many Canadians; the middle market itself comprised an astonishing range of incomes; and to a degree, tastes and aspirations remained structured by ethnicity, region, gender, and other factors. In retrospect, analysing this 'new middle class' seems a distraction, one often based on the erroneous assumption that class is a cultural choice about taste and style rather than a web of social and economic experiences.[82]

Whether or not the great middle class actually existed, donut shop owners positioned themselves to exploit the growing middle market of consumers, starting with their core product itself. As a discretionary and impulsive purchase, eaten as a snack not a meal, donuts were consumed by people doing well but not too well. A 1959 study by Fleischmann discovered that middle-income families bought 62 per cent more donuts (measured in dollar volume) than lower-income families, but that donut consumption trailed off in the upper-income range. In other words, the poor bought the fewest donuts, the middle-income spent the most, and the wealthiest somewhat less. Seven years later, Mister Donut's marketing research suggested that 'donut purchasers were usually clustered in average income groups.'[83]

Donut chains sought out areas where the local population inhabited this broad mass market: the expanding middle-income areas on the fringes of cities. These market areas – generally considered to be within a two-mile radius of the shop – were typically populated by households whose 'family heads' were somewhere on the middle rungs of the occupational ladder: semiskilled workers like truck drivers, tradesmen like electricians and printers, low to middle-range professionals like salesmen and teachers, small business owners like car dealers, and white-collar managers like principals and bank managers.[84] Like many mass marketers at the time, donut chains usually assumed that this middling market was composed of nuclear families. Thus, every shop that opened in Toronto between 1965 and 1970 was in or close to a census tract with an above-average percentage of preteens – a market that the chains actively courted with special Walt Disney souvenirs, tie-ins to children's movies like *Batman*, and donut-eating contests.[85]

Then as now, consumer culture was a fascinating riddle. Anyone driving past the plazas, supermarkets, and restaurants that lined commercial streets like Scarborough's Eglinton Avenue, Oakville's Lakeshore

Road, or Welland's Niagara Boulevard could see that the mass market was a real thing, an economic formation that had been carved into the landscape by countless public and private decisions. Yet at the same time, words like 'mass' and 'consumer' were little more than rhetorical inventions, part of a convenient shorthand to draw together people with different incomes, tastes, and backgrounds, and thus constantly dissolved into more specific identities like gender, class, age, and ethnicity. By the mid-1960s, retail experts were starting to notice that the mass market was falling apart. 'Why should there not be a mass-produced consumer?' wondered Morgan Reid in 1966. 'Not so long ago the large-volume retailer ... drew assurance from his market evidence that there was a growing, dominant market of middle-income people who would mainly want the same goods ... [but] the mass merchandiser who wishes to improve his competitive position in the future must meet the demands of an increasingly fragmented market.'[86] Donut shops had not quite figured out how to segment their customers into more precise categories: many donut entrepreneurs often sought out the mass market simply by looking for suburban locations or car traffic. Yet in their daily patterns, customers seemed to segment themselves. Donut shops were not a single social space and never served one homogenous taste.

As much as they drew consumers together into a broad middle market, as donut chains spread across space they had to take account of local tastes and social differences. As a chain that spanned many regions in North America, Mister Donut noticed this problem on a continental scale: plum fillings were popular in Milwaukee and cheese fillings in Canada, for example.[87] The precise nature of this pattern is intriguing: the chain tended to construct these sorts of local wrinkles less in terms of national boundaries and more in terms of cross-border regions. Company president Dave Slater suggested that regional boundaries *within* each country were harder to cross than the 49th parallel. 'I can go into Alabama and feel more out of place than I do in Canada,' he noted.[88] French Canada further complicated the question of unity in national markets; the chain realized it would have to adjust its menu in order to succeed in Quebec. 'In French Canada, people's tastes and demands are different from the rest of North America,' admitted Joseph Lugossy in 1970. 'We will have to adjust to them to make progress there – we cannot expect them to adjust to Mister Donut.' Tim Hortons discovered that sweeter tastes spilled over into areas of high French population in eastern Ontario. 'Honey-dipped doughnuts, apple fritters, and Dutchies with raisins are preferred in this area,' Ron Joyce told an

Oakville newspaper. 'Around Cornwall, where there are many French Canadians, the cake type is popular. In the Waterloo area they like the cream-filled doughnut.'[89] Though indicating a certain tenacity in local tastes, few of these differences were problematic for donut chains. Indeed, offering variety within a standardized format reduced such local complexities to adjusting fillings and dips, making more cake donuts than fritters, or more maple-dipped than raised chocolate.

Class was another tension. Despite the middle-market aspirations, the owners, servers, and customers I interviewed often portrayed the donut shop as a working-class institution. 'I just thought that we had to open one in Hamilton,' recalled Jim Charade of his decision to open the Ottawa Street Tim Hortons. 'It's a worker, blue collar kind of worker, and they come out of there at two–three o'clock in the morning and they have no place to go for a cup of coffee.' Such descriptions spoke of practical and unspectacular connections based on mundane daily rituals and conveniences rather than social status, cultural image, or grand claims about working-class families joining the postwar middle market. Workers also appreciated the informality of the shops, which, unlike restaurants popping up in plazas, had no pretensions about offering full meals. The first Ideal Donut in Winnipeg drew in a lot of workers from the nearby sugar plant: 'They would come in with boots and overalls and the place would clean up easily ... They felt comfortable, almost like a small town diner atmosphere ... they wanted to know all the girls' names and they would joke around with each other.' Workers on the road congregated at donut shops: salesmen, hydro workers, cabbies, and truck drivers came up as the core business quite often in interviews and newspaper stories. 'The bulk of the business in the early days were truck drivers,' recalled Linda Lalonde of her Cornwall Tim Hortons outlet. 'I can remember taking calls for them in the early days. I felt like a dispatcher for Williams Transport, because all those guys came in and I'd say, "Call the shop, somebody's looking for you."'[90]

In interviews, almost everyone used the term 'working class' to mean 'working men.'[91] 'There were a lot of men in there,' remembered Sandy Willard of a Tim Hortons outlet in east Hamilton. 'When I went in, I was usually with my father or brother.' Smoking reinforced the male character of the shops – a characteristic not necessarily appreciated by people who had to spend long hours in the shops. 'Ninety-nine percent of the people who came in smoked, no question about it,' recalled one Tim Hortons owner. 'In the store, the donuts were tasting like smoke ... it was just awful.' Smoking had two effects. First, it made the place dingy and dark, no matter how much daily cleaning was performed. Costas Kiriakopoulos remembered 'ashtrays all over the counter' of his family's Country Style outlet at Lawrence and Weston in Toronto. The smoke got so thick that they had to periodically wash down the walls, which had become brown with nicotine. Second, smoking also reinforced the general maleness of the place, at least for some customers. 'Men smoked. It was the manly thing to do,' Ed Mahaj recalled of the Ottawa Street Tim Hortons in the early 1970s. 'You'd go in there if you had some time to kill. You'd order a coffee and light up a cigarette ... Everyone would be smoking ... The one on Ottawa Street was always men.'[92]

The sit-down counter was the hub of male culture in the outlets, carrying considerable symbolic weight in memories of donut shop socializing. More than any other feature, the counter made the shop a social space, linking the donut shop with lunch counters and coffee shops even while distinguishing it from other drive-in restaurants. At Red Barn and McDonalds, customers were handed their food by an efficient male worker behind a cash register; at the donut shop, you could get service at the counter. 'It was a coffee shop, not a restaurant,' remembered Lori Broadfoot, a server at Winnipeg's Ideal Donut in the early 1970s. 'You would serve a person and then you could stand and talk to them.' Even the shortest conversations across the counter, or seemingly trivial events like a server remembering a daily order, enhanced the donut shop's role as a social space. When repeated as part of a daily routine of working, commuting, or travelling, such cross-counter rituals allowed consumers to graduate from the status of customer to that of regular. The pattern of attracting regulars from local businesses was common, even in drive-in institutions: along Eglinton Avenue in Scarborough, employees of the nearby Red Barn Hamburgers often dropped in on the Mister Donut when the hamburger stand closed.[93]

The employment policies of donut shops cemented the male character of the sit-down counter. Fast food companies like Red Barn and McDonald's deliberately avoided hiring female cashiers, fearing they would attract unruly teenage boys. Servers at donut shops, on the other hand, were exclusively female in the early days. Brief, informal conversations across the counter occasionally passed into longer flirtations. Jenny Bryce made it clear that there were many attractions to being a high school student working the counter at Tim Hortons #7 on Queenston Road in Hamilton. She remembered young men 'who came crawling out of those holes after Friday night's adventures. Actually, I went out with

Interior of Tim Horton Donuts, Kitchener, 1970. With counters, stools, and simple menu boards, early donut shops borrowed designs from lunch counters and coffee shops. (*Kitchener-Waterloo Record* Photographic Negative Collection, The Library, The University of Waterloo)

a couple of them that I'd met there – a couple of them at the same time ... I didn't know they knew each other.' One day, she needed a ride home from work, so she asked 'one of those guys in the leather jackets. He used to just ride for pleasure and drink Coca-Cola and eat ice cream cones – he wasn't your real hood ... I guess I vaguely knew who he was, but I knew [my friend] didn't think much of him. So I got a ride home from him one afternoon and the next thing you know, four months later [we got] engaged and a year later married. That was twenty-six years ago.'[94] No doubt for many servers, flirting across the counter was an annoying (and perhaps, at times, disturbing) part of the job, but Bryce obviously thrived on it.[95]

Flirting between servers and customers was a stereotype of the earlier lunch counters. Though donut shops were a novelty in the 1960s, many of their key features were familiar to customers. Continuities between lunch counters, diners, and donut shops were mentioned in interviews almost as often as references to novelty. Sometimes, the connection was direct. Tom Busnarda, who grew up on Ottawa Street in Hamilton, described the way the first Tim Hortons picked up on but also reformulated the social function of existing neighbourhood restaurants:

> Around the corner and up a couple of blocks was a restaurant called the Bright Spot. The Bright Spot was a twenty-four-hour restaurant that predates Tim Hortons. It was a hangout for all this element ... that was ... associated with the east end ... of Hamilton, which of course is working-class poor. And slowly, Tim Hortons started to take that element from the Bright Spot and you could see a movement to Tim Hortons ... The Bright Spot was probably a better place to be, because there was a full menu, but Tim Hortons was more accommodating in some ways of having people sit and not do much of a purchase, and having some place to go.

But sometimes, the connection between the lunch counter and the donut shop was more abstract, focused not on a specific restaurant but on the idea of the diner itself. Allan Asmussen, co-owner of Kitchener-Waterloo's Donut Queen, remembered:

> When the cities were downtown oriented, you had like a Woolworth's or a Kresge's and you had your lunch counter there with specials, and the guys would go in there in the morning from different businesses and have a coffee and get a donut, and some of the donuts they made were just out of the machines and they really weren't much, but others got into a bit more ... Every morning you'd go there for coffee – some guys would have coffee and toast – but you sat there. You went to spots like that.[96]

Consumers like Busnarda and entrepreneurs like Asmussen built cultural connections on a sense of both product and place. Before the advent of donut drive-ins, lunch counters and coffee shops had been a key market for donut wholesalers like Val's and Margaret's as well as for companies (like CDC and Hol'N One) that sold compact automatic machines. For his small lunch counter in east Hamilton, Rita Browne's father purchased a small CDC machine in the mid-1950s, figuring donuts would compliment the existing menu of chilli, soup, toast, and sandwiches, prepared in the family kitchen and transported to the restaurant by car.[97] In more abstract terms, it was not so far from tea and toast to donuts and coffee: both were cheap snacks that fit with a broad pattern of petty consumption, where customers traded small purchases for time.

A sense of place reinforced these associations. The staples of early donut shop design – small, utilitarian interiors with stainless steel and arborite fixtures, menu boards over the cash register, a straight or U-shaped counter with stools, and a few small tables in the corner – were also the mainstays of the coffee shops and lunch counters that had been common in urban neighbourhoods and fringe areas since before the war. There were quite practical reasons for adopting these layouts. Restaurateurs had known for years that stools encouraged a quick turnover of customers – as much as four times the rate of tables.[98] Moreover, it was economical for equipment companies to build to standard designs, and their prices and advice structured the decision making of both chain and independent restaurant owners. Indeed, designing a low-priced, fast-service restaurant in this period was as much a mass phenomenon as making donuts: companies like Ontario Store Fixtures manufactured the same basic stools, counters, and fittings in varied colours, types, and sizes.[99] Most lunch counters, diners, and donut shops, then, developed a distinctive look not through dramatic innovations in layout or design, but by choosing blue instead of green, vinyl instead of plastic, straight instead of rounded counters, or booths instead of tables and chairs. But from these practical and economic decisions grew a sense of cultural familiarity and social similarity, one that connected donut shops with lunch counters and diners in a seamless architecture of informal eating out.

Yet from a consumer's perspective, features like menu boards and sit-down counters were more than simple design decisions; they were also cultural cues, as much a part of the donut shop's commercial speech as advertisements and promotions. Indeed, in many ways the appearance of an outlet was *the* key element of its commercial speech, since few donut chains advertised heavily in the early days. Ron Joyce, for example, was quite explicit about viewing the outlet itself as the primary promotional vehicle for Tim Hortons.[100] From this perspective, the design and atmosphere of donut shops expressed the complex cultural dynamics of the postwar mass market. If the outlets were familiar to blue-collar consumers, they also spoke to a broader customer base. According to American historian Andrew Hurley, the middle-income market was created by two developments in postwar consumption: the adoption of the discretionary consumerism of the middle class by working families with increasing amounts of disposable income; and the attraction of sanitized versions of working-class institutions for a middle-class market.[101] Thus, the American diner was redefined in the postwar period from a working-class institution to the precursor of the middle-market family restaurant when its owners – anxious to draw upwardly mobile suburban families – cleaned up their outlets, expanded their menus, installed tables, and relocated to sites with ample parking.[102]

The situation in Canada was roughly similar, although the term 'diner' was never common here.[103] In 1956, Jeff Purvey took over a small lunch counter in Peterborough, Ontario, sporting twelve stools and three folding tables, and serving 'hamburgers, coffee, light snacks, and other lines' to factory workers in an industrial area outside the downtown core. A year later, he expanded the building and opened a standard restaurant to supplement the diner, offering a broader menu of southern fried chicken, oysters, shrimp, fish and chips, and other items, aiming to attract families on weekends as well as 'industrial plant officials, office workers, and other customers,' who would spend more money on full meals.[104] Though donut shops had more limited product lines, their interior designs and imagined markets reflected a similar cultural dynamic. Mister Donut, in a typical approach, distributed thirteen pages of instructions on cleaning to its franchisees, and ruthlessly enforced these policies through regular inspections.[105]

By the 1960s, these two trajectories of mass marketing made for a confusing and complex mix of donut shop patrons. On the one hand, the shops often acquired a reputation as male, working-class institutions; on the other, by adding tables to the lunch counter design, enforcing standards of cleanliness, serving the roadside market, pitching their advertising at baby-boom families, and seeking out locations in shopping plazas and middle-income neighbourhoods, they aimed for a broader clientele. The surviving evidence suggests that overall, the early market was only slightly tilted towards men and that the social use of the shop could depend on time and location.[106] Donut shop owners and workers often spoke of a basic rhythm to the day: truck drivers in early morning, salesmen later, housewives doing shopping in the afternoon, youth in the evening, bar patrons after midnight, cabbies after that. These memories may be too neat, but they do speak to the way that time could alter the basic character of the shop. Space mattered as well: despite being organized on a chain basis, one donut shop was not necessarily like another. One Mister Donut marketing study found that men comprised almost 70 per cent of customers at a typical freestanding outlet on a busy commercial strip, while a shopping centre location had the highest proportion of female customers. Location also affected the class character of the shops. Chris Pappas owned a number of Country Style Donut shops around Toronto in the 1960s and 1970s, and found that no matter how much they targeted the transient, car-driving market with big parking lots and easy access, the social composition of the neighbourhood affected the customer base. 'It depended on the area where you were, of course,' he explained. 'If you are in a blue-collar area, then you get that type of people ... But over here at Dundas and Islington, we had a better clientele ... So it depends where you were.' This point reinforces the importance of local residents to the shop's profitability.[107]

What Pappas described was less a grand blending of different social groups into a broad middle class than the strategy of selling to what might be called a 'middle market in aggregate': different locations might attract different sorts of customers; cabbies and truckers might sit at the counter while families stuck to the tables; the morning might be given over to salesmen and the afternoon to female shoppers. Across the chain and through the day, customers spanned the middle market. How else to make sense of Country Style locations beside an industrial park in Scarborough and in the heart of Canada's most affluent community in Oakville? Two different places, same commercial institution. Even a single outlet, drawing on a market of two miles or more, could sew together increasingly segmented suburban neighbourhoods. Few construction workers, after all, lived next to surgeons: even if early postwar suburbs drew together the diverse middle market on the same street (a highly debatable point), by the 1960s, residential developers were pitching subdivisions at much more segmented markets, more and more separating income niches within the middle range of the economic ladder.[108] For donut entrepreneurs, however, changing residential dynamics were less important than convincing everyone in the area to drive in and buy donuts. Yet the desire to blend middle and working class in the middle market of the donut shop did not necessarily succeed in the long run: by the 1980s the biggest donut chains would begin to lament their male, blue-collar customer base and would seek to reinvent their shops to attract a still broader clientele.[109] But in the 1960s, class rarely arose as the key marketing problem. Their biggest challenges lay elsewhere.

'They Were Selling Drugs out of the Washrooms'

In early July 1970, during a confrontation in front of the Country Style on Lakeshore Road in Oakville, nineteen-year-old Peter Simpson was arrested by Constable Roy Bonham and charged with obstructing a police officer. The next day, no doubt to his horror, Simpson found his late-night confrontation on page one of both local newspapers, on the Metro page of the *Toronto Star*, and even on the TV news. All the commotion wasn't really about Simpson, however. It was the place, not the person, that attracted the attention. Judging by media reports around the time of Simpson's arrest, the Country Style at Brock Street and Lakeshore Road was a veritable snack food Sodom and Gomorrah. 'Violence, Sex on Oakville Street,' screamed an *Oakville Beaver* headline on July 2. 'A "circus" that includes amusements like stomping heads until bloody, sexual intercourse on lawns, and urinating on sidewalks came up before council last night,' the *Daily Journal Record* reported of the goings on around the Country Style outlet.[110] Clearly, the shop had become the site of one slice of nighttime youth culture, but there was more going on than bad behaviour. As the events around the outlet took on the trappings of a moral panic and spun into a broader discussion about civility and rights, matters soon became explicitly political. At their root, however, the problems were commercial, growing from the inherent tensions of the early donut shop form.

Donut shops attracted young people like magnets. 'The Donut Hole ... has become an informal drop-in for a cross-section of youths between the ages of 15 and 21,' reported Don Mills youth worker Jesse Dean in 1971, noting that the shops filled a gap in local recreational space. Oakville youth largely agreed, complaining of restricted movies, conservative parents, and few other leisure options than donut shops and fast food outlets. If the typical outlet became a sort of commercialized drop-in centre, the parking lot became a kind of park. The horseplay at the Lakeshore Road Country Style was matched at the Tim Hortons across town. 'A group of eight boys were tossing a Frisbee around the parking lot of Tim Horton's donut shop until the cops came to break it up,' the *Journal Record* commented. 'What Oakville needs is some kids space ... Just unstructured, open space to gather.'[111] Informal styles of leisure and complaints about alternative options had been staples of youth culture for much of the postwar period.[112] As they proliferated through the late 1960s, donut shops also served as sites of the emerging underground economy. 'We did have a problem with teenagers,' Anita Halaiko, who owned a Mister Donut with her husband in St Catharines, recalled. 'There was a drug problem there. They were selling drugs out of the washrooms, and they were very disruptive.' Drug culture in donut shops seemed to vary: during his summer in Don Mills in 1970, Jessie Dean found many stoned teenagers – 'speeders' especially – in the Donut Hole, but relatively little actual drug selling (in contrast, 'deals were made openly' at Edward Gardens park up the street).[113]

Youthful behaviours like horseplay, rowdyness, and drug selling were products of the age, but they were triply encouraged by the donut shop form. As informal institutions of petty consumption entailing all-night hours, small purchases, a minimum of supervision, and an informal setting, donut shops naturally attracted young people looking to socialize. In building outlets that emphasized automobile convenience, moreover, donut chains built large parking lots that became spaces in their own right, facilitating all kinds of alternative activities. Finally, because of their locational strategies, donut shop neighbourhoods were teeming with teens. By 1970 the baby boom had subsided, but the peak of its demographic bulge was aging into and out of their teenage spending years. Young people were a lucrative market of their own, with abundant leisure time and – at least in the minds of marketers – considerable amounts of discretionary income, which they were more than willing to spend on fast food, especially if it bought them a period of socializing with friends. At the chain level, Mister Donut recognized the value of pitching advertising to the 'youth component' because donut eating was inversely related to age. At the outlet level, owners knew they needed youth spending. Chris Pappas, who took over the Oakville outlet amid the troubles, knew that most local youth had cash in their pockets and were heavy spenders at the outlet.[114]

In a broad sense, these demographic, social, and economic forces brought Simpson to the front of the Country Style that evening in early July, but his confrontation with Constable Bonham flowed from the difficulties of regulating the geography of youth culture, a complex tangle of public and private jurisdictions. A donut shop parking lot was an open and accessible public space in appearance, but in law it was private property with a fairly simple regulatory regime: misbehaving youth could simply be banned from the lot by the owner. Legally, this strategy relied on the Petty Trespass Act, which allowed the police (with written permission) to act as the agent of private property owners. 'That's private property,' judge James Butler lectured one Scarborough youth (who had 'long hair and a chin beard') before fining him $50 and warning him of possible jail time if he ever returned to Parkway Plaza. 'I like to play pool, but I'm not a troublemaker,' the youth replied, explaining his presence in the parking lot at 1:20 a.m. on 16 October, despite having been previously warned to stay away. 'I was only near the doughnut shop, which is within 50 feet to the entrance of the pool hall.'[115]

But as a form of social control, the Petty Trespass Act relied on co-operation between business owners and police. Back in Oakville, Tim Horton dealt with news of the goings on around the Country Style by making a special trip to his nearby outlet to set a firm rule: 'no hippies.' Meanwhile, over on Lakeshore Road, the Country Style's owner and local police engaged in a public war of words about responsibility for the troubles.[116] The owner claimed that many problems actually occurred on town property, but regulation around the periphery of the shop was complicated. Outside of parking regulations, which the Oakville council quickly amended to declare Brock Street a No Stopping zone after 9:00 p.m., there wasn't much the local constabulary could do about young people congregating on public streets. Transferring residents' concerns from moral panic to legal regulation was a difficult proposition, and the council referred the matter to the town solicitor for study.[117] On 7 July 1970, acting on the solicitor's report, the Oakville council passed the only bylaw in history known to be aimed specifically at a donut shop, although naturally the language was much broader. 'No person,' the bylaw declared, 'shall by himself or with another or others, loiter on any sidewalk ... so as to occupy more than one-half of the width thereof ... [or] so as to interfere with any person's access to or from any private premises.' The bylaw further empowered the police, after delivering suitable warnings, to arrest 'any person apparently loitering' in contravention of the regulation, making that person liable for a fine of up to $300.[118] That evening, Simpson was arrested when he joined thirty-five youths hanging out on the sidewalk in front of the shop.[119]

Though not so surprising in a town that one academic called the 'last outpost of WASP society' and a 'place where observable reactions are almost sure to be at the maximum possible,' the bylaw could easily be read as an extension of broader adult attacks on youth leisure, running from legal regulation through 'no hippie' policies to informal harassment by police. As such, it expressed the links between generational discord, consumer culture, and the most powerful political discourses of the day. Indeed, once Brock Street residents arrived at council, the debate quickly moved to first principles, playing on notions of freedom, rights, and order. Specific complaints from small to large – from squealing tires, horn honking, and shouting to swearing, sex, violence, and 'immodesty' – ran together into a version of what Kenneth Cmeil has called the 'politics of civility.'[120] Angry adults lamented the breakdown of authority and decorum. Councillor Michael Boyle blamed 'permissiveness' for Country Style's problems. A *Beaver* editorial lamented excessive freedom: 'Yes, this country is free and under our democratic system so are the people who live in it. Our country is so free that a certain segment of our population choose to do exactly what it pleases, regardless [of how it] affects others ... what happened at the Country Style Donut shop ... [is] an example of the type of freedom that is too often allowed.' In response, the paper urged more police and stiffer laws for the 'hoodlums and hooligans who have nothing better to do with their time.' The *Daily Journal Record* joined the chorus, arguing that 'law and order are prerequisites of representative government and indeed of all civilized societies.'[121] Youth responded to such attacks on their leisure habits with their own dramatic rhetoric. One youth reporter condemned Tim Horton's 'no hippies' policy by appropriating the language of civil rights: 'In the early 60's,' he reminded the great defenceman, 'many restaurants in the southern states had similar policies dealing with black people.'[122]

This kind of language suggests that the politics of age and style were genuinely heated, but generational dynamics are easy to exaggerate. In fact, adult responses varied, and efforts at social control took many forms. Across suburban areas, some municipal officials preferred a softer approach to moral regulation, dispatching youth workers like Jesse Dean, who spent the summer and fall of 1970 trying to reach alienated teens in the Don Mills Donut Hole.[123] Nor did the regulatory politics of civility divide neatly between old and young. Many adults openly ridiculed the law-and-order approach. The *Toronto Star* called Oakville's antiloitering legislation the 'bonehead bylaw.' Canadian Civil Liberties Union counsel Alan Borovoy told municipal officials that the bylaw was sure to be found unconstitutional, musing sarcastically that the provisions discriminated 'between the stout and the lean.' Oakville Labour Council president John Kane had more serious concerns, worrying that the regulations empowered employers to break up legal pickets during a strike.[124]

Few councillors or editorialists were inclined to take these complaints to their logical conclusion – a motion to repeal the bylaw received only three votes – but as time passed and tempers cooled, the Country Style debate showed more ambivalence. After Borovoy's visit, the *Beaver* featured a photo of a paunchy local cab driver munching a donut in front of the outlet, blocking a good deal more than half the sidewalk with his bulk, and facetiously invited the police to lay charges. Though admitting that the antiloitering law was reasonable and that 'the general unrest and turmoil ... has made a shambles of law and order,' the *Journal Record* nonetheless cautioned against the 'tendency today, particularly where the young are concerned, to attempt to apply repressive laws and retrogressive tactics simply because of what they wear and how they look, rather than what they do.'[125] Even at Council, underneath heated generational rhetoric and hasty regulatory action, motives seemed multiple and complex. Many councillors anticipated an outright crackdown, but not all of the bylaw's supporters had such clear motives. 'All we were trying to do was clean up the situation on Lakeshore, but not give the people involved a criminal record,' insisted councillor Michael Boyle. From this perspective, the bylaw served a dual purpose, arming police with a tool that was at once more forgiving and more effective than existing regulations. More forgiving because a loitering charge promised a fine with no permanent record, unlike existing criminal laws against rowdyism, which could saddle a teenager with a life-long record for what many saw as a youthful indiscretion. More effective because without the threat of long-term consequences, the police might be more willing to lay charges.[126]

These nuances were probably of little comfort to Simpson, who was charged not with loitering but with obstructing a police officer. For the police, criminal charges and antiloitering bylaws were probably most useful in terms of on-the-ground discretion and intimidation. Controlling youth culture in 'public' was usually just a question of simple, day-to-day disruption, using the threat of formal charges (and the officer's own intimidating physical presence) to push young people out of their regular hangouts. In Oakville, one anonymous youth interviewed by the local paper in the Country Style parking lot complained that police came by looking for conflicts, turning up music before declaring it too loud, engaging in ongoing harassment, and so on.[127] Editorialists and councillors often called for more police on the beat,[128] but even informal disruption raised problems of enforcement, as Councillor William Reaume found during a confrontation with a group of youths in the Country Style parking lot. 'I was ready to have them charged,' he said, 'but they took off right after I called police.' From a law-and-order standpoint, new bylaws and informal harassment were all well and good, but the police could not be everywhere. 'Last night, a bunch of hot-rodders were tearing around Tim Horton's donut shop for most of the evening,' the *Journal Record* complained in 1971. 'Finally the police arrived. But all was quiet.'[129]

In the absence of effective strategies of regulation and control, shop owners were left to balance moral peril and economic promise on their own, generally using masculine bravado and informal negotiation rather than formal police action. Dave Ambeault, who owned a Tim Hortons in North York, spread the rumour that he was a former professional boxer, a claim that his impressive size made easier to believe. Even when they threw their weight around, it is hard to see shop owners as agents of generational social control: most had put their houses and mortgages on the line and were working long hours to build sweat equity in the business, and many recall being terrified and stressed out by problems with misbehaving youth. When the Halaikos tried to crack down on youthful misbehaviour at their St Catharines Mister Donut, angry youth exercised their political agency not by deploying the language of civil rights but by vandalizing the family's house, a strategy somewhat difficult to romanticize as counter-hegemonic. For Chris Pappas, as bad as the Oakville situation got, his Etobicoke outlet was worse. 'We had the same problem down at Dundas and Islington. It was even worse down there ... I used to park across the street with my partner ... watching at three or four o'clock in the morning ... You had to get up in a few hours to start baking and serving the people, so you had only a few hours' sleep. It was stressful.'[130]

Two weeks into the troubles at the Oakville Country Style, Pappas took over the outlet at the behest of the chain's head office and proceeded to assure local residents that he would not tolerate rowdy behaviour. 'I have my mortgage tied up in here,' Pappas told a *Journal Record* reporter, 'so there won't be any trouble.'[131] For donut shop owners, questions of civility were refracted through their own economic interests. Everyone wanted youth to behave, since rowdyness caused trouble for neighbours and drove good customers away, but notwithstanding the occasional 'no hippie' policy, few owners were willing to ban them outright. Young people had money, and donut shops were almost perfectly suited to the patterns of youthful pleasure. In this sense, Peter Simpson stood at the margin between attempts to exploit the consumer power of youth and efforts to control and reform their behaviour. But the dynamics of age were at once rhetorically simple and practically complex. Generational politics were consistently cross-cut by other ideas and impulses: economic interests, uncertain regulatory strategies, and commitments to liberal rights. Some adults, after all, were inclined by their professional equipment to see youth hedonism in terms of economic potential rather than moral regulation, while others struggled to define a legal regime capable of institutionalizing civility without disrupting a young person's future.[132] In the end, these tensions were almost inevitable, built into the donut shop form, its market, its atmosphere, and its parking lots.

'Oakville Needs Something Like This'

Four years before Oakville's infamous bylaw, Country Style Donuts built its new 'palace of donut pleasure' at Brock Street and Lakeshore Road with asphalt, mortar, bricks, and arborite, but the *place* it assembled was constructed from the building blocks of postwar consumer culture. Donut shops were one attempt to capitalize on the growing middle market of consumers. This market was not just the dream of the sophisticated retail expert: less erudite entrepreneurs understood that tapping car culture meant reaching consumers with money to spend, and their decisions about locations carved the dream of reaching the middle market consumer into Canada's commercial landscape. Yet in offering customers a counter, some tables, and large parking lots, donut shops became social spaces, assembled out of broad changes in space and time, architectural informality, cheap products, and the cultural categories of customers, who fit these new places into their daily routines and into their mental maps of informal eating out. In doing so, entrepreneurs and consumers created places that attracted many working men, but that also served a broader market of families – women, children, and teens, who found their own uses for these mass commercial institutions.

As the residents of Brock Street discovered, these differences were real, but to the donut shop owner, the middle market never had to be a single or unified social group. Did it really matter whether youth hung out with cab drivers or afternoon shoppers with salesmen, so long as everybody bought donuts? Though never consciously expressed in these terms, the strategy of early donut entrepreneurs was to both recognize and mute social differences, offering informality and cleanliness, variety within standardization, fun without rowdyness. Where time and space could not resolve such tensions, they became the stuff of local politics. In the end, though, it was usually left to the shop owners themselves to manage the social dynamics of consumption. 'We'll make sure there is no trouble,' Pappas promised as he surveyed his new outlet in 1970. 'We'll stay here ourselves 24 hours a day if we have to.'[133] From the perspective of small entrepreneurs like Pappas, balancing the tensions of the middle market in aggregate meant hard work and less sleep, but it also could be a lucrative business.

3 'He Must Give Up Certain Things': Franchising and the Making of the Donut Shop, 1960–1980

'I was an entrepreneur, that's what I was,' William Stockwell declared confidently as he described his jump from waged labour into business ownership. In the late 1960s, he was living in London, Ontario, and in his fifteenth year working at Richards-Wilcox, a metal fabrication plant, where he was making a decent living as a foreman. But when his brother-in-law asked him to come in as a partner in the donut business, Stockwell sold his car, scraped together some money, and made the plunge into the new venture. For Stockwell, selling his car and scraping for funds were the costs of leaving waged labour to pursue one of the great dreams of the twentieth century, small business ownership. Entrepreneur or not, however, Stockwell gave no thought to pursuing his own vision by finding a spot, mounting a sign saying 'Bill's Donuts,' and trying to build a customer base by word of mouth and clever promotions. Instead, he bought into Country Style Donuts, at that time an upstart chain comprising a baker's dozen worth of outlets around Ontario.[1]

For Stockwell, Country Style had much to offer, starting with the fact that it was cheaper – he was sure – than opening his own shop. At the time Stockwell signed on, buying into Country Style required a down payment of $14,000 on a total cost of about $40,000. 'I actually wasn't even able to [start my own shop because] ... I didn't have enough money,' he remembered. 'You could buy a franchise [for less] – you didn't have to pay the whole $40,000 cash.' Besides, he knew absolutely nothing about making donuts, let alone running a whole donut shop, and Country Style had already compiled a 'system' of management and production into an inch-thick operating manual, knowledge it might have taken Stockwell months to acquire on his own. In this sense, Country Style seemed to combine the best of big and small business: the knowledge and stability of the chain and the independence, pride in ownership, and individual initiative of small entrepreneurship. The promotional materials Stockwell received from Country Style enumerated the many aspects of setting up a business that were handled by the company, emphasizing the standardized nature of the operation. Country Style promised its expertise in site selection, building design and construction, equipment, suppliers, training, and ongoing supervision, all in exchange for an upfront franchise fee and 2 per cent of Stockwell's monthly gross revenues. His main reason for choosing the company, however, was the family connection. His brother-in-law was already a successful operator in London and Sudbury, so Stockwell was confident the business would do well: 'In the late sixties, we were fairly close, a fairly close family, and [Marvin] suggested that I might want to go in with him.'[2]

'An Ideal Blend of Big and Small Business'

By joining his brother-in-law in a franchised operation, Stockwell had jumped on one of the most dramatic retail revolutions of the twentieth century. By the late 1990s, franchising would eat up almost half the retail dollar in Canada, providing a business model for products as diverse as automobiles, hamburgers, hardware, and photocopying.[3] In the 1960s, however, franchising seemed a new and novel method, despite its long history. In strictly business terms, the idea developed in the nineteenth century as a kind of contract or agent system. Manufacturers like Singer Sewing Machines and McCormick Harvesters found that there was a national demand for their products, but limited transportation networks made far-flung distribution expensive and impractical. Both companies found it more efficient to license 'agents' in different areas across the country to manufacture and market products to company specifications. It was a successful system that later spread to beverages, automobile and petroleum retailing, and other industries. America was well into a genuine 'franchise boom' by the late 1950s. Canada was somewhat behind but was experiencing a minor boom by the middle of the next decade. Franchising included a wide range of relationships, but much of the new energy in the postwar years came from 'business format franchising,' where an entire plan of operation – a 'system' including detailed rules on everything from production and marketing to hiring and housekeeping – was offered for sale by a franchisor to a franchisee.[4]

In its boosters, franchising inspired an almost poetic devotion that far exceeded matters of economic efficiency. By defining a system of production and marketing from the centre and then selling it to small and scattered entrepreneurs, franchising combined the two great longings of twentieth-century capitalism. 'Franchises give the small businessman a chance to participate in the financial resources, promotional ability, guidance, training and servicing of a large parent company, yet maintain individuality and pride in ownership,' A.L. Tunick, the Montreal-born president of the International Franchise Association declared in 1960.[5] This statement was perfectly in tune with the economic culture of the age, which was caught between admiring the sophistication and efficiency of large enterprises and romanticizing the contributions and experience of individual entrepreneurship.[6]

These two impulses expressed broader threads in economic culture. For much of the twentieth century, Canadians held apparently contradictory visions of the economy. On the one hand, small business was celebrated as an economic form, social institution, and community pillar. In strictly economic terms, small business was thought by some to benefit the consumer, because the small, independent operator was more responsive, provided personalized service, and (unlike a corporate employee) possessed the motivation to really nurture a business. In broader terms, the health of small business could serve as a sort of economic barometer, in that independent operations were thought to produce, reflect, and reinforce 'real' competition in the marketplace. More often, the economic role of small business was connected to some broader social or cultural purpose, such as political democracy or community stability.[7] Many of these threads of small business mythology flowed into the parliamentary debate on Canada's Small Business Loans Act of 1960, which aimed to guarantee credit for small enterprises. Members on both sides of the House spared no efforts in revering small business as the 'backbone of the Canadian economy,' the 'mainstay of free enterprise,' the symbol of 'economic democracy,' and the 'lifeblood of any community.' Even the Liberals, who had been relatively uninterested in the difficulties of small business throughout the 1950s, did not dare question the motherhood status of the small enterprise.[8]

Larger enterprises were not without defenders, however. If nothing else, big business provided a greater abundance of cheap products to purchase, which benefited the consumer and, by extension, all of society. 'From the point of view of the consuming public,' the Canadian Chain Store Association commented in 1937, 'the great achievement of the chain-store system of merchandising has been the reduction ... in the cost of living ... Chain stores have increased the purchasing power of the consuming public.'[9] Yet big business mythology also went beyond questions of economic calculus. Even cultural critics like John Kenneth Galbraith found much to praise in bigness, portraying large firms as reliable and stable.[10] The image had a broad reach. When Allan Asmussen told his family that he intended to open an independent donut shop in 1968, they thought he was crazy: 'If you worked, like my father did ... for a big corporation, you'll have a pension plan, you've got a paycheque. Why would anybody want to have their own business?'[11] The most common (and likely the most powerful) defence of big business, however, was simply that it was inevitable – a notion that infected even the small business myth. 'I am not going to say that this development toward largeness is not a good thing,' W. Thomas sheepishly informed the House of Commons in 1960. 'I believe it is a good thing in some respects. At any rate, it is a development in our economy ... which is here to stay.'[12]

As Thomas implied, these two impulses – the celebration of bigness and the romanticization of the small – did not have to be polar opposites. Though populists, small entrepreneurs, corporate managers, and industrial magnates might fall on one or the other side of the debate, many Canadians were more conflicted. Writing in *Canadian Business* in 1948, R.A. Mahoney trumpeted the symbolic value of small business: 'Because small business provides an opportunity for any man to become an entrepreneur, it makes our free enterprise system a reality. Moreover, this psychological effect applies to many people who never will go into their own business.' Yet he made sure to remind his readers that the 'large organization with its huge capital assets and its research facilities is just as necessary to our economic welfare as is the small business.'[13] From this perspective, by laying claim to both modern business practices and romantic notions of small ownership, franchise boosters like Tunich almost perfectly expressed the conflicted economic imagination of North America. Franchising was a kind of in-between system, offering both the efficiencies of corporate capitalism and the advantages of small business.

In editorials and speeches, this sort of franchise boosterism was an effective rhetorical strategy, but it could never perfectly connect the various threads of economic culture. Critics marshalled their own poetic metaphors, and like boosters, worked to put them into practice. In Ontario, a minister's committee headed by G.M. Grange investigated franchising in 1970, tabling a damning report that enumerated problems ranging from arbitrary termination of contracts to secret profits on franchisee purchases, to discrimination between franchisees with regard to prices and services and financial irresponsibility by franchisors. The language was often dramatic, playing on symbols of capture and dependence. 'There are many happy franchisees,' the report noted, 'just as in feudal days there were many happy serfs.'[14] Around the same time, four partners in a Mister Donut franchise (whose company was called 'Jirna Ltd.') sued the parent company over the practice of secret rebates on bulk purchases – a case the press reported with considerable zeal, picking up the dramatic metaphors of the court's ruling rather than the more subtle legal details. 'It appears to me,' wrote Justice Stark in awarding damages to Jirna, 'that franchisor and franchisee are bound together over a very long period of years in a relationship which in many respects is almost as close as that of master and servant.'[15]

Yet franchising was more than just an idea in the public sphere of newspapers, government bodies, and business college seminars. In operations, the blend of big and small engendered a powerful code of behaviour. On a grand scale, claims about modernizing small capitalism and injecting entrepreneurial energy into corporate procedures competed with metaphors of capture and subordination, but in franchised outlets, these questions were rendered less as poetry than as practice. For new franchisees like Stockwell, dramatic claims often gave way to the day-to-day problems of production, supervising employees, and balancing the demands of business and family; practical issues like these then shaped, and were shaped by, broader ideas about economic possibilities and their relationship to social connections and community networks. It was a family connection, after all, that pulled Stockwell into donuts. Yet the symbolic thrust of franchising – its vision, its possibilities, its perils – was never far beneath the surface.

'She's the Brain and I'm the Worker'

Not long after William Stockwell moved from London to Windsor to open his new donut shop, Lynda Lalonde made the long, tedious trek down Highway 401 from Cornwall to Hamilton, a drive the Group of Seven quite rightly left out of their celebrations of Canada's scenic wonder. With her husband and two partners, she was going down the road to check out Tim Hortons' modest but growing chain of donut shops. 'We were interested in getting into a business so we wouldn't have to work for anybody,' she recalled of their decision to investigate the chain. 'We were all, I guess, ambitious young people at the time.' The partners eventually returned to sign the necessary documents and exchange ritual handshakes, sealing their place as owners of the chain's eleventh franchise.[16]

Lalonde's story is typical of the initial experiences of many early donut franchisees, both in execution and conception. Franchisees' stories of their first plunge into the donut business often end with a journey to the head office to put in an application, to check out a prospective outlet, or to finally sign the contract. These accounts almost always begin with a straightforward, relatively unreflective assertion of small business aspirations. Indeed, in interviews, most franchisees simply stated in a matter-of-fact way that they bought a donut franchise because they were, or wanted to be, an 'entrepreneur,' that they aspired to have a 'business of their own,' that they wanted to be 'independent' or to be 'their own boss.' Despite the best efforts of generations of scholars to distinguish between dynamic entrepreneurs and run-of-the-mill small business owners, franchisees typically used these descriptions synonymously, and did so to describe a variety of experiences.[17] For franchisees like Stockwell and Lalonde, running a donut shop was their first entrepreneurial venture. Others remembered their plunge into the franchised donut business as simply a new way to 'make a buck,' part of a longer process of plucky, if modest, ambition. 'We were always on the lookout – or my younger brother was – for something you can make a buck at,' reported Sam Shneer, who bought a Mister Donut franchise with his brother Harold in 1962. This was hardly the first jump into entrepreneurialism for the Shneer brothers. Indeed, Sam saw his move into donuts as one more step in a career of clever salesmanship:

> Originally we started off ... selling Bibles ... door to door ... We hooked up with a company in North or South Carolina and we bought these gorgeous Bibles. Oh, beautiful Bibles! We were buying them for about two bucks a piece, and we were selling them for about thirty dollars [laughs]. So we got smart – or my brother did – he said ...'We'll go see ... the head honcho at every diocese, we'll give him a few bucks, and he'll give us a letter of recommendation in the bibles.' ... We got this letter recommending these Bibles and, man, we had crews going from Newfoundland to Alaska selling Bibles.[18]

Just as there were different routes *into* the business, there were a variety of paths *through* it. Indeed, the range of what it meant to be your own boss was frustratingly wide. Some franchisees left the business fairly quickly, finding that the reality of donuts did not match their original aspirations, or discovering that their real passion lay elsewhere. George Etzel left Mister Donut soon after he joined in the early 1970s, but ended up in another small business.[19] Other franchisees owned one shop for twenty years; still others acquired two or three at various times; some grew to a handful of shops, sometimes with partners. A few took entrepreneurialism even further, building impressively large mini-empires of a dozen or two outlets within their chain.[20] Still another group of franchisees eventually started their own chains.[21] None of these roles were watertight compartments. Franchisees could pass back and forth between focusing on one shop and owning several or between being an operator and being an investor. At Country Style, Chris Pappas started as a baker, became an owner-operator, then had an independent shop, and then continued on as a silent partner to help other franchisees buy outlets in various chains.[22] 'Entrepreneurialism' and 'small business identity' were not fixed roles, but evolved and shifted over time in response to growing confidence and experience as well as to new business opportunities.

Yet franchisees often explained their leap into the donut business as a product of fixed personality traits. 'Always having been a bit of an independent cuss, I wanted to get into my own business,' Dave Ambeault said of his decision to buy a Tim Hortons franchise in 1970.[23] Few reported any particular passion for donuts. Most franchisees simply wanted some sort of business and ended up in donuts almost by happenstance: through family, friends, or work; by spotting an advertisement at just the right time; or just tripping over a successful shop one day, perhaps after attending the theatre or having dinner at a nice restaurant. If they showed any emotion for the business at all, the feeling was generally phrased as generic 'ambition' rather than passion for the specific product. Many franchisees' memories of their work and business lives – both before and after they bought a franchise – highlight their hard work and ambition rather than passion, creativity, and inspiration. Ron Hewitt started as a factory worker as a teenager, then worked as a salesman before buying a Tim Hortons. 'I sold vacuum cleaners door to door [for] ten years,' he told me with a grin. 'I was ambitious ... In those days, you walk and talk and make money. That's a hard business but if you work hard, you make money.'[24]

Understanding the relationship between entrepreneurial identity and the franchise experience is further complicated by the inconvenient reluctance of many independents to act the part of the tragic 'little guy' fighting the good fight against the invasion of chains.[25] Independent owners reported small business desire in much the same way as franchisees, with ritualistic references to a desire for 'control of our lives.' This desire for independence was sometimes framed in explicit opposition to the franchise experience. Gerry Etkin, a former jeweller, opened King Donut near Toronto in 1963. Though he initially investigated an American chain, he eventually rejected the franchise route because of the stringent conditions for operations, supplies, and promotional ideas. Moreover, the initial cost was higher than opening his own shop, and Etkin was not convinced that the chain had sufficient strength north of the border to warrant the expense. 'I'm glad I went it alone,' he told *Canadian Baker*. 'If I'd taken the conditions offered by the U.S. company I'd probably still be struggling for my first profit.' But even in Etkin's case, the line between franchisee and independent was blurry. Etkin did not reject franchising out of hand in the name of some dogmatic commitment to independence; he simply found the specific conditions undesirable.[26]

Many independents first considered opening a donut shop when they encountered a chain store, and often reported becoming attracted to the donut shop idea in the same terms as franchisees (spotting one on a trip, seeing one at the side of the road, or hearing about it at a club meeting), but for various (often serendipitous) reasons, deciding to copy the franchise rather than buy it. 'I forget where it was that I came across a donut store,' Eugene Pechet recalled of his decision to open Dolly Donuts in 1970. 'I think it was Montreal or New York ... I came back to Edmonton and discovered that we didn't have a donut shop. So I decided to open one.'[27] Some psychologists might draw a firm line between a cooperative franchise personality and a creative entrepreneurial mind;[28] in the donut business, however, the border between franchisee and independent operator was sometimes related not to self-conception or preference, but simply to financial or other reasons. 'We went to a meeting which discussed franchising, and they used Mister Donut as the example,' Deborah Asmussen of Donut Queen in Waterloo recalled. 'Unfortunately, we couldn't afford the [Mister Donut franchise], and we began to query: What does it take to run a donut shop? What do you have to buy in a franchise that you can't figure out yourself?'[29]

As in the case of franchise operators, there were varied meanings of 'independent.'[30] Two examples illustrate the varied development of independent shops and the difficulty of trying to apply simplistic notions of independence in this period. Calvin LeDrew represented one configuration of independent owner with his Donut Queen in Sydney, Nova Scotia (no relation to the Donut Queen in Waterloo). Like many franchisees, LeDrew remembered his work life in terms of independence, ambition, and energy. As a young man in the early 1960s, he and a friend toured central Canada and the northeastern United States in a Volkswagen Beetle, looking for promising business opportunities to bring to Cape Breton. They checked out a number of operations, including a Dairy Queen franchise, but LeDrew eventually settled on the idea of opening a donut shop. His father-in-law was the manager of Eastern Bakeries in Moncton, 'so there certainly was some encouragement from that side of the family to get into the bakery business ... and he put me in touch with the [suppliers].'[31]

Although he opened a second outlet for a short time, LeDrew's donut operation remained small, largely because of financial problems. Money was a constant struggle. LeDrew took a job selling real estate while he ran the business, and his wife worked as a teacher, did the books for the shop, and spent evenings in the family kitchen baking pies to sell in the Donut Queen the next day. The LeDrews added other products, including hot dogs and sandwiches, but the shops never seemed to make money. 'A big day was a hundred and fifty bucks,' he remembered. 'We were just paying our bills and it was tough, tough going.' After seven years, LeDrew sold the shop to concentrate on real estate.[32] In retrospect, LeDrew felt his problem was not competition from big chains – there were no franchised operations in Sydney until years later – but the lack of it. 'We were at least ten years away yet,' he mused thirty years later. 'People were not conditioned to the donuts. They were certainly not conditioned to the prices.' In Sydney back in the 1960s, most people were still excited by the cheap minidonuts churned out by the progeny of Levitt's original automatic machine and sold at the Woolco lunch counter. In LeDrew's mind, unlike other cities where some independent operations thrived during this period – southern Ontario cities like Waterloo and Niagara Falls – the Sydney consumer had not been trained to go to donut shops and was not primed to pay a premium for big, fresh, hand-cut donuts.[33]

It is an interesting theory, although some other independents thrived in relatively undeveloped markets, even growing to multiple outlets. At Ideal Donut of Niagara Falls and later Winnipeg, Vladimir Ududec forged a different route through the independent donut business. In the mid-1960s, Ududec was a Downsview factory worker who earned extra money by doing some bookkeeping on the side and soon opened a donut shop in Oshawa. The first outlet failed, so Udedec tried again in Niagara Falls, then moved the family to Winnipeg, where he opened freestanding shops on two of the city's main automobile arteries, Pembina Highway and Portage Avenue. Through the 1970s and early 1980s, Ideal grew to eight outlets, six of them satellite locations in shopping mall food courts.[34] By the time the larger chains like Tim Hortons and Robin's arrived in Winnipeg in the late 1970s, the Ududecs had a well-established donut business with multiple locations. Like the franchise operators they often copied, then, independent donut entrepreneurs found different routes through the business.

Like the ideal postwar consumer of washing machines, television sets, new cars, and subsidized mortgages, franchisees were pulled from a broad spectrum of semiskilled workers, skilled trades, and middling professional occupations: salesmen, real estate agents, accountants, police officers, factory workers, foremen, bakers, and similar occupations.[35] Few came from the lowest or the highest rungs of the occupational ladder. The downsized middle managers and corporate executives who streamed into franchised businesses after the late 1980s were nowhere to be found in the donut business's early days; nor were many unskilled labourers making the jump to franchising – likely because they lacked the financial means. In the mid-1960s, donut franchises cost $35,000 to $40,000, with about one-third of the amount as a down payment. Until the late 1970s, banks were often reluctant to lend money to new franchise operations, so franchisees were often forced to pay higher interest rates at finance companies.[36]

Prospective franchisees often tried to combat these problems by bringing in a friend or family member as a partner. Chris Pappas overcame his financial limitations by hooking up with his brother-in-law, a waiter at a private club. Family members were also approached for loans. Spencer Brown, Tim Hortons' first franchisee, who had been working as a bank teller in Scarborough, borrowed money for the down payment from his uncle. Even when bringing in partners or drawing on family members for support, franchisees clearly had to scrounge for money to afford the move. Typically, they did not draw from a single large source of funds; instead, they sold possessions, collected small sums from family, borrowed, and so on. 'I sold my car and scraped around,' remembered William Stockwell in a typical description.[37]

Of course, the franchise market was no less undifferentiated than the mass market. Scraping together money was obviously much harder for a semiskilled worker like a baker than it was for a stable professional like a real estate agent. Though almost all franchisees emphasized the financial hardship of buying the business – especially the difficulty securing cheap and reliable financing and still having money left over to pay for housing and daily expenses – it was clear that professionals-turned-franchisees had easier access to funds. One former real estate agent sold his house in a suburb of Toronto and bought a donut franchise in a city with cheaper housing. Though he stressed the difficulty of securing financing, his living standards didn't suffer considerably when he became a franchisee: 'Today, Royal Bank, Toronto Dominion: you need $100,000 for [a donut shop]? You'll get it. [Back then,] not a nickel ... I sold my house ... [and] that was quite a bit of money. I borrowed money from a friend, and that was the way I bought it. [Luckily, houses were] cheap like hell in [the city where he bought his outlet] at that time ... Beautiful homes for peanuts.'[38]

Recruitment into the business was often based on personal relationships – that is, on community links, family groups, and other social networks. Donut shops expanded in Greater Toronto partly on the strength of the entrepreneurial ambition of the city's growing Greek population.[39] Country Style's first franchisee, Chris Pappas, arrived in Canada from Greece in 1956 and got a job in a bakery in Peterborough, then later at the second Country Style outlet at Weston Road and Lawrence Avenue. He eventually took over the outlet, and two years later sold it to the Kiriakopoulos family. The subsequent decade is a sort of mini-directory of Greek immigration to the GTA after the Second World War: Bill Douras, Hercules Kelefas, Ted Panagakis, Steve Mavros, John Goulas, and Mike Sotos all became early Country Style franchisees.[40] At Mister Donut, nine of the chain's twenty-seven Ontario outlets were Greek-owned by 1977, including seven of the eleven shops in the GTA.[41]

The presence of so many Greek franchisees in the donut business was partly a by-product of the traditional concentration of Greek immigrants in food service,[42] and once it developed, donut chains could draw in new franchisees through a kind of 'chain migration' based on kin or (less commonly) village ties. Gus Anastakis became a Country Style franchisee in the mid-1970s, having done factory work since coming to Canada in the early 1960s, eventually rising to the position of foreman. Though he had been in Canada for thirteen years, Old World village ties were his path into the donut business. 'A friend of mine – we come from the same village back home – used to have a

Mister Donut,' he recalled. 'He told me, "Come over and I'll teach you about donuts and you can get a store." I was a manager at a factory and my wife was at home with the kids, and I didn't want to leave the job.' Later, two Country Style franchisees – who had 'married girls of my neighbours back home' – persuaded Anastakis to join the chain. Having the made the step into the business, Anastakis became the conduit for others to come in. By the early 1980s he was ready to take on another outlet, and joined one of his former bakers as partners in the venture. To sort out the early history of chain donut shops in the GTA one must marshal the skills of the genealogist, ferreting out kin and village connections over multiple generations.[43]

This process of kin and chain recruitment should not be romanticized as a by-product of ethnicity. While a few native-born Canadians answered recruitment ads in newspapers or in the outlets themselves, many others followed various social networks into the donut business. At Tim Hortons, Ron Joyce recruited a notable percentage of early franchisees from the Maritime diaspora to industrial southern Ontario, one of the most significant but understudied migrations of the postwar era. By 1961 there were almost 10,000 Maritime-born people living in Hamilton, which made them a significant though certainly not dominant contributor to the local migrant population.[44] Joyce himself arrived in Hamilton along this well-worn path. A native of Tatamagouche, Nova Scotia, he left home at fifteen in search of work, landing in Hamilton at the beginning of its postwar industrial boom, finding jobs at American Can, Firestone, and later with the local police. At the helm of Tim Hortons by 1967, Joyce tapped the local Maritime population to help build the chain. Ed Mattatal, an old friend of Joyce's from Tatamagouche and an eighteen-year employee of American Can, was one of the chain's earliest franchisees. Al Murray, also a Tatamagouche native who had worked with Joyce at Firestone years before, bought store number six on Hamilton Mountain. New Brunswick natives George and Dorothy McGlinchey, whom Joyce met while moonlighting as a produce driver (George, an employee of Stelco, was doing the same), took on the outlet in Cambridge. In 1974, Joyce sold the first Maritime outlet, in Moncton, to Gary O'Neil, a Hamilton steelworker whose father was from Tatamagouche.[45]

Family and friendship was another early route into the donut business. Dave Ambeault first heard about Tim Hortons from a family friend, Eldon Fawcett, who owned the chain's outlet in Burlington. Ambeault joined the chain in 1970. Tim Hortons' second Maritime outlet, in Dartmouth, Nova Scotia, was owned by Joyce's brother Willard, who returned east after stints in Oshawa and St Catharines. Family and friendship connections were common at the other chains as well. After Marvin Wallace opened a Country Style outlet in London, his brother-in-law Thomas Majerle became a Mister Donut franchisee with his wife.[46]

Kin was more than a path into the business; it was woven into the very fabric of operations, albeit in a variety of ways.[47] At Country Style's Calgary outlet, Sylvia Cultrera covered the front of the store, supervised the 'girls,' and did the bookkeeping and payroll, while husband Nello took care of production, baking, and ordering supplies. But in other cases, there seemed to be a lot more 'pop' than 'mom' in both the initial decision to enter the business and in the day-to-day operations, even when women spent a lot of time in the shop. In 1967, Walter Halaiko was more enthused about buying a Mister Donut franchise than his wife, Anita. 'I was still not in favour of it, but I figured if I didn't go along with it, I probably wouldn't hear the end of it,' Anita Halaiko laughed. 'I had no idea what it would be like, but I knew that our life would change.' Once the outlet was open, however, the whole family joined in: Walter worked at the outlet full time, doing the books, ordering supplies, supervising bakers and servers, and running the back of the shop. Anita worked evenings (after a full day teaching elementary school) and weekends; daughter Judy took shifts at the counter on weekends; Walter's and Anita's parents cleaned the outlet every Sunday.[48]

Family participation in the shop was not just an economic proposition, but was tied to (often gendered) notions of skill and ability and to emotional relations within families. In North York, Harold and Rose Bonaparte divided up tasks in much the same way as the Halaikos and the Cultreras, although Rose was less involved in the day-to-day operations. Harold Bonaparte loved to bake, having spent a lifetime working with his hands, including designing and building furniture. He felt he had a natural gift for skilled manual work. 'If a carpenter is making something,' he said, 'I can almost put myself in his spot and take over what he's doing. As long as I watch what he's doing, then I can do it.' His wife Rose was more of a thinker. 'She's the brain and I'm the worker,' Harold told me. Part of the Bonapartes' family economy involved Rose bringing in income to supplement the profits of the donut shop. Rose worked as a secretary at an insurance company and did the books and paperwork for their Mister Donut outlet at Wilson Avenue and Jane Street in North York, while Harold handled the day-to-day operations. In the early days, the Bonaparte children were involved in the business as well, mainly chipping in when needed rather than working every day. Their daughter, who was born in 1961, covered the counter on holidays even when she was a child. Eventually, Harold brought his son into the business full time – a move he remembered not in terms of economic necessity, but of fatherly duty:

> My son, who turned sixteen, decided that he didn't want to go to school anymore ... He was a rough kid, he missed school ... He didn't want to learn. So, my wife says, 'You've got to take him in, where else is he going to get a job?' ... So I did take him in, I did teach him the business. I taught him how to bake and I guess after about two months my wife came in and she looked at the donuts and said, 'I see you baked today.' I said, 'No, I didn't bake today ... Jeff baked today.' She said, 'They look like yours.' I [said], 'I know. He wants to show me that he can be as good as his father.' He was great. I mean, he took over ... I had other things to do. I had to check the orders. I had to check this, check that. So, he was the biggest help I could get.

For Bonaparte, bringing both his son and his daughter into the business was part of teaching his children important life skills. The product was a coffee and donut, but the paternal project was to teach a work ethic and an ability 'to get things done.'[49]

Not all franchisees brought the whole family into their outlets. Some male franchisees understood the shop's place in their family economy through the lens of male breadwinner ideology, which meant their wife covered domestic duties to allow the franchisee to spend long hours on the business. Families might be expected to chip in if necessary, but they were not seen as key to the operation. Dave Ambeault remembered his wife helping out at the counter on occasion, but looked at me blankly when I asked him to elaborate on the 'mom and pop' nature of his outlet. 'No, it was a business. It was a retail business,' he stated with bewilderment. Sam Shneer was distressed that his unreliable staff meant his wife had to cover the counter on occasion. '[It was a] twenty-four hour business, girls don't show up, my wife had to go in sometimes,' he complained. For Shneer, having his wife working in the shop with him was not a romantic archetype to be embraced, but a labour problem to be solved. For these and other reasons, he eventually decided to hire an 'older married woman,' one who lived close by, for each of his two all-night outlets. He put both of them in charge as managers.[50]

Of course, the significant difference between the independent shop and the chain was that the franchised operation channelled the entrepreneurial ambition and family economy of the small investor into the corporate philosophy of the chain. 'Our most successful owners,' Mister Donut informed its prospective franchisees, 'are those who understand that they must relinquish some of their own independence to preserve the standards of the chain and to profit most from our management experience ... He must give up certain things.'[51] Franchisors like Country Style and Mister Donut were churning out two different products: on the one hand, they borrowed, defined, or refined a system for producing large quantities of specific commodities like donuts. On the other hand, by developing detailed business plans, they were creating systems for producing and controlling small business people such as William Stockwell. The most coherent summary of the system defined by donut chains was the Manual of Operating Procedures, called 'the Bible' by almost all franchisees. The Bible set out procedures for virtually all aspects of running the business, combining scientific management, well-defined cost controls, motivational strategies, and codified common sense. For the ongoing operations of the shop, the manual laid out a system with two interrelated parts: a production process and a management system. To explain the experience of the franchisee, it is useful to understand these two aspects of the system.

'Son of a Gun, Anybody Can Do That!'

By 1966, Otto Seegers' future was being pinched on both sides. For two years, he had built the business of his five Kentucky Fried Chicken outlets in the Chatham area through a combination of good locations and clever promotional stunts. After securing a choice site on St Clair Street, the main automobile route through the city, he advertised his first Chicken Place by begging residents to stay away, declaring that the store was already too crowded with customers and that his staff simply could not handle any more. His strangest promotion joined Colonel Sanders and an elephant named Tulsa (which Seegers imported from Michigan) in a bizarre parade to his new outlet in Wallaceburg. The plan almost ended in disaster when Tulsa was temporarily lost somewhere near the American border – a development so astonishing in the safarilands of southwestern Ontario that a Canadian wire service picked up the near disaster as a 'believe it or not' story. In a photograph on the wall of Seegers's apartment in North York, the colonel gets a lesson in lost elephant geography from a bemused OPP officer in the parking lot of the new outlet.[52]

By 1966, with no more KFC territories available, Seegers started to cast around for a new business opportunity. 'I saw a Country Style Donut store in London,' he remembered. 'I watched these bakers bake the donuts and I said, "Son of a gun, anybody can do that!" So, over a period of a time, probably a year and a half or two years, I put my own donut shop package together.' Seegers soon discovered, however, that donut shops were fundamentally different from other drive-in operations. From the outside, the locations looked tantalizingly similar: all you needed to make a fortune in the drive-in business was a simple product, a high-traffic location, a 1,200-square-foot building, adequate parking, and an efficient flow of customers in and out the door. But there was a big difference that neither the customers nor Seegers could see. In the back production area lurked a set of procedures entirely unlike fried chicken, hot dogs, hamburgers, or any of the other classic drive-in foods. In these operations, labour was totally deskilled and interchangeable, but donut production was another matter. 'It's the baking that's the killer,' Seegers complained in hindsight, 'I could teach you or anybody how to fry chicken in five minutes ... and you could come up with chicken that even if it's not done a hundred percent right, it still comes out good ... You need a skilled baker to bake donuts. It is a *trade*. I didn't know that – I got caught.'[53]

The production system of donut shops was not only different from that of other drive-ins; it was also unlike traditional mass production in the donut industry. Industrial producers like Val's and Margaret's adopted a Fordist production process, aiming for the continuous flow of the mechanized assembly line. Donut shops relied much more on hand labour but still embraced mass production ideas, looking to that other prophet of capitalist innovation, Frederick Taylor, to codify and regulate the labour process and to define a 'system' for controlling production. In the early twentieth century, Taylor conducted a series of studies of work processes, measuring and charting the exact movements required to complete a task, seeking to minimize effort, to define rules for performing hand labour, and to separate the processes of planning and executing an operation. Both Ford and Taylor were hoping to maximize efficiency and deskill labour, but where Ford applied the pace of the machine through the assembly line, Taylor sought to control human movement itself through study and regulation.[54]

Tim Hortons baker, 1970. Unlike the Canadian Doughnut Company, donut shops relied on hand labour. (*Kitchener-Waterloo Record* Photographic Negative Collection, The Library, The University of Waterloo)

Taylor's ideas attracted considerable attention during his lifetime, but they were not widely applied until later. In the postwar period, visionaries like Ray Kroc, who built McDonald's into a North American empire, often boasted of 'putting the hamburger on the assembly line,' but in fact his restaurants owed more to Taylor than to Ford. Small physical plants and the nature of the product made mechanized assembly lines impractical in the fast food industry, but they seemed perfectly suited to Taylorist production: hand labour, rigidly controlled by exact rules of preparation defined, enforced, and refined by management. At McDonald's, teams of (initially) young men did specialized tasks in choreographed unison, producing the hamburger step by step to company specifications.[55] In broad terms, donut shops fit into the mainstream of these developments in food service, forming a modern version of a cottage industry: a combination of mass production ideas and small workshops dispersed across geographical space. The typical daily production of a donut shop in the 1960s was around 200 to 350 dozen a day, only one-tenth or less of the average volume of wholesalers. Except for mechanized mixers, most of the work was done by hand.[56] But as Seegers discovered, however much owners tried to regulate the labour process, the donut was not a hamburger or a fried chicken, and skill continued to be an important part of donut production.

In a donut shop, jobs were divided between bakers and servers. The baker did the primary production: mixed the dough, rolled it out, cut the donuts, proofed the yeast product, and fried the rings. Besides covering the counter, servers took care of secondary production like finishing: icing, glazing, and pumping fillings. Depending on the size of the store, this finishing job might be a separate task, but usually finishers passed back and forth between production in the back and serving in the front. The system built its division of labour on a foundation of gender and skill. Bakers, both in design and practice, were typically men. At this time, want ads were still divided by gender, and bakers generally appeared in the 'Help Wanted Male' column. The work was heavy, involving picking up fifty to hundred pound bags of flour and fifty-pound blocks of shortening, although franchisees indicated that they simply assumed it was a male job. 'It was just the way it went,' said one.[57] The servers were always female, even though some fast food chains, notably McDonalds and Red Barn, relied exclusively on male counter staff throughout the 1960s.[58] Wants ads explicitly advertised these server jobs for women, although any man with a pioneering spirit would no doubt have been discouraged from applying by the standard uniform, which included a skirt and apron. Serving and finishing was not heavy, but it could be hard:

> Working at Tim Hortons was a lot of work for someone fifteen years old. The students were responsible for doing a lot of the heavy cleaning work ... We were ... responsible for cleaning the bakers' racks, which at the time were taller than me and full of grease. This was an awfully messy job. I remember having to use a special cleaner to cut through the grease. I also recall slipping in the mess and hurting myself, but back in those days I recall being afraid of management and never said anything.[59]

Skill overlapped with gender in the shop's division of labour. Servers were considered less skilled than bakers, even though working the counter required a certain flair and personality.[60] The 'girls' were urged to practise 'suggestive selling,' subtly encouraging customers to get a donut with their coffee, for example.[61] Manuals instructed franchisees to be on the lookout for servers with certain attributes, especially in terms of appearance and comportment, and further ordered servers to keep fingernails clean and to gargle mouthwash to avoid bad breath. 'Poise' seemed an especially appreciated characteristic. Servers were ordered to stand straight, to face the counter, to work quickly without looking rushed, and to smile constantly.[62] Poise, beauty, and hygiene were not recognized as skills in the conventional sense of the term. More often, at least in want ads, they fell into vaguer and less material categories like 'mature,' 'friendly,' or 'attractive' – attributes that were rewarded with minimum wage. While the traditional argument for low pay for servers in food service was the compensatory value of tips, donut companies typically enforced a 'No Tipping' Policy as a standard part of operations, mainly to limit employee theft. At the sit-down counter at least, the policy was widely ignored by servers and customers alike.[63]

The situation for bakers could not have been more different. Manuals made a point of highlighting the craft of the baker, even while laying out a baking process that was thoroughly regulated and quantified.[64] Indeed, the labour process of the baker was not craft work; it combined Levitt's innovations in raw material and mixing with Taylor's vision of scientific management and the smaller physical plants of traditional retail bakeries. Cutting and frying were done by hand, but little judgment was required to perform these tasks, which used premade mixes and predetermined times, temperatures, weights, and so on. Measured quantities, precise timing, and prescribed temperatures could not eliminate all the judgment and discretion from baking, however. Many of the steps, like rolling the dough, required experience and practice to do efficiently and quickly. Moreover, the weather, especially humidity, could affect the proofing of yeast donuts, which meant that a certain feel for the dough was helpful. 'You have to work by feel,' recalled Ron Joyce of his early trials with baking. 'Heat and humidity affect everything you do; even after you think everything is figured out the weather could change and you are back where you started from, struggling to make a consistent product.' Donut manuals, trade magazines, and mix companies tried to offer help with troubleshooting guides, but the solutions usually came back to the experience and judgment of the baker.[65]

The nature of these 'skills' placed the baker in an ambiguous position. Companies like Mister Donut might make rhetorical concessions to their craft abilities, and would reward bakers with higher wages than servers, but ultimately, the donut baker was a classic semiskilled worker, one who exercised rudimentary judgments within a thoroughly codified production process.[66] Their judgments were very specific to the donut industry, and recognition of their skills often eluded them outside the shops. Steve Furgeson, who started as a baker in Tim Hortons in Toronto and later managed a company-owned shop in Surrey, related his running conflict with the local branch of the Canada Employment Centre, which offered to subsidize the wages of any employee receiving training for a skill, but refused to include donut baking in the program.[67]

Still, inside the shops, the semiskill of bakers made them an expensive nuisance.[68] Workers did not normally move from city to city in search of jobs in donut making, so to secure reliable bakers, franchisees had to take their chances in difficult local labour markets. 'Back then ... people my age were going to university or the factories were hiring and paying very good money,' remembered Judy Halaiko, who helped her parents run a Mister Donut in St Catharines in the late 1960s. 'Guys would be quitting Grade 12 and going to work for [General Motors] in the factories, so to find somebody for those middle-of-the road positions [like baking], it really wasn't that easy ... You'd have kids ... getting on with the paper mill or [General Motors], especially in our area.'[69] To each franchisee, the problem seemed local, but finding good bakers was a problem across the industry throughout the 1960s and 1970s. Tim Hortons eventually prohibited poaching of bakers from other outlets, while Country Style became involved in efforts to expand the pool of applicants by developing educational programs at community colleges (part of a larger effort to improve training in the food service industry) and by encouraging franchisees to hire female bakers. Al Watson, president of Country Style, argued that female bakers were more loyal than male bakers, who tended to move from shop to shop in search of 'more and more money for less work.' The most common way to encourage bakers to remain on the job was paying them under the table. 'Bakers ... weren't paid by the hour, they were paid by the bake,' noted Ron Ansett, who worked in the head office of Country Style and Mister Donut in the late 1970s and early 1980s, 'and in those days if you were getting forty bucks a day and ten bucks under the table, or twenty bucks under the table, you were doing great.'[70]

Companies also continued efforts to deskill bakers and to move production closer to the factory model that had dominated the donut industry in the 1950s, without losing the advantages of freshness and quality offered by on-site production. In a 1968 report to its franchisees, Mister Donut laid out its plan for 'Emancipation Through Automation.'[71] The report made it clear that the anticipated freedom was for the franchisee, not the worker, and targeted two particularly troubling facts about bakers: their expense, and their lack of reliability. From 1962 to 1968, labour costs for baking a dozen donuts increased about 15 per cent, even for the most productive baker. More troubling, though, was the number of bakers who fell below company standards of productivity. Good workers hardly relished being buried on the night shift, the report noted, which meant they drifted away and the franchisee was left to hire any 'warm body' who was available. The report especially lamented the high rates of absenteeism and the lack of concern for product quality.[72]

Franchisees were remarkably frank in interpreting this bureaucratic language. 'They're all drunks,' claimed Sam Shneer. 'Every last one of them ... All the professional guys who were old-time bakers, they all drank ... Not the young guys ...The young guys tried to fool around with the girls ... We frowned on that, but what can you do?' But the franchisee, like other owners employing semiskilled workers, was reliant on the baker's knowledge and experience, however limited his craft ability. 'We had a fridge in back and you'd come in and there was bloody booze in there,' Tom Majerle recalled of one of his night bakers. 'You'd say, "You been drinking?" The guy'd say, "No," but he could barely stand up. You need a baker, though, you know. If he takes his apron off, you say, "Oh, I've done it now, I have to start baking." Because once you start you can't come back tomorrow and finish up.'[73] Whether specific complaints about drinking were true or not – such drunkards may have been memorable exceptions – the stories highlight the reliance of franchisees on the semiskills of bakers.

The new procedure, then, must have seemed a godsend for the beleaguered franchisee, in that it promised – for a mere $2000 in new equipment – 'emancipation' from these problems.[74] The specifics of the new system fell somewhat short of its philosophic vision, however. The plan essentially mechanized the forming of the donut – using a machine cutter for yeast and an automatic extruder for cake – a part of the process that was more time consuming than it was skilled. Mechanized cutting eliminated some labour costs and ensured a better schedule for bakers, but it neither emancipated the capitalist nor automated the process. Some franchisees were just as happy to do the baking themselves, but this was not realistic for multi-outlet owners. The best solution remained hiring inexperienced bakers and training them. 'We hired guys and trained them,' recalled Lynda Lalonde of Tim Hortons, in a typical bit of Taylorism (which she combined with unquestioned assumption about the gendered nature of the job). 'For the most part, they had to be trained by whatever method we wanted done. [Experienced bakers] had bad habits.'[75]

Donut executives were relentless millenarians, however, and continued to dream of being liberated from enslavement to the inebriated night baker. In the 1970s, some of the chains began to investigate frozen donuts. Working with one of the chains, Margaret's Donuts tried to design a new freezing and microwaving technology, a development that Margaret's Tom Brazier claimed 'would have revolutionized the donut stores. By having this box in your stores, you are eliminating your bakers, so you're not relying on bakers, [and] you probably have better control over freshness because you would bring it out as you need it, as opposed to baking at night and selling all day.' The project never quite worked, though Margaret's did come out with a line of frozen donut shells, promising that 'your unskilled staff can be fully trained in a single day.'[76] But few operators were happy with the taste of the frozen shells, which did not simulate the fresh-baked standard in donut outlets. The shortage of cheap and reliable night bakers continued to be a problem throughout the 1970s and into the 1980s. Country Style eventually moved towards a central commissary system for its new Toronto-area stores, producing donuts at a central plant and distributing them to non-baking outlets on a daily basis. Others opened satellite locations where donuts could be shipped from nearby outlets. But most donut shops continued to rely on the semiskilled baker.[77]

'You Name It, It Was There'

There were striking parallels between the situation of bakers and the position of franchisees. In company policies, franchisees came off as 'semiskilled' entrepreneurs who exercised rudimentary judgments within a thoroughly codified and standardized management system. Donut chains applied Frederick Taylor's mass production ideas to the manufacture of the entire donut shop. Mister Donut's manual was especially developed in this regard, laying out (in more than a half-dozen binders) detailed instructions on the duties, responsibilities, and behaviour of franchisees and managers, including such details as a step-by-step, chronological enumeration of the daily routine for managing a Mister Donut shop.[78]

The management system had obvious value in two crucial areas: cost control and portion control. Material costs were the single biggest expense in a donut shop, running at 30 to 40 per cent of gross revenues, so controlling portions and costs was the bread and butter of the business. The chains set prices for the franchisee based on a formula for production costs, labour costs, operating expenses, and so on. Keeping an eye on day-to-day costs was left to the franchisee, although the procedures were stringently defined. Franchisees were given company forms on which to calculate costs relative to labour and output, required to fill out exacting paperwork on all items sold, instructed on proper ways to stack inventory, and even told where to place their office in the shop to better facilitate inspection by the chain. Prices, costs, materials, and labour were precisely calculated by the franchisor, leaving the franchisee to simply monitor the inputs to cut down on waste.[79]

Some of these activities required good planning by the franchisee. Analysing labour needs at a particular time for a particular store, for example, was easier with preprinted company forms, but franchisees had to use their experience to deal with local wrinkles. Yet, as in the case of bakers, these 'skills' were rudimentary and were structured by the rules and regulations of the system. Indeed, there was much in the franchise experience that might be called semiskilled or quasi-entrepreneurship, with franchisors recruiting inexperienced small entrepreneurs and training them to company specifications. Prospective franchisees were quite aware that they needed the greater knowledge and experience of the franchisor, at least initially. Though one of the advertised advantages of joining a franchised operation was superior strength of marketing and exposure, donut chains were still fairly small in this era (certainly, much smaller than other franchised operations), and most franchisees remembered joining the chain not for the power of collective advertising but to acquire basic knowledge of operations, in terms of both production and management. 'Well, at the time there was no way that [you could] open your own,' remembered Costas Kiriakopoulos, who helped his parents run the Country Style at Weston and Lawrence in Toronto in the late 1960s, 'because you didn't know how to start it, how to put this concept together.'[80]

Indeed, training was one significant advantage for the franchisee over the independent, who often had to scramble to acquire knowledge from flour companies, family members, and rival bakers, as well as by borrowing from existing chains. Rudimentary baking knowledge could often be learned fairly easily, especially from flour companies like Jo-Lo and DCA, which offered training in donut making in order to increase their own sales of donut mix. At Donut Queen in Sydney, Calvin LeDrew relied on 'other bakers and suppliers' to get his business established. Other independents simply hired good bakers who already knew the procedure. '[I] hired a baker,' Eugene Pechet of Dolly Donut in Edmonton remembered. 'He came from England and he worked in the bakery that provided the cake for the Queen's Coronation, and I felt he was quite experienced.' Other aspects of donut operations, like true expertise in baking, were more complicated to learn, and independents had to be inventive in adapting, borrowing, and outright stealing ideas from other shops. To set up the Donut Queen in Waterloo, the Asmussens visited more than twenty-five donut shops in southern Ontario, surreptitiously measuring counters and stools, examining light fixtures, and so on. Deborah Asmussen even posed as a health inspector, complete with clipboard, to trick her way into the back of shops, where she could examine the baking equipment. For ongoing help, independents relied on family, experienced employees, and salesmen from the flour companies.[81]

With applicants unwilling to go to such lengths to acquire knowledge of the business, the process of moulding the would-be entrepreneur into a franchisee began with the training procedure. The shaping of the franchisees to the system began the moment they walked in the door of the training facility. 'You walk in on the first day,' one recalled, 'you put on a white uniform and they gave you a mop. "Clean the toilets," they tell you. Now hold it, I just gave you a hundred and fifty thousand dollars, [and] I'm cleaning toilets? And he said "Ya, for a reason, because if you hire a porter, you want to teach him the right way." Now think about that: They were right. There, they were right.'[82] This was not just a practical move (although chains did seem rather obsessed with small matters like toilet brush choreography); it was a kind of psychology, a jarring message to the franchisee that every aspect of the business, no matter how mundane, had a procedure designed by the head office. From that lesson, training moved up the ladder of tasks, growing more complex as it went along: serving, finishing, and finally baking. Some franchisees already had baking experience: both Sam Dimakis and Chris Pappas, for example, had started as bakers in the chains they eventually joined as franchisees. But for most, even training in the most rudimentary production skills was appreciated. 'Keep in mind that I knew nothing about the donut business,' Tom Majerle told me, 'I didn't know the first thing about it.'[83]

For the American companies like Dunkin' and Mister Donut, training was steeped in the language of professionalism and managerial expertise. 'There is no more professional business training program in the U.S. than Dunkin Donuts University,' Dunkin' Donuts declared. 'The curriculum is intensive, varied and absolutely complete. You can learn to make a perfect product, hire personnel, handle finances, maintain equipment, merchandise, profitability, establish administrative procedures, and, in all, run a successful donut shop.'[84] Until the late 1970s, the upstart Canadian operations had less developed training processes, mainly relying on experienced franchisees to train new ones in existing outlets. Costas Kiriakopoulos trained many incoming Country Style franchisees at his family's outlet at Weston Road and Lawrence Avenue in Toronto.[85] This type of in-store training covered the technical aspects of baking, cleaning and maintaining machines, and so on, but some franchisees complained that they lacked a clear idea of the chain's finance and administrative controls.[86] For their part, franchisors worried that in-store training 'kept us from having a consistent standard across the chain. Deviations between stores would creep in, depending on whom the owner had trained with ... This method of training meant that there was a wide variety of acceptable standards.'[87] Over time, the training in Canadian chains became more formalized. Tim Hortons, for example, set up a separate training centre in 1977. The new facility represented a change in approach as well as location: 'All of our training ... has been carried out in existing outlets up to now,' company president Ron Joyce told the *Hamilton Spectator*. 'The new facility ... will be a working classroom in which we can train people in all facets of the business ... In addition, there will be a series of lectures by our own management and by outside experts in such areas as administration, operation maintenance, financing and inventory control.'[88]

Notwithstanding its limitations in the early days, the training procedure did more than teach practical skills; it also conditioned the franchisee to think in terms of the system. Franchisees came out of training knowing the basic system so well that they rarely consulted the manual in their day-to-day business. Yet they knew its contents with considerable precision. 'The manual was the complete history of the donut business,' recalled one, 'starting off with how to hire a person, to how a hire a janitor, how to show him how to clean, train bakers, how to do advertising, how to buy product – you name it, it was there. It was a complete manual ... You name it, it was in the book.'[89] In many ways, training was a form of indoctrination as much as it was a teaching of skills: a way to ensure that franchisees internalized the system and made it a basic part of their thinking about the business. Reinforcing this process of indoctrination was the organization of space in the shop. Franchisees usually bought a 'turnkey operation': they paid for a key to the front door of a fully equipped outlet that was ready and waiting to churn out donuts. In locating, designing, building, and equipping an outlet, the franchisor literally built much of the system into the physical plant of the shop, handling most of the typical activities of setting up a small business. Once a location had been secured (usually by lease, although Tim Hortons and, to a lesser degree, Country Style often bought property), the franchisor's construction and engineering department typically built the shop (or in some cases, arranged to have it built) and subleased it to the franchisee. Even once the building was up and the business was running, some controls were entrenched in the organization of space, requiring only maintenance by the franchisee. Equipment was placed in proper order on the counters to minimize the number of steps by staff; shelves were set at the correct angle for proper display; small items like ashtrays, spoon holders, and sugar dispensers were supplied in preset numbers (six, two, and eight respectively); and signage was preprinted to reflect the image, colours, and policies of the chain, right down to the 'No Tipping' sign. Coffee machines came preset to deliver a standardized quantity of the optimum brew. Even cream and sugar were controlled and standardized.

With the system built into the shop and indoctrinated thoroughly into the franchisee, it seemed there was little left for the franchisee to do. The system did not run automatically, however, and human realities continued to mute the effect of the franchisor's designs. Franchisors still had to supervise their outlets effectively, and franchisees were not completely passive. They spent hours in their shops, maintaining the system, squeezing out profits, and even resisting the control of the franchisor. Control continued to be a complex and dynamic issue within the chain.

'They Should Have Gotten Rid of Me Long Ago'

'You get up in the morning and you go to work,' William Stockwell explained, describing the typical day of the donut franchisee in the late 1960s. 'You go down there and you check your receipts, get the banking done and all that kind of stuff, and you always had a little time with staff, because [you had] a lot of part-time staff. And you kind of arranged to make sure that you've got all the shifts covered. And sometimes you did a little baking.' Franchisees put long hours into their shops, baking, serving, cleaning, repairing, chasing down tardy employees, covering shifts of absent bakers or servers (often on short notice), keeping track of inventory and cost controls, ordering supplies, and generally keeping an eye on things. If there is a dominant memory that comes out in interviews, it was the hard work and the fact that the donut business was a twenty-four-hour, seven-day-a-week proposition.

Much of this activity seemed to involve the careful supervision of employees, some of whom were considered unreliable, if not dishonest. Beyond paperwork, franchisees spent much of their time making sure their workers weren't wasting or stealing. But the main motivation for close supervision was that with cost controls so carefully defined, labour and materials were the one place where franchisees could squeeze more profitability out of their shops. Yet cost controls went to the heart of the contradictory position of the franchisee. On the one hand, cost control formulas made the operation profitable, especially when it was difficult to directly monitor employee waste or theft for the entire day. On the other, they were used to calculate royalty payments and thus were one foundation for oversight by the chain. The franchise agreement required the franchisee to keep records available for inspection and allowed franchisors to enter the store to check operations and inventories, ostensibly to ensure standards across the chain. Franchisors employed field representatives to perform regular inspections, checking an outlet's inventory room, for example, to ensure that the shop was using the raw materials from designated suppliers.[90]

Franchisees sometimes believed that the line between preserving standards and making money was fuzzy. The most famous example of this was the case of *Jirna v. Mister Donut*, where a group of Toronto franchise owners discovered that their franchisor had been demanding substantial kickbacks (up to 20 per cent) on purchases from designated suppliers, indirectly collecting extra money from the franchisees. The news of this case spread quickly through the Canadian donut business (and the larger franchising community), both through extensive media coverage and informal contact between franchisees. 'The other store at Wilson and Bathurst – they were the ones that were taking Mister Donut to court,' remembered Harold Bonaparte, who owned the Mister Donut at Jane and Wilson at the time. 'They would keep us up to whatever they were doing, so we knew what was going on all the time. They, myself, and Sam [Shneer] were like a triangle and we kept together.'[91] Other franchisees reported already knowing about the practice, having discovered it from the supply salesmen who came by their stores. The kickbacks were deeply resented by the franchisees, who saw it as an unfair attempt to skim money off every transaction instead of just being satisfied with the 4 or 5 per cent royalty. Some franchisees did their best to buy what they could from other suppliers on the sly.[92]

A few franchisees admitted that they tried to fudge their reported gross revenues for the month, though even years later, they were reluctant to speak openly about these activities. One simple strategy was to lie about cigarette sales, which were somewhat difficult to verify, since they didn't appear on the cash register tape. The franchisee would report a deflated total, pocket the difference, and buy new supplies directly from the vending machine salesman. Such techniques, as with buying unauthorized supplies, often depended upon the informal relationships that developed between operators and salesmen, who were both out in the field on a daily basis. Another strategy was to make some sales 'off the tape.' The trick here was to leave the cash register open all day and only ring in a fraction of the sales. On the register tape that the chain inspected, the day would look slow and the franchisee could pocket the difference. Selling cans of coffee by the pound on a cash basis – again off the register tape – was another way to deflate revenue reports. At the best of times, none of these techniques was especially lucrative, since they involved seeking out tiny crevices in the cost control system, and in chains like Tim Hortons, which had its own distribution system for most supplies, it was even more difficult.[93]

For the most part (although it is often difficult to tell), these franchisees seemed to believe that such operations, though violating the contract, were legitimate. They described a kind of moral economy in which franchisors were blamed for acting 'surprised that somebody else wanted to make a buck.' The same logic applied to buying unauthorized supplies. While many didn't mind that franchisors collected kickbacks from suppliers, others considered the practice morally indefensible, even if technically legal. Franchisors who used kickbacks, they argued, were making money without offering any real service, besides taking advantage of their contractual power without providing any real benefit to the franchisee. 'They didn't even *see* the stuff,' complained one, 'because [the flour company] would collect the money off us and then send [the donut company] a cheque.' Yet there were limits to this moral economy, especially if a franchisee was thought to be threatening the reputation of the entire chain by lowering quality.[94]

This was risky business, since violating the terms of the franchise agreement was grounds for termination of the contract. Every franchise agreement had a 'termination clause' that allowed the franchisor to take back the business.[95] Critics of franchising aimed the bulk of their attacks at this clause, since the wording was extremely vague; they also contended that the power required no standard of reasonableness or fair play to be exercised. Yet the power of the franchisor was as much a human question as a legal and economic one, in that it depended on the degree of oversight they were able and willing to exercise. Donut companies were still modest in size at this point, and technology had not advanced enough to allow the sort of computerized monitoring of sales and revenues that is common in franchising today.[96] Donut franchisors, then, relied on human inspectors to keep an eye on franchisees. These structural realities opened space for conflicts over control. Over the course of the 1970s, Mister Donut gradually acquired the reputation as being too loose with franchisees.[97] Tim Hortons and Country Style were considered to be more exacting, but even then, human relations and other factors intervened. Ron Joyce recalled that his brother Willard developed a side business selling donuts to navy ships docked in Halifax: 'Of course, he didn't report any of these sales to me ... I knew it was going on, but the company looked the other way. After all, we were still making money shipping all the ingredients and packaging ... and he wasn't the only one not reporting all the sales to avoid paying royalties and other charges.'[98]

Control within the chain, then, was not simple, and franchisees were not the passive victims that the system's critics like to portray. Termination was a brute force contractual tool that could be met with equally brute resistance. In London, Marvin Wallace engaged in decade-long trench warfare with Country Style Donuts. By all accounts, Wallace was a free spirit who bought supplies where he liked, sold unauthorized products,[99] and generally ran his four outlets as he liked. In 1974, having proven through 'tests by independent laboratories' that Wallace was using an unauthorized coffee supplier, Country Style terminated his franchise and seized Wallace's Adelaide Street shop at five o'clock one morning. Wallace refused to vacate his other London outlet, secured an injunction against the occupation of his stores, and threatened to sue the chain for two million dollars. This particular dispute was eventually settled, but the ongoing conflict continued until 1981, when the two parties 'negotiated a joint settlement' whereby Wallace sold his outlets. He eventually left London and settled in Florida.[100] Though termination was clearly a significant power that controlled franchisees' actions, it was not absolute.

Another weapon in the franchisor's arsenal was the threat of non-renewal. Since franchise agreements typically lasted twenty years (but could be renewed by the franchisor at the time of expiry), the patient franchisor could simply wait until the twenty-year period elapsed and sell the franchise to someone else or, in the interim, use the threat as a bludgeon. This was a significant, if not especially immediate, power. After twenty years, the experience of being forced to give up outlets was not merely a matter of calculating investments and accounting for sweat equity – it went directly to the heart of a franchisee's sense of family and community. Mister Donut refused to renew Harold Bonaparte's franchise in 1983 after a dispute over some extra items he sold in his outlet at Wilson and Jane. When he split from his original partner in 1963, his wife Rose, who took over doing the books, had discovered the outlet was deeply in debt. The Bonapartes started adding extra items (key chains, bagels, sandwiches and so on) without permission in order to help him climb out of the hole. Bonaparte claims he included sales of the items in his gross revenues to the head office. Years later, he says, the chain asked him to remove the items, and he refused. A few years later, the chain denied his renewal request. Seventeen years later, he was still visibly upset when describing his last day:

> The day I closed up the shop, all the young guys came into the store who had grown up with us, and they all sat at the counter ... The place was packed, and everybody was having donuts, and my wife was there, and my son was there, and my daughter was there, and I think some of my in-laws, and I was giving out free coffee and whatever donut was on the shelves. I was telling them, 'Take whatever you want,' and about 11:30 at night time, I said to the fellas, 'Okay, we're closing the doors,' and they all came over and shook my hand, and I was ready to cry. Cause all of these guys grew up with me ... So, we closed the store.

Bonaparte sold his equipment and retired.[101]

This case involved a rather raw exercise of power by the franchisor, but the issue of renewal points to a much subtler dynamic of control and consent. For the most part, the ongoing relationship between chain and operator was based not on raw force but on a series of more subtle trade-offs and negotiations. The promise of renewal could be used as a positive reinforcement, when the franchisor made it clear from the beginning that there were rewards for being a 'good operator' who played along with the system. Larry Keen discovered this fact at the time he entered the Tim Hortons chain in 1969, when it was only a fledgling chain of a dozen outlets:

> I remember Tim [Horton] saying to me at the time we signed [our first fran-chise agreement in 1969], 'This is the franchise agreement. I want you to take it to your lawyer. Your lawyer's going to tell you that it is all in favour of Tim Hortons, and it is, and we're not changing a thing.' And he went on to say, 'This is our standard agreement, and it's a twenty-year agreement. We want you to sign, put it in a filing cabinet, and you won't have to take it out for twenty years when it's time to renew it.' And he was right.[102]

Moreover, even while resisting the franchisor by buying unauthorized supplies or fudging gross revenues, franchisees clearly accommodated themselves to the oversight of the franchisor. Few franchisees wanted to be left fully alone. After all, they had joined the chain to get assistance running a small business. Franchisees were as likely to bemoan the lack of support from the chain as they were to complain about the burdens of oversight – a contradiction that went right to the heart of the fran-chise experience. 'The franchisor allows you to operate independently,' a Mister Donut franchisee complained to the Grange Commission. 'If problems arise and you cannot make any money the franchisor seems to dream up all kinds of reasons why you cannot make money.'[103] The two impulses – to own a business and to join a chain – were not opposing poles of the franchise experience: they were reflected in all its aspects. One franchisee condemned the *lack* of oversight even while declaring his desire to be left alone. 'Once you had the formula, what the hell [did] you need them for?' he asked. But only a few moments later, he dis-missed his chain's head office for its lack of oversight. 'I think [they] were trying, but ... they didn't have the courage ... They didn't police it and what they should have done was say, "Look, you don't toe the line, you're out." That's what they should have done, but they wouldn't do it, you see. Like, they should have gotten rid of me a long time ago. But they didn't ... They should have terminated me a hundred times.'[104]

Consent could coexist with the recognition of the power of the fran-chisor, especially since the chain, however burdensome its demands could be, was facilitating the genuine entrepreneurial desires of people of relatively modest means. Profits at a well-located and well-run shop could be impressive. Jirna reported annual gross revenues of $450,000 at its three shops, a figure that likely would produce profits in the $70,000 to $90,000 range. Eldon Fawcett, who joined Tim Hortons in 1967, recalled making a profit of $27,000 in his first year, a princely sum compared to the $7,000 he had earned at Westinghouse in Hamilton the year before. In the early 1970s the average Tim Hortons was grossing about $130,000 a year, with profit margins running up to 20 per cent.[105] Chris Pappas admitted that, in law, a franchisee had few rights and little protection, but he still made a positive assessment of his time in the donut business: 'We were small people who came from another country, we didn't speak the language too well. We were happy. We made our living, a good living. When I used to work for Woolworth's Company [as a baker], I used to make twenty-six dollars a week. When I went to Country Style, I worked for myself. I was making a decent, a good wage for the week. So even if it bothered us, it never stopped us from buying another store.'[106] In such cases, recognition of the franchisee's vulnerable position was combined with a more fundamental acceptance of the system, expressed in terms of a desire to earn a living profit.[107]

'The Big Money Was Gone, but I Don't Regret It'

William Stockwell left the donut business in the early 1970s for the same reason many got in: the pull of family life. 'I got out of it mainly because, well, I fell in love with a lady here in London,' he said near the end of our conversation, 'and ... well, she didn't want to live in Windsor.' He was happy enough to get out when he did, and not just because of his love life: 'I was getting a little bit concerned about things in Windsor because it was quite a motorcycle gang area. And the motorcycles wanted to take over the donut shops if they could. So the opportunity to get out of it came and I did, and I don't regret it. The big money was gone, but I don't regret it.' Stockwell sold the shop and returned to London, where he took up selling real estate.

In the donut business, the franchise system was more than ideas of boosters and critics, duly recorded by journalists, politicians, and courts. It was a web of relationships and interconnections, standing between rhetoric and reality, system and practice, chain and franchisee, franchisee and family. Franchising was unquestionably a vessel for small business identity, both in terms of the romantic ambitions of various salesmen, bakers, and factory workers, and in its complexity as a daily practice that marshalled gender, kin, ethnicity, and other resources. Yet having channelled their entrepreneurial ambition into the security of the chain, franchisees found themselves running their businesses by making rudimentary judgments based on codified procedures. They needed the chain, especially in the early days, but they resented their loss of control. They might risk their franchise to shave a few dollars off their gross reports for the month, but their own profitability required them to ensure that their employees did not exercise a similar agency. They might be frustrated by the demands of the chain, but ultimately they were satisfied with the social mobility it could provide. Ultimately, then, franchisees were quasi-entrepreneurs in an in-between position of power. They were living the life of an entrepreneur within the confines of a mass production system, serving (sometimes happily) as the raw material in a grand scheme of mass retailing that was slowly spreading its vision across postwar commercial geography.

4 Expansion and Transformation: Colonizing the Canadian Foodscape, 1974–1999

In September 1977, Howard Advertising, a Toronto advertising and public relations firm, announced that it was resigning from its $350,000 account with Tim Horton Donuts. Howard had hooked up with the growing chain eighteen months earlier and seemed positioned to roll with the expansion of Tim Donut Limited, which was already the largest donut company in the country. But by late 1977, the relationship had turned sour. In announcing the resignation of the account, Greg Howard, creative director at the ad company, told *Marketing* magazine that 'his agency and the chain's former ad manager had attempted to make Tim Hortons "the McDonald's of the Doughnut Business,"' complete with jingle, TV spots, radio commercials, and promotions for the concept 'A friend along the way.' The slogan, a first in the Canadian donut business, was intended 'to create a strong corporate image for the chain (like McDonald's and other large chains in the fast food industry).'[1] Though his vision for Tim Hortons did not work out, Howard had coined an insightful metaphor. Hortons moved in the period after 1977 to a position where the company could rightfully be called the McDonald's of the Donut Business. Indeed, by the turn of the twenty-first century, Hortons would surpass McDonald's and rise to dominate the quick-service restaurant sector.

But Howard's vision also serves to remind us that in the mid-1970s, companies like Tim Donut could only aspire to the status of McDonald's. By this time, donut chains had defined efficient systems of production and franchising, but they did not even command donut selling. In 1976, the *Bakers' Journal* estimated that donut shops accounted for, at most, 17 per cent of Canadian donut sales, with the bulk produced by industrial bakeries and sold through supermarkets.[2] The three largest franchisors – Mister Donut, Country Style, and Tim Horton Donuts – ran chains of forty to sixty outlets with impressive regional reach in central Canada, and they were growing at the moderate rate of six to twelve outlets per year. Remarkable enough for a decade-old business, but it was hard to be too impressed by these figures or with the donut shop's regional base when McDonald's was adding forty or fifty outlets per year and was spreading across the country with remarkable speed. In *Foodservice and Hospitality*'s annual survey of the biggest restaurant chains, donut companies occasionally squeaked into the bottom quarter of the list, but they were more likely to be tagged as 'Firms Worth Watching.'[3]

This designation, as it turned out, was perfect: after the mid-1970s, the donut shop moved from minor player to an almost ubiquitous institution on the Canadian foodscape. This development had four key aspects. First, most of the original donut franchisors made an effort to grow nationally, although only Tim Hortons really succeeded, and even then its national growth came in phases. Second, though all the major franchisors continued to grow, Tim Hortons emerged as the dominant presence in the industry in the 1980s, before rising even higher in the following decade. Third, the donutscape became much more crowded as underneath the original franchisors, several new chains emerged, often spreading one or two dozen outlets across metropolitan or regional markets, supplemented by a veritable explosion of independent shops. Finally, donut chains and independents reinvented the donut shop form itself, adding new products, redesigning the physical space of their shops, adopting new ways to increase convenience and speed of service, exploiting new kinds of locations to seek out tiny crevices in the marketplace, and attempting to remake the image of their shops to attract a broader clientele. Throughout this process, donut chains and consumers confronted the original tensions of the donut shop form of the 1960s: tensions between drive-in culture and sociability, as well as between the shops' mass market aspirations and their male, working-class character.

'A Bid to Become Established Nationally'

Up until the mid-1970s, no donut company had taken decisive control of the industry. Mister Donut got off to an early start after arriving in Canada in 1961, aggressively opening outlets in Montreal and southern Ontario, and growing to twenty-two by 1968. After International Multifoods, a Minneapolis-based food conglomerate, took over Mister

Figure 4.1   Growth of largest donut chains in Canada, 1961–1998

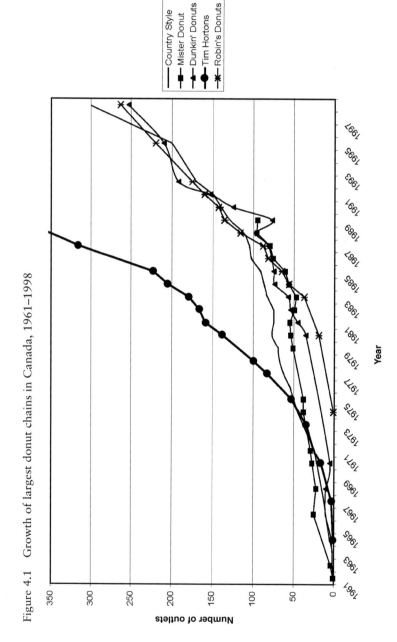

Sources: *Bakers Journal, Foodservice and Hospitality, Canadian Hotel and Restaurant, Canadian Baker*, Tim Hortons Media Kit.

Figure 4.2   Growth of Tim Hortons, 1964–1998

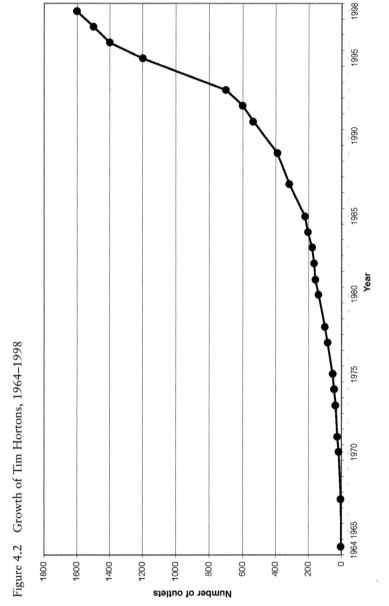

Source: Tim Hortons Media Kit.

Donut in 1969, the Canadian operation announced aggressive expansion plans, forecasting fifty new outlets across the country. But the chain soon found itself tied up in legal wrangles with its Toronto franchisees, and its Canadian growth slowed considerably in the 1970s.[4] At fifty outlets, Country Style had moved into the lead position by 1974, only to be passed by Tim Hortons two years later. In 1977, Tim Hortons' seventy-six stores and $20 million in annual revenues placed it well above second-place Country Style (at sixty-three outlets and about $13 million). By this time, Hortons had already started to accelerate its growth, based partly on an infusion of capital from the Mercantile Bank of Canada, which offered $1 million in credit contingent on the chain opening several stores in short order. With this new money on top of solid operations, the company reached one hundred outlets by the end of 1978.[5] (Country Style took seven years to reach this level; in Canada, Mister Donut never attained it.) While all the original franchisors accelerated their growth in the mid-1980s, Hortons kept pulling away from the competition. By 1986, the chain had more outlets than its nearest three rivals combined (figures 4.1 and 4.2).

Ron Joyce oversaw Hortons' rise to supremacy. A former Hamilton police officer and Dairy Queen franchisee, Joyce became a Tim Hortons franchisee when he took over the chain's outlet on Hamilton's Ottawa Street in 1965. Two years later, the chain's founder (and Tim's first donut partner), Jim Charade, encountered financial problems, and Joyce stepped in to become co-owner and vice president of Tim Donut. A year after Tim's death, in circumstances that would later become the subject of a lawsuit, Joyce bought out Tim's widow and became sole owner of the company.[6] Joyce was considered a smart business owner as well as a workaholic with a careful eye for detail. Certainly, he seems to have been relentless about operational efficiency. In 1977 the chain improved its training procedures, opening up a centralized franchisee training facility in Hamilton, dubbed 'Doughnut University' (similar to McDonald's first training facility, known as 'Hamburger U'). The focus on operations was lucrative: by the mid-1980s, Joyce claimed that per outlet revenues were 'significantly' higher than those of other chains. Figures are difficult to come by, but in 1985 the *Financial Times* estimated that Hortons' per outlet sales were almost one-third higher than those of other chains.[7]

Joyce also transcended the chain's Ontario base – a project that enticed all the major chains in the mid-1970s. Since the advent of donut chains, building a national network of shops had been a goal much talked about but never achieved. As early as 1965, for example, Mister Donut had announced its intention to build a national network of stores, but it managed to open only a few scattered outlets in the West.[8] Around 1974, however, the largest operators began to make more serious moves into other regions. Country Style opened outlets in the West in the mid-1970s, growing to Calgary and Vancouver, but many of these outlets did poorly, and the chain never established a consistent or substantial western presence outside Alberta. Its eastern outlets, opened in the early 1980s, suffered a similar fate and closed within two years of opening. Country Style expanded west again in the 1980s, but its Alberta outlets remained its most consistent presence in the region into the 1990s.[9] For its part, Mister Donut experimented with outlets in the West and East, first in the 1970s, then again in 1980s. The western outlets soon closed, although the Maritime operations did better, carving out decent markets in Nova Scotia and Prince Edward Island.[10] Most disappointing was Dunkin' Donuts. Despite its head start in the 1960s, the deep pockets of its American parent, and its ambitious plans to expand, the chain experienced only stunted growth through the mid-1970s, never expanding beyond a handful of outlets in Ottawa and Montreal. The company attacked the Quebec market more aggressively in the late 1970s, and beefed up its marketing program in 1980 in anticipation of 'a move into the Ontario market in a bid to become established nationally in Canada.' But more than a decade later, over 90 per cent of Dunkin's 198 outlets were located in Quebec.[11]

Tim Hortons, in contrast, built the first permanent national network of shops, but it did so slowly and in phases. Initially, the chain looked east, opening outlets in Moncton, New Brunswick, and Dartmouth, Nova Scotia, in the summer of 1974. The company moved into Quebec three years later and then jumped west the following year, with outlets in Penticton and Surrey, British Columbia.[12] Hortons' initial growth to the East and West relied on family networks and connections from the chain's Ontario base. The first Nova Scotia franchisee was Joyce's younger brother, Willard. Moncton was developed by Gary O'Neil, a Hamilton steelworker (and Nova Scotia native) who agreed to relocate. Hortons initial moves into Quebec relied on existing Ontario franchisees. In the West, the Surrey outlet was owned initially by Ed O'Reilly, a former teacher from the Hamilton area. The chain's first outlet in Greater Edmonton, opened 1983, was owned by a couple from Simcoe, Ontario. Hortons accelerated its national growth in the early 1980s, relying more and more on less personal connections to draw in

Table 4.1   Regional distribution of outlets, Tim Hortons, Country Style Donuts, and Robin's Donuts

	1979/1980*			1994		
	TH	CS	RD	TH	CS	RD
Ontario	86	54	9	425	169	60
Quebec	1	4	0	91	5	0
Atlantic Prov.	14	3	0	189	0	10
West**	3	8	10	119	25	126
North†	0	0	0	2	0	0
Total	100	69	19	826	199	196

*Tim Hortons figures estimated for December 1978, Country Style for February 1979, Robins for June 1980.
**Manitoba, Saskatchewan, Alberta, British Columbia
†Yukon and Northwest Territories
Sources: Ron Buist, *Tales from under the Rim* (Fredericton, 2003); A. Victoria Bloomfield, 'Tim Hortons: The Growth of a Canadian Coffee and Doughnut Chain,' *Journal of Cultural Geography* 14 (Spring/Summer 1994), 4; *Foodservice and Hospitality*, February 1979, 29; *Directory of Restaurant and Fast Food Chains*.

franchisees. It completed its coverage of every province with an outlet in Saskatchewan in 1986. Yet even into the 1990s (and to a lesser degree, into the new century), Hortons' coverage continued to be heavily weighted towards central and eastern Canada (table 4.1).[13]

In trying to build national chains, the major companies confronted the regionally divided nature of Canadian food service. Even during their initial growth in central Canada, the donut companies recognized that local and regional tastes affected sales and product lines.[14] These differences only intensified as donut shops spread across the country. In western Canada, for example, customers initially complained that Tim Hortons coffee was too strong. The chain adjusted the brew to aim for a milder taste, but eventually returned to a single national standard.[15] Notwithstanding adjustments like these, Tim Hortons' western outlets continued to underperform for many years, while the efforts of other companies in the region failed. It was not simply a matter of maintaining standards or adjusting one or two specific products to regional tastes – the donut shop concept, after all, did well in Atlantic Canada. 'It is almost as if you could draw a north-south dividing line, from the western boundary of Ontario, straight down through the United States; certain types of restaurants work well east of that boundary, but fail to

Table 4.2   Regional distribution of Mister Donut locations in North America, 1977

Region	Outlets
Total Northeast U.S.	117
New England	52
Middle Atlantic	65
Total Midwest U.S.	134
East North Central	81
West North Central	53
Total South U.S.	97
South Atlantic	86
East South Central	4
West South Central	7
Total West U.S.	12
Mountain	10
Pacific	2
Total Canada	37
Ontario	27
Quebec (all in Montreal)	10
Total outlets, North America	397
Total in eastern North America	325 (82%)
Total in northern North America	290 (73%)

Note: U.S. regional definitions from U.S. Census Bureau, Census Regions and Divisions of the United States, http://www.census.gov/geo/www/us_regdiv.pdf.
Source: Mid-Atlantic Mister Donut Advisory Council, Mister Donut Phone Directory, 1977.

connect with customers west of it,' Joyce noted in his inside account of Tim Hortons. Another observer described a kind of 'Denny's Line' running athwart the continent, dividing consumers into areas where Denny's taught them to expect free refills or donut shops trained them to pay by the cup.[16] While not precisely accurate in empirical terms (Denny's and similar restaurants are actually common in the east), these regional rules of thumb contain a certain truth. Like Tim Hortons in Canada, both Mister Donut and Dunkin Donuts had difficulty building strong operations in the western United States, despite their powerful hold on the Northeast and Midwest (see table 4.2).[17] In the end, only Tim Hortons succeeded in transcending regional divides, but it was a painful and difficult process, one based partly on willingness to decentralize, splitting the day-to-day operations into geographic regions.[18]

Table 4.3   Donut chains founded in Canada, 1974–1994

Founded	Chain	Based in	Max. # of outlets (to 1 Jan. 2000)
1975	Robins Donuts	Thunder Bay, ON	246
1975	Donut Castle	Toronto	9
1976	Maison du Beigne Inc.	La Salle, QC	7
1976	King Donut	St Catharines, ON	10
1976	Donut World	Toronto	11
1977	Dutch Master	Toronto	7
1977	Bakers Dozen	Mississauga, ON	109
1978	Nuffy's Donuts	Vancouver	10
1978	O'Donuts	Bramalea, ON	18
1979	Donut Café	London, ON	13
1979	Donuts & Things	Toronto	11
1980	Nectar Donuts	Welland, ON	N/A
1980	Global Donuts	Sarnia, ON	11
1981	Cross Country	Toronto	10
1982	Coffee Time	Toronto	300
1982	Coffee Way	Toronto	22
1983	Mr. Mugs	Brantford, ON	23
1985	Donut Delite	London	30
1985	Fine Donuts	Hull, QC	4
1985	Holey Donuts	Toronto	11
1985	Donuts Plus	Toronto	N/A
1985	Mister C's	Markham, ON	65
1988	Donut Diner	St Catharines	28
1988	Donut Gallery	Toronto	15
1994	Eddie Shack Donuts	Caledon, ON	N/A
N/A	Swiss Pantry	Kitchener, ON	N/A
N/A	Delight Donut	Saskatchewan	N/A

Note: Only companies with outlets in more than one city were counted.
Sources: *Foodservice and Hospitality*; *Bakers Journal*; *Directory of Restaurant and Fast Food Chains in Canada*, 1985–2000.

'New Spots Are Rising as Quickly as Yeast'

The growth of Tim Hortons was only one part of the increasing saturation of the Canadian foodscape by donut shops after 1975. As Hortons
built a large national chain, it was pulling away from an industry that
was increasingly crowded and complex. In the first phase of the donut
shop business in Canada (from 1961 to the mid-1970s), save for a smattering of independent shops and small local chains like Hol'N One in

Vancouver, four franchisors constituted much of the Canadian industry: Mister Donut, Country Style, Dunkin' and Tim Hortons. In the following decade and a half, however, more than twenty chains were founded. Indeed, by the late 1970s, it seemed that everyone wanted to combine donuts with some prefix, suffix, geographical feature, building type, proper name, or royal title in the hope of business success (see table 4.3).

New chains came from three directions. Some grew out of existing donut operations. Robin's Donuts, for example, was started by two Tim Hortons employees, who left the company in 1975 to open a shop in Thunder Bay. Both O'Donuts and Cross Country were founded by former Country Style franchisees.[19] Others began as extensions of food service operations with no connection to donuts. Donut Diner was founded in 1988 by a partnership that included a former restaurant operator and the owner of a chain of variety stores. Howard Rosenberg started Donut Café in London after working as an accountant for Grandma Lee's, a soup-and-sandwich chain that opened several outlets in the late 1970s and early 1980s.[20] Yet a surprising number of these new chains were led by entrepreneurs with no experience in either donuts or food service, who were drawn by the popularity of the donut shop form, the apparent simplicity of the operation, and the promise of financial reward. Joe and Carla Garagozzo knew nothing about donuts before they started Donut Delite in 1985, having spent ten years in the women's clothing business. The chain began when the couple was looking for a new investment; they tripped over the donut shop idea when a developer friend offered them a location in one of his plazas. As soon as the Garagozzos saw the numbers, they were hooked. 'Joe was very business minded,' recalled Carla Garagozzo. 'When you are business minded, you can run any kind of business, because business is business. We never made the donuts, naturally. It's just financial. You make sure that your numbers work.' Over the next decade, the couple opened more than thirty Donut Delite outlets across Ontario.[21]

Most of the new chains found regional or local niches in the market and grew to one or two dozen outlets by the mid-1990s, forming a second tier of companies operating between independent shops and the larger, original chains.[22] Some second-tier chains found room in the established markets of urban Ontario, while others focused on carving out niches in underdeveloped areas. Robins Donuts consciously pursued a regional strategy. The chain's founders, Harvey Cardwell and George Spicer, started with a sense that donut shops, while a good business, hadn't penetrated the West. They opened their first outlets in Thunder

Bay, Ontario, a place they saw as 'a more isolated market. We needed a trial area where we could work out the equation of the franchise. Find out what works and what doesn't.'[23] From there, Robin's spread outlets as far as British Columbia. When the chain arrived in Vancouver in 1981, for example, it found long-established Hol'n One concentrating on indoor shopping malls, three Tim Hortons shops, and upstart Nuffy's Donuts slowly spreading freestanding outlets across the area. Robin's quickly opened additional outlets in Vancouver, growing to nine by 1985 before levelling off. In Winnipeg, Robins literally steamrolled across the landscape after its first outlet in 1978, growing to ten shops within two years and to an astonishing forty-two outlets by 1999, leaving local chain Ideal Donuts in its wake. 'Winnipeg's just phenomenal,' Cardwell bragged in 1980. 'We thought we'd have to develop our market here. We didn't. It took immediately.'[24]

In Ontario, markets were more competitive and niches harder to find, at least in urban areas. 'When I opened my first [O'Donuts] store [in 1979],' Costas Kiriakopoulos told me, 'everybody told me that I was a little bit out of my mind, opening a donut chain, because there were so many around.' Yet with a background as a Country Style franchisee and almost a decade as a commercial real estate agent, Kiriakopoulos found excellent locations for his O'Donuts outlets, even in the crowded Greater Toronto area. This was a general pattern – new chains found room to grow in the 1980s, even in already crowded markets. Using real estate brokers and few operational controls, Coffee Time opened more than 300 outlets in the Greater Toronto area (notably targeting downtown Toronto with an almost endless network of shops). In 1988, Donut Diner started in St Catharines – a city that was already claiming to have the most donut shops per capita – and grew around the Niagara Peninsula, reaching thirty outlets and $8 million in annual revenues. Other second-tier chains combined a few urban locations with outlets in small towns (even those under 10,000 people), where large chains were reluctant to open outlets. Southwestern Ontario was an especially popular area, but second-tier companies spread outlets across a network of small towns from one end of Ontario to the other.[25]

While the large chains grew and smaller franchisors arrived on the scene, independents expanded almost exponentially in the late 1970s and early 1980s. 'New spots ... are rising as quickly as yeast,' declared the Toronto Star in the first of an endless string of (increasingly tedious) dough metaphors, profiling the success of new independent operators in a city already crowded with more than fifty big-chain franchises.[26]

Across Ontario, statistics backed up this kind of anecdotal reporting. In Windsor, for example, the number of independent shops steadily increased after 1974, peaking around 1993 (see figure 4.3). Besides exploding into established urban markets, independents, like second tier chains, found niches in smaller communities. 'The big franchises, generally speaking, will not go into a town under 30,000 population. To me, that's one fantastic market,' said the new owner of Northwood Donuts in New Liskard, Ontario, in 1982. These new independent operators followed a number of different business models. Northwood was opened by a Barrie businessman who saw investment potential in donut shops but who relied on managers to cover the day-to-day operations. Others operated as 'mom and pop' businesses. Gus and Petra Pantasis took over Global Donuts in Sarnia in 1980 and put in long hours to build up the business. Gus worked the midnight shift, while Petra arrived in the early morning to bake pastries and cakes. The couple struggled to balance the demands of the business against family commitments, including bringing their children into work with them, rocking the cradle and filling the donuts at the same time.[27]

The growth of the original chains, the emergence of second-tier franchisors, and the proliferation of independents meant a much more crowded market by the late 1980s, especially in Ontario. 'Kitchener-Waterloo appears to be experiencing a doughnut-and-coffee shop "explosion" reminiscent of the fast-food outlet growth of the late 1960s and the pizza expansion of this decade,' the *Kitchener-Waterloo Record* reported in 1986. 'Twenty years ago, K-W had only a few donut and coffee shops ... [Now] there are seven Tim Hortons, three Donut Queens, two Coffee Grinders, two Donutland By Girls and Co., and two Sir Donuts. There's a Donut Castle, Donut King, Donut Place, Donut Plus, Swiss Pantry Donuts, Hart to Hart Donuts, and a Kaffeehaus. The list goes on and on.'[28] Four years later, the *London Free Press* estimated that the number of donut shops in the city had increased fivefold in a decade. The local market was *very* crowded: four donut shops competed for customers along a 1.2 km stretch of Dundas Street, while in another section of the city, customers could 'look out the window of the Tim Horton Donuts shop ... and see people sipping coffee at the Country Style Donuts across the street.' Even smaller communities were becoming more crowded. Owen Sound, Ontario, with population of 27,000 (although the tourist trade expanded the local market considerably during the summer), was supporting *six* donut shops by 1989, including two Tim Hortons, one Mister Donut, two second-tier chain outlets, and

Figure 4.3   Donut shops in Windsor, Ontario, 1971–1999

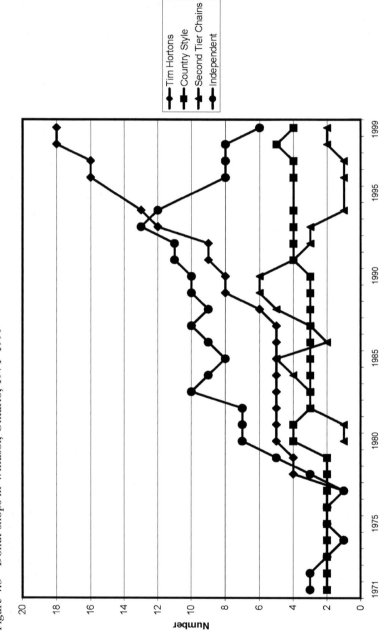

one independent shop. It was no surprise, then, that many observers declared that the Ontario market was saturated. 'People will admit that Ontario, and especially the Toronto region, is now getting saturated with doughnut shops,' commented *Bakers Journal* editor Ernest Naef.[29]

Other regions remained less developed, however. Even as late as 1985, Bill Rankin of Robin's could reasonably observe that the 'Western market is virgin to the concept of doughnuts and coffee.' Independent shops, for example, seemed less common in the West, although there was considerable local variation. Though Edmonton had fourteen independent shops by 1989 (almost half the total outlets in the city), Saskatoon and Regina had only one each, and Winnipeg's donutscape was similarly dominated by chain outlets.[30] Nor were the western provinces so crowded with second-tier chains. While they proliferated with alarming speed in Ontario, typically only one or two emerged in each main western city: Delight Donut in Saskatchewan, Nuffy's in Vancouver, and Robin's right across the Prairies and into British Columbia. Even the big chains, though expanding, remained concentrated in particular regions: even into the 1990s, Tim Hortons was deepest in Ontario and the East; Robins in the West; Dunkin in Quebec; and Country Style in the Greater Toronto Area (table 4.1).[31]

However regional its structure, the donut shop entered its golden age in the decade and a half after 1975. Existing chains expanded both numerically and geographically, new entrepreneurs joined the business, even small operators found markets to exploit and room to manoeuvre, and donut shops expanded across the country in an uneven patchwork of large, transregional chains like Tim Hortons and Mister Donut, second-tier companies like O'Donuts and Nuffy's, and an increasing number of independents. What made these developments more remarkable was the way they defied economic trends. In the mid-1970s, after three decades of fairly steady growth, the Canadian economy followed its American counterpart into a period of 'economic challenge,' initially characterized by the anomaly of runaway inflation *and* high unemployment. Over the following two decades, North Americans witnessed ongoing crisis, inconsistent consumer confidence, regular labour disputes, high interest rates, deep recessions in the early 1980s and early 1990s (with an uneven boom in between), and dire warnings about deindustrialization, globalization, and the end of postwar economic security.[32]

At first glance, these developments hardly suggested an imminent golden age for donut shops. Gasoline prices skyrocketed in 1973 and

Nuffy's Donuts, New Westminster, British Columbia, 1980. By the early 1980s, several smaller chains had entered the donut business. (Vancouver Public Library, Special Collections, 53387)

1979, leading many to fear the end of North America's drive-in culture while runaway inflation pushed up the cost of eating out.[33] In the case of coffee, rising prices were exacerbated by a disastrous frost in producing countries, making the donut shop's connection to the world's economy all too clear. In the United States, coffee consumers rebelled and organized boycotts, while north of the border the media followed rising retail prices closely. Donut companies worried that customers would vote with their pocket books, especially when increased unemployment during recessions and longer-term industrial decline promised to rob the male, blue-collar consumer (a core customer for donut shops) of his discretionary dollars. 'You have to be sympathetic to your customers' feelings,' said Allan Asmussen, owner of four Donut Queens in Kitchener-Waterloo. 'I'm positive they're not prepared to pay any more.

We've been charging 25 cents for awhile and I guess we'll stay there.' World coffee prices soon returned to customary levels; even so, the broader economic trends promised danger for donut shops.[34]

As institutions of petty consumption, however, donut shops had never relied on prosperity or affluence. At Robin's Donuts, the average purchase was just over one dollar in 1980, so even in uncertain economic times, the trend was upwards. 'As the economy gets tougher, our business gets better,' said Country Style's Alan Watson, noting that Sudbury's Inco strike had increased local business dramatically, since strikers had more time on their hands and less money in their pockets. This was not simply wishful thinking. Five years later, at the other end of the early-1980s recession, the company's vice president made the same point: 'We're at the low end of the scale ... If you can't afford a doughnut, you can't afford any snack.' Nor did the deep recession of the 1990s do the industry any great harm. Indeed, donut companies were more likely to complain about government policies than hard economic times. Tim Hortons found that the introduction of the federal goods and services tax in 1991 affected sales (a problem across the restaurant industry), but that revenues continued to rise during the early 1990s recession. Some smaller operators in Ontario, who relied heavily on low-income customers, were hit hard by the deep cuts to welfare initiated by the Harris government in 1995.[35]

Indeed, in many ways, donut shops seemed perfectly positioned to ride the economic trends, and they entered the Canadian foodscape at a much faster rate than other kinds of eateries, even in markets where the industrial worker was said to be facing declining fortunes. In Windsor, an automakers' town, for example, the number of donut shops grew fourfold in the decade after 1976, while the total number of restaurants grew by a more modest 47 per cent. (In the subsequent decade, restaurants stagnated overall while donut shops grew by 53 per cent).[36] On the business side, economic insecurity seemed a particular boon to chain operations, since a bad economy created a larger pool of potential donut shop franchisees. By the 1980s, downsized middle managers had become staples of franchise recruitment, joining the bakers, salesmen, and police officers who had dominated the business in the early days. 'So many people have been laid off. Many people in their 40s and 50s, whose houses are paid for, their family grown up, want our business,' Marlene Storry-Nicholson, Country Style's vice president of franchising, pointed out, noting that many were attracted by the apparent economic security of a large franchise operation.[37]

'They Could Survive in the Middle of Lake Ontario'

Even as donut shops rode out the recession of the early 1990s, the business was entering a new phase. While attending the annual meeting of Wendy's hamburgers in 1992, Ron Joyce noticed company pens stamped with the slogan '5000 by 1995,' referring to Wendy's goal of reaching 5000 outlets. Joyce was taken by the idea, and declared that his own chain would aim for one thousand outlets by the same year. It was a bold prediction, since it meant doubling the size of Tim Hortons in three years. Many people in the donut business recall being astonished – and more than a little amused – by Joyce's target, since most knowledgeable observers figured that the donut business was already thoroughly saturated. But Hortons' growth accelerated, and the company reached the goal with an outlet in Ancaster, Ontario, in late 1995. Joyce then set an additional goal: two thousand outlets by the year 2000. Though he was increasingly turning the day-to-day operations of the chain over to his heir apparent, Paul House, and though he sold Tim Hortons to Wendy's in 1995, the chain took the new target to heart, missing it by only a few weeks.[38]

This accelerated growth marked a new phase in the donut business. In virtually every conceivable market in the country, Tim Hortons took control after 1995. The company deepened its coverage in areas it already controlled, like Ontario and the Maritimes; and it moved ahead in areas, like Quebec and Greater Vancouver, where it had been competing with well-established companies like Dunkin' and Robin's. In the 1980s, Tim Hortons had been growing along with many other companies; now, in the 1990s, the company was growing at a time when no new second-tier chains and few independents were entering the donut business. Hortons' growth in some places, like the West, actually increased the total number of donut shops in many communities; but in others, especially in southern Ontario, growth meant an increasing share of an already saturated donut market. In St Catharines, for example, Tim Hortons accounted for only 5 of the city's 36 donut shops in 1989 but 14 of 38 a decade later; in Windsor, the company had 8 of 27 shops in 1989 and 18 of 30 in 1999 (figure 4.3).[39]

Depending on the city or region and the timing of events, the victims of Tim Hortons charge to its new targets varied; but across the country, the basic story was the same. At the bottom of the industry, independent owners had been locked in struggles against larger chains for some years, but more and more, the target was specific. '[The chains] are trying to kill the small doughnut shops,' declared Ron Burke in 1988, the year he converted his donut shop in St Catharines to a full breakfast and lunch restaurant (and saw his sales triple). 'That's why I'm glad I got out of it.'[40] From the perspective of small business history, Burke's claim was unremarkable, since independent operators in almost every retail industry had been complaining about chains for decades, marshalling a 'folklore of retailing' that celebrated the small and condemned the large.[41] What is most interesting about Burke's statement was its generic target: in the late 1980s, an independent might get angry at any of a number of chains; a decade later, the enemy was more singular. 'As soon as they put their sign up, I'm dead,' declared Bill Siscos of Canadian Style Donuts in Hamilton, on hearing that a Tim Hortons was opening across street. Even larger chains had problems. In 1999, Robin's, by then a well-established company with almost three hundred outlets across the country, pulled out of donut-loving St Catharines. 'It hasn't been a good market for us,' said the company's vice president. 'We just can't compete.'[42]

This was not just an urban problem. Once second-tier companies like Mister C's and Donut Delite had proven that small towns could support donut shops, Hortons, relentlessly charging toward one thousand outlets by 1995, began conquering smaller communities. Ron Hewitt ticked off small towns where Mr Mugs originally thrived: 'We did [Aylmer]. We did Grand Bend in southern Ontario: no Hortons. Caledonia: no Hortons. Hagersville: no Hortons. Port Dover: no Hortons. Everyplace I went, I didn't expose myself.' This strategy was no longer possible by the 1990s: in December 1991, Hortons reached five hundred outlets by opening in Aylmer, the site of Hewitt's first Mr Mugs. Other chains had similar problems.[43]

As soon as Tim Hortons began filling urban markets and targeting small towns, the writing was on the wall for second-tier chains. It was one thing to compete against another chain of similar size, but who could stand against Hortons' rolling empire? 'Everybody – Mr Mugs, and Mister C – were going into the small towns, so they were doing well,' noted Carla Garagozzo. 'You had room to grow. [Then] Tim went everywhere and killed everybody ... Mister C by then had died. Swiss Pantry was gone. Mr Mugs had the same [problems]. If you weren't big, you couldn't survive.' By the 1990s, many second-tier chains were being swallowed up by larger companies or simply going bankrupt. Mister C's, Donut Delite, and then Robin's Donuts were snapped up by the Afton Food Group, an investment company that was consolidating franchise concepts.[44]

In the end, few companies, whether independent, second-tier, or established franchisor, could stand up against Hortons. Afton itself went bankrupt in 2003. Two years before that, the once mighty Country Style had filed for protection from its creditors and moved quickly to eliminate marginal stores and abandon unprofitable leases. 'There's no plan on our part to overtake the number one leader,' Country Style's new president admitted. 'We're going to be a very solid number two.'[45] With a national network of stores and penetration into big cities *and* small towns, Hortons had not simply saturated the donut business by the 1990s, it had transcended it. McDonalds was now its only real competitor, and even that chain fell behind in the franchise race. At two thousand outlets – almost double the number of McDonald's – Tim Hortons was simply everywhere. 'I thought they wouldn't bother coming here because it wouldn't be viable for two doughnut shops,' said Jimmy Davé, owner of the independent Donut Stop in Hamilton since 1987. 'I was wrong. They'll go anywhere. They could survive in the middle of Lake Ontario.'[46]

How the Bagel Became White Bread

Donut shops proliferated across the foodscape at a time when the form itself was being redefined. Beginning in the mid-1970s, menus expanded from the donut-and-coffee staple to include donut holes (the most famous, of course, was Tim Hortons' Timbits, introduced in 1976), pies, cakes, brownies, tarts, danishes, croissants, bagels, and cinnamon buns. Few of these new products were true innovations. In some cases, donut chains looked to the United States for new ideas. Tim Hortons added cinnamon buns after company executives toured a growing operation in Kansas City.[47] In other cases, products were borrowed from businesses closer to home. Muffins were first popularized by two Toronto companies. The largest, Mmmuffins, was the brainchild of Michael Bregman, who had experimented with the product while working at Loblaws, a large Canadian grocery chain. While rethinking the product line of the chain's in-store bakeries, Bregman discovered that oversized muffins were a big hit with affluent customers, who were willing to pay more for premium products. Bregman realized the product had 'mass appeal' when they sold in blue-collar Oshawa. He opened his first outlet in the Eaton's Centre, a large indoor mall in downtown Toronto, and the chain grew quickly.[48] Muffin stands were often portrayed as upscale versions of the donut shop – one report called the oversized muffin the 'yuppie donut'[49] – even though the muffin outlets typically located in shopping mall food courts, which donut shops avoided in favour of outdoor strip malls and freestanding locations. Nonetheless, donut companies responded to the challenge by adding muffins to their menus. It was a great product: considered (incorrectly) to be a healthy snack, the muffin attracted new customers, kept old ones, and, most importantly, increased the average donut shop purchase.[50]

A decade later, new concerns about health also pushed bagels onto donut shop menu boards and into the mainstream of eating habits. Though a stereotypical Jewish culinary icon, bagels had actually flirted with a more diverse market for most of the twentieth century. Historian Donna Gabaccia has pointed out that after the bagel was brought to America by Jewish immigrants from Eastern Europe, it quickly crossed over into the diets of other urban dwellers, eventually becoming a symbol of 'New York deli' cuisine rather than an icon of one particular ethnic group.[51] In Toronto, Lou Bregman (Michael's father) opened Bagel King as a retail coffee and bagel outlet in 1957. Ten years later, he was selling four to six million bagels a year from three outlets in Toronto's suburbs, including one at Yorkdale, a large regional mall at the intersection of two highways northwest of Toronto. According to Bregman, only about one-quarter of his customers were Jewish. 'There aren't enough Jews in Toronto to eat all the bagels I make,' he told the *Toronto Star*.[52] But it would be exaggerating to say that the bagel had mass appeal: even Bregman's shopping centre outlet was located in an area with a high concentration of Jewish consumers, many of whom had settled in a suburban corridor in the northwest of the city after the war. Locating all three outlets in this corridor, Bregman could draw a diverse crowd but still rely on a heavily Jewish population.

The pattern was similar when donut shops began flirting with bagels in the 1980s. Some of the Toronto Mister Donut franchisees started buying bagels from bakery wholesalers and offering them as part of their product line, but the company found that the product had little appeal outside certain urban neighbourhoods. The company planned to 'take each market individually,' offering them in markets with 'a high Jewish population' like Toronto and Montreal, but not in places like New-foundland or Cape Breton, where they sold poorly. Robin's had a similar view, noting in 1988 that the bagel was 'only successful in certain markets.'[53]

The bagel underwent a startling transformation over the following decade. Between 1988 and 1995, bagel consumption increased more than 88 per cent, and by the end of that time, more than half a dozen bagel chains were eagerly franchising across the country. The largest, Great Canadian Bagel, was founded in 1993 and expanded quickly. By 1996 it was selling more bagels in a month than Lou Bregman's Bagel King had in a year. Even Great Canadian's president, Neil Shopsowitz, was amazed by the product's mass appeal, noting that he had expected to do better in large cities where the product was 'less foreign,' but that he ended up doing very well in some small centres. 'Regina was probably not a spot we would have done right away,' he commented, 'but we opened there and that store really took off from day one.' The company soon opened five more shops in Saskatchewan. Jumping on the latest trend, Michael Bregman, now chair of Second Cup, bought a 24 per cent interest in the chain in 1996. 'The bagel used to be considered a pure ethnic type of product,' he declared. 'Today, it's very much mainstream.'[54]

Even more startling was Tim Hortons' announcement of a full bagel program that May, including television, radio, and point-of-purchase ads announcing 'Yes, we have bagels.' 'There's currently a demand in the marketplace,' Tim Hortons' marketing vice president noted at the time. 'It's obvious from the popularity of the product and from the influx of U.S. bagel shops.' The chain had been serving bagels at some outlets for five years, but the new program – and the marketing campaign – put the humble bun in more than 1,200 outlets across the country and straight into the public imagination. Great Canadian even noticed that *its* sales increased during Hortons' bagel campaign. Other donut companies quickly improved their bagel programs, installing toasters and adding the many varieties of cream cheese typical of the product mix at bagel chains. Country Style integrated the bagel into its new breakfast program, developing a breakfast bagel with scrambled eggs, an idea borrowed from Burger King.[55]

Not everyone was happy to see the downtown Jewish icon making inroads into suburban institutions like Tim Hortons and Country Style. As an ostensibly ethnic food, the bagel was steeped in ideas of history and authenticity. For years, bagel lovers had debated the relative merits of its local and regional versions. 'There are people who seriously love Montreal bagels, and they'll taste the New York bagels, but there's no way they'll ever say they're better,' noted Randi Adler, a transplanted New Yorker who cofounded BagelWorks in Halifax. 'Part of it is a question of what you've grown up with.'[56] These sorts of family squabbles seemed a quaint distraction now that a rigidly uniform bagel would be served from Victoria to St John's, and more shockingly, in 'white bread' flavours like blueberry and chocolate chip. Mass consumers, unlike bagel connoisseurs, preferred a lighter, sweeter taste and texture, which – not coincidentally – was also easier to manufacture in large quantities. Like most mass-produced bagels, the donut shop version was steamed rather than boiled before baking, and connoisseurs feared the loss of the authentic bagel, which was heavy and crusty, manufactured as an art not a science. 'We're not big wholesalers or mass marketers,' scoffed Irwin Shlafman, whose family had been in the bagel business in Montreal since 1919. 'We're not trying to do what these others are doing. These people are making a product anyone can make.' Mocking the crossover, which by 2001 saw Tim Hortons selling one of every two bagels in Canada, an ad for a Vancouver bagel bakery hit all the highlights of the urban chic appeal to authenticity: 'Warm conversation, candlelight, jazz, sweets, somewhere to go ... Relaxed, Hip, memories of New York, big city, small café. No Donuts.'[57]

By the mid-1980s, then, donut shop customers could partake of a wide range of baked goods, and the shops had become much less dependent on their core product at a time when donut consumption was falling across Canada. In the fifteen years after 1975, the donut declined consistently in both dollar volumes and units purchased. According to Fleischmann's Consumer Panel Report, the average Canadian household bought 4.7 donuts in October 1975, but only 3.4 six years later and 2.3 three years after that. Average spending declined as well: from 47 cents in 1981 to 37 cents in 1984. The percentage of households buying donuts also declined, from 18.3 per cent in 1981 to 13.7 per cent in 1984. In response, donut shops scaled back production. 'Ten years ago, each shop pumped out about 200 dozen a day, now we're down to about 150 a day,' reported Peter Mertons of Country Style.[58]

Changing ideas of good health drove the donut's decline, but hidden underneath the diversity of new products was the singular reality that donut shops had become a coffee-driven business. At Country Style, donuts made up as much as 80 per cent of an outlet's sales in the 1960s; by the 1980s, coffee was almost half the business and by far the most profitable item in the shop. 'We are looking for new products that can be baked quickly, cheaply and can be eaten in the car,' commented Anne Marie Vanier of Country Style in 1983. 'The product must also compliment a cup of coffee.' In one sense, this focus was ironic, since overall coffee consumption had been generally static for two decades – a situation that showed little potential for change (see Figure 4.4). But coffee

Figure 4.4   Apparent per capita coffee consumption in Canada

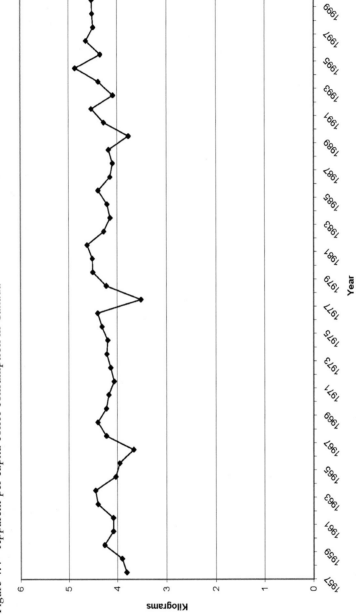

Figures reflect 'disappearance rate' (coffee available for consumption on average as of July 1), not actual consumption.

Source: DBS, Cat. 32-229, Apparent Per Capita Food Consumption in Canada, 1957–1980, 1995, 1999.

had always been incredibly profitable at the retail end (somewhat less so for producers), and the general drift away from donuts and toward coffee paralleled, reflected, and reinforced the increasing importance of the morning trade. In the early days of Canadian donut shops, the typical customer bought donuts on the way home from work; by the late 1970s and 1980s, most of a donut shop's sales occurred between six and eleven in the morning.[59]

Increasingly, donut chains looked for products to extend their sales past 11 a.m. Tim Hortons opened a sandwich, chili, and soup operation in 1977, called Break Away, which was run as a separate operation out of one end of a few existing outlets. These menu extensions accelerated in the 1980s. Mister Donut tried pizza and soup and biscuits. Country Style rolled out what it called a 'soup and savory' program, including products like sausage rolls, meat pies, salads, and soups. Hol'n One started serving hamburgers. Some small operations went in other directions. King Donut in St Catharines secured a liquor license and set up a small bar at the back of one of its outlets.[60] Others served different varieties of 'ethnic' foods, often drawn from the owner's culinary tradition, making for some interesting combinations in surprising places. 'Sandy's Donuts' in Milton, Ontario (a small town near Toronto), served Indian food; others combined donuts and halal food or Chinese food.

'Hockey Players, Construction Workers, and Suburban Wasteoids'

The reinvention of the donut shop went beyond food. As they grew in the 1980s and 1990s, donut chains continued to seek roadside sites for their standard outlets, but they also experimented with new types of locations. 'Satellite outlets' allowed the larger companies to open outlets in busy downtown neighbourhoods. A satellite outlet was small, comprising only a serving area and seating, with products shipped from a nearby outlet, usually one owned by the same franchisee. The idea was an old one – Mister Donut had a few even in the 1960s, and Mister Donut and Country Style brought the idea downtown in the mid-1980s. Tim Hortons was more aggressive with satellites in the subsequent decade, opening several outlets in the downtowns of cities across Canada. 'Kiosks' (modular units, as small as 200 square feet, with serving facilities but no seating) were an extension of the satellite idea. In the early 1990s the largest companies began to experiment with kiosk locations at Canadian Tire stores, shopping mall food courts, universities, and hospitals. Tim Hortons was particularly aggressive in this area.

By 1997, kiosks comprised 369 of the chain's 1,578 outlets across Canada. Hortons also innovated with 'twinning': opening large outlets that shared seating space (but had separate kitchen facilities) with other fast food concepts. The chain opened its first 'twinned' outlet with Wendy's in 1991, hoping that the hamburger chain's strength in the afternoon and evening would complement the morning focus of the donut shop. The two companies opened a dozen more combination outlets over the next four years, and the arrangement was so successful that when Joyce was looking to sell his company, Wendy's seemed a natural fit. 'We know where their company is going,' Joyce told the *Hamilton Spectator*. 'All the pieces fell together.'[61]

As the major chains moved to broaden their markets, they eliminated many of the core symbols of the donut shop's early status as a working man's social space: most notably, the sit-down counter and smoking. Most of the major companies were altering designs during this period, but Tim Hortons made the most dramatic changes, rolling out several new models in the late 1980s and early 1990s. The new outlet was larger (at least 2,000 square feet compared to the traditional 1,200) and brighter (with more windows and warmer-coloured bricks replacing the older dark brown), and significantly, it had no sit-down counter. Customers now expected to sit at standard fast food tables. And the updated design was not just for new outlets. The company undertook an aggressive, decade-long renovation program for all of its shops.[62]

Tim Hortons also gradually eliminated smoking. Smoking had been a core feature of early donut shops, but also a source of considerable complaint. Constant smoking did not do much for the atmosphere, figuratively or literally: donut shops often smelled bad, looked dingy, and served products that sometimes tasted more like tobacco than glaze. After 1975, many foodservice experts argued that greater accommodation should be made for non-smoking customers, and a few restaurateurs responded by setting aside tables for a non-smoking section.[63] Though designating a few tables in a restaurant for non-smokers was not a perfect solution to the problem of second-hand smoke, it was especially unworkable in donut shops, which were too small for any meaningful separation of smokers and non-smokers. Regardless, the donuts would absorb the smell as soon as the bulk of customers lit up. Hortons' initial solution was to open completely non-smoking outlets, the first one in Hamilton in 1983, another in Kitchener two years later.[64] Later, the company built outlets with completely closed-off smoking sections, dividing the smokers from non-smokers with a glass wall and installing separate ventilation systems for the two sides of the store. Non-smoking outlets became increasingly popular in the company during the 1990s, and in 1999 the company banned smoking in all of its outlets outside Quebec.[65]

Other companies followed Hortons' example, both in smoke-free stores and new designs. Country Style had been working to brighten its stores since the mid-1980s, but many of these changes had been cosmetic: adding plants and brick walls and moving the counter back from the serving area. In 1992 the company launched a complete repositioning program for its outlets, including a brighter new design. Earlier renovations had moved the counter away from the serving area, a compromise between the need for larger and more efficient serving areas and the attachment of customers to the counter and stools. The company soon discovered, however, that the compromise did not work: few customers sat at the counter, which was now an island in the middle of the shop. The counter and stools were eliminated completely from the new design, which Country Style planned to use for all new outlets. It intended to renovate all its stores to the new design by 1997, and to simply close some of the older, low-volume stores.[66]

These changes remind us that cultural categories like gender and class are implicated in changing business strategies and economic markets. The major donut chains were hoping to improve the overall image of the donut shop, especially their reputation as 'smoke-filled hangouts' for working-class men, in order to appeal to a broader clientele – a notion that seemed synonymous with attracting women and families. Though his company was leading the donut business by the early 1980s, Ron Joyce was fond of telling colleagues that Hortons was simply 'the best of a bad lot,' too dependent on what one journalist later called 'aging men in baseball caps looking for a caffeine and nicotine fix.' At the time, the ratio of men to women in Hortons' customer base was about 55:45. At Country Style, market research and franchisee observation suggested that the ratio of men to women could reach as high as three to one.[67] Though women were entering the paid workforce in numbers greater than ever before, they remained a small part of the donut shop's business, largely because they found the shops intimidating. Remembering her days as a high school student in the early 1980s, one Kitchener native wrote of needing a 'male guide' to enter the 'domain of hockey players, construction workers, and suburban wasteoids that populate[d] the average donut shop.' No single feature was more distasteful than the sit-down counter. During a Country Style focus group in 1990, one woman declared her reluctance to visit the washroom (since it required a trip past the counter), which she likened to running a gauntlet of 'construction workers and truckers.'[68] The chain eliminated the sit-down counter from its future designs.

All the chains constructed 'broader clientele' in terms of gender and class. Indeed, the typical donut executive made almost no distinction between 'broader market' and 'family.' Robin's renovation program was intended to reach 'a market we'd lost over the years,' including families, women, and white-collar workers. This was a significant shift from earlier marketing efforts, which aimed squarely at a 'primarily male target audience who work in driving-related jobs and make the bulk of Robin's purchases.'[69] Tim Hortons justified its own efforts to revamp stores and limit smoking as a way to 'attract a larger female clientele.' 'We get a lot of families here who don't want to expose their children to smoke,' noted Brigette Regenscheit, who owned the company's first smoke-free outlet. 'It's a completely different clientele.'[70]

The fact that Tim Hortons added new products and brightened its stores has now become a widespread journalistic shorthand to explain the company's tremendous success in conquering the Canadian foodscape. To a degree, Tim Hortons did move more decisively in redesign and reinvention, especially in the case of non-smoking shops. Yet it is easy to exaggerate the company's pioneering vision, since these changes were widely discussed by observers and extensively implemented by owners throughout the 1980s. If Hortons was more decisive, its advantage was less its innovative approach than its size and resources: smaller companies could not afford to renovate as thoroughly as the major ones, nor could they compete with the diversity of designs emerging from the larger companies. By the early 1990s, besides opening eighty new outlets a year, Hortons was renovating fifty stores a year as part of a $12 million dollar effort to renovate and expand all of its shops. This figure was more than double the *total sales* of most of the second-tier chains: Donut Delite, for example, had gross revenues of $5 million in 1992.[71] Independents were even worse off: one study of sales tax records for 1987–8 found that franchised donut shops reported average annual sales returns more than twice those of independents.[72] For small chains, brightening up meant little more than a few plants, some new wallpaper, or a paint job. It's all they could afford.

Reinventing the shop was not simply about having more resources to renovate, but having sufficient sales to forgo alternative sources of revenue. Further down the economic ladder, some independent shops relied on features – such as video games and pinball machines – that drew misbehaving youth, raised neighbourhood ire, and exacerbated the shop's seedy image. Many municipal officials and members of the public associated arcades with drug dens – an image that was easily extended to donut shops, with their all-night hours, transient populations, and informal atmosphere. 'I'm worried that drugs could be passed in this place,' complained one high school principal in Toronto, who faced a combination donut shop and video arcade right next door. 'It's going to be open 24 hours a day.'[73] This was not simply moral panic: as we saw in chapter 2, donut shops were (and continued to be) sites of underground market activity. In the case of video games, however, the problem was refracted through the economic structure of the industry. The chains had long ago eliminated features like jukeboxes and pinball machines, and while everyone, from big chains to small independents, had problems with bad behaviour, few smaller operations could afford to be purists. When city council in Etobicoke (a Toronto suburb) passed a bylaw limiting businesses to two arcade machines, local donut shop owner Maryann Akit complained that she needed her $250 to $300 a week share of the revenue to survive: 'The doughnut shop doesn't make that much money, so I have to bring in something else to subsidize it.'[74]

Nor were non-smoking outlets (which ensured fresh air and helped establish a less seedy, family atmosphere) a realistic option for smaller companies. Initially, the non-smoking strategy exploited Hortons' saturation of the marketplace. In 1985, 80 per cent of Tim Hortons' customers smoked, so opening smoke-free outlets could easily become a zero sum game: you might attract non-smokers, but smokers would simply head down the street to the competition. Since Hortons often had a cluster of outlets in a particular area, smokers were just as likely to find another Tim Hortons as a Country Style or Donut Delite. Significantly, Hortons' first non-smoking outlets were in Kitchener and Hamilton, cities where the company had several outlets located close together. Indeed, Hortons made it a point to remind customers that there were two other Tim Hortons within a mile of its first non-smoking outlet.[75] In fact, once Tim Hortons converted all of its outlets to non-smoking, many independents and smaller chains positioned themselves, or were positioned by customers, as smokers' alternatives. 'We allow smoking,' Saint John Donut Queen's Marjorie Lake bragged in 1997. 'It's getting so that there's nowhere for smokers to go.' This was a sensible strategy in the short term (although it made them dependent on a shrinking pop-

ulation of smokers), but it became a major problem after some municipalities forced all restaurants to ban smoking.[76]

Revisiting the Geography of Convenience

In the 1990s, 'drive-thru' lanes became the latest extension of attempts
to broaden the donut shop market. The drive-thru lane was a long-
standing concept in fast food, having been part of efforts to serve the car
almost from the beginning of drive-in food service after the First World
War. The first versions of the drive-thru might be better described as
'drive up' windows: customers would drive up, order, and be handed the
food through the same window. By the 1950s, technological developments had allowed this system to be modified into the modern drive-
thru. To reduce costs, car hop drive-ins began to add two-way speakers
and numbered stalls, a system that allowed orders to be taken from the
kitchen, cutting down on trips back and forth to the car. The new technology fit nicely with the drive-up idea, and thus the drive-thru was
born: with a menu board and speaker strategically placed at the entrance
to the lane, customers could place an order and then proceed to the
window to receive it. In Canada, the drive-thru was never as popular as
car hops (as at A&W) or self-service (as at McDonald's), but a few operators used the system in the 1950s and 1960s. No donut companies
adopted the idea. Drive-thru momentum picked up in the mid-1970s.
Wendy's first Canadian store, opened in 1975, included a 'pick-up
window,' complete with speaker for ordering. McDonald's and other
chains struggled to catch up, and the drive-thru lane quickly became a
standard part of Canadian fast food. One suburban planning study in
1980 noted that drive-thru customers were generating 51 per cent of the
vehicle trips to the area's two Wendy's restaurants and 37 per cent to
McDonald's.[77]

Though the Canadian donut business was growing rapidly, drive-
thrus hardly took the industry by storm. Some American donut shops
adopted the idea in the early 1980s, but Canadian chains were dragged
into the idea by franchisees following local developments. In 1984,
Country Style's Sault Ste Marie franchisee, Jim Fitzpatrick, borrowed
the drive-thru concept from the McDonald's up the street.[78] Despite
the increasing popularity of the idea in fast food and its apparent fit
with donuts, Fitzpatrick's idea was greeted with little enthusiasm by
Country Style's head office. At the time, Country Style seemed more
interested in developing outlets that brought the donut shop to cus-

tomers rather than the other way around. The company was hard at work developing a fleet of mobile donut shops, aiming to move into the coffee truck business, serving construction sites, factories, and special events.[79] But there was more to the company's reluctance than excitement about a different concept. Country Style's lukewarm reaction was typical of the entire industry. Tim Hortons opened its first drive-thru window at about the same time, but it came by accident when the chain took over a Church's Fried Chicken outlet on Hamilton Mountain in 1985. The window was there, but the company was not enthusiastic about using it. 'We had trouble selling Mr Joyce on it,' remembered franchisee Stew Galloway. Mister Donut was dragged into the drive-thru business by a franchisee, John Wheatley, who in the mid-1980s convinced the company to develop Prince Edward Island. Wheatley had seen the concept working in American fast food operations, and he was sure it would work for donuts, but Mister Donut, like other chains, hesitated.[80]

Donut chains were reluctant to install drive-thrus because the idea clashed with their established business model in several ways. Drive-thru lanes required bigger properties, and existing outlets were often too small for them. Besides, many donut shops weren't properly sited on the lot to add a drive-thru lane, especially given the advent of stricter zoning regulations regarding 'stacking' space (the distance allowed for cars to line up so that they didn't pile into the street and disrupt traffic). Based on their experiences with hamburger chains, municipal councils began instituting stacking requirements in the early 1980s, even before donut shops turned to the idea.[81] Even in the absence of such regulations, adapting existing lots to the drive-thru lane could make for awkward configurations. At the site of Tim Hortons' third outlet (University and Weber in Waterloo), which had been taken over by Donut Queen in 1982, the only way to add a drive-thru lane was to go out the back wall and have cars approach the window through the alley behind the building. This was symptomatic of the problems of adding drive-thrus to existing outlets: though a practical accommodation in a building not designed for this type of service, it was hardly an ideal set-up for a business selling access and convenience.[82]

A more difficult – and more nebulous – problem was the idea of the donut shop itself. From a business perspective, profitability was thought to depend on getting customers inside, since talking to the servers and seeing the products encouraged impulse buying. From the beginning, as we saw in chapter 3, servers were instructed to practice suggestive selling, encouraging customers to make an add-on purchase or to 'up-size' (i.e., order a larger size or greater quantity than originally intended).[83] Another way to encourage impulse buying was to con-stantly adjust displays: if maple dip donuts were on the bottom shelf on Tuesday, they would be moved to the top shelf on Wednesday, forcing customers to look around for their usual order, which exposed them to the outlet's complete product mix. Donut companies also relied on the smell of on-site baking to further tantalize the consumer – an induce-ment that would be lost if customers never left their cars. '[Ron Joyce] said customers wouldn't get to see and smell the product. He worried that we wouldn't get the add-on sale,' commented Stew Galloway of Tim Hortons' reluctance to embrace the drive-thru concept. Moreover, the donut shop's status as a social space proved difficult to abandon. Some donut executives felt that a drive-thru would tilt the donut shop away from its 'base' customers, who sought a particular balance of con-venience and sociability. In 1987, Country Style's franchising manager expressed doubts about the concept: 'People regard a trip to a coffee shop as a bit of a break – a chance to relax and get in from the hot or cold. It's a coffee *break*.'[84]

So, while drive-thru lanes spread quickly through hamburger chains in the 1980s, they remained a small part of the donut business. Three years after Fitzpatrick opened his window, his drive-thru was the only one in the chain, and Country Style stated somewhat unenthusiastically that it was 'monitoring' the idea.[85] Mister Donut was the most enthusi-astic about the concept; yet in the end, it developed only a dozen drive-thrus (mainly in the Maritimes and Quebec) before Dunkin' Donuts took it over in 1989.[86] For its part, Dunkin' already had drive-thrus in the United States when it started adding them in Canada in 1988, but it was not overwhelmed by the concept. The company's six drive-thrus did 'anywhere from excellent to poor, depending on the market,' according to a company official.[87]

In the 1990s, however, the drive-thru window became an important part of the donut business. Drive-thru ordering was only one-quarter of the industry's total business in 1999, but could account for up to 70 per cent of the business of a particular outlet.[88] Tim Hortons began devel-oping drive-thrus with deliberate speed in the early 1990s, renovat-ing old stores to include the windows, building them as a standard part of new outlets, and even relocating existing shops to accommodate a drive-thru lane.[89] The concept even changed the way the company looked at property. Simply finding a high-traffic site was no longer enough: the lot had to be large enough to accommodate a drive-thru lane. Borrowing an idea from fast food chains in Florida, the company also adopted drive-thru-only outlets, modular units that included two drive-thru lanes and no seating and that took up only a few hundred square feet of space, making them easier to fit onto small lots along heavily developed suburban strips. Hortons opened its first unit in 1993; four years later, forty-two double drive-thrus were serving Tim Hortons customers across Canada.[90]

Like remodelling, the drive-thru drove a wedge between big and small companies. Other large donut chains struggled to catch up to Hortons in drive-thru serving. Country Style, for example, built sixty-one windows between 1993 and 1998, and Robins was not far behind. Smaller, second-tier companies found it difficult to adopt the idea. Equipment was expensive, and the original decision to develop strip plaza locations – made in the mid-1980s, when plaza developers were hungry for donut shops, and before drive-thrus became a necessary part of the business – ultimately sealed the fate of the second-tier companies. 'I had corner units in plazas, sometimes centre units ... and then it became difficult,' Ron Hewitt told me at a Mr Mugs in a Brantford, Ontario, strip plaza. 'Like here,' he continued, waving his hand at the parking lot, 'we looked at this store and could never figure out how [to put in a drive-thru] ... I think now, or from that point on, seven or eight years ago, I would not have built a store without one.' But money was an issue as well. 'All day long I see that drive-thru going non-stop,' complained Mr Mugs franchisee Curtis Mitchell. 'If I had money in my pocket, I would build one tomorrow.'[91] The inability of small chains and independents to adapt to drive-thru serving reinforced their broader helplessness in the face of the redefinition efforts of the large chains. A drive-thru lane was more than a new way to speed up service. The idea turned out to be especially popular with women, and thus fit into the overall project of attracting a broader market. Women cited safety and convenience when travelling with children as the main reasons why they preferred using the drive-thru lane to entering the store.[92]

As donut shops reinvented themselves after 1977 – adding new products, brightening stores, installing drive-thru windows, banning or limiting smoking – a few long-time customers worried about what was being lost. Some Hamiltonians responded to the city's first drive-thru-only outlet by pulling up to the window and sarcastically ordering Big Macs, suggesting that ultra-convenience was somehow out of place in a donut shop.[93] Others griped about non-smoking sections, complaining that they felt like zoo animals behind the glass, or that non-smoking outlets violated their human rights. One customer presented a petition to Tim Hortons' head office, signed by 2,200 of her fellow customers, imploring the company not to ban smoking at her regular outlet.[94] Many simply moved to other locations. 'I used to go to the Tim Hortons on King George Highway,' Colin Regan told me between puffs on his cigarette at a Robins Donuts in Surrey, B.C. 'I used to go every day and see people from all walks of life. You knew them by 'Dave the Electrician' or 'Bob the Bus Driver,' by what they did, you know ... They changed to non-smoking a year ago, and I haven't seen any of those people since.' Many more made peace with the changes, sitting at the new-style fast food tables, nostalgic for the old donut shop. 'They say now that the donut stores have turned into restaurants,' Al Stortz lamented near the end of our conversation in Welland. 'There's one down the road here near where I used to work ... It says 'Donuts and More.' So, in other words, you can go in and get a hamburg or whatever ... I don't think you'll likely find an actual donut shop anymore.'[95]

'The Donut Stores Have Turned into Restaurants'

In the two decades after 1975, Canadian donut culture was remade. While the country entered a period of economic challenge, the donut shop idea penetrated more deeply into the Canadian foodscape, and spread out across a more extensive geography. Throughout this process, the expansion of donut shops reflected the ambivalent continental dynamics of Canadian economic culture. On the one hand, chains grew outwards from central Canada along the existing east–west linkages of the national economy. Though Country Style and Tim Hortons made some inroads into the United States, they devoted most of their energy to spreading across Canada, imagining a business space that was national in scope and scale.[96] At the same time, the Canadian donut business continued to operate as one part of a continental business culture that, for much of Canada's history, had emphasized the north–south flow of commerce and ideas. Mister Donut operated as though Canada was a region within the North American market, and even Canadian chains like Tim Hortons and Country Style kept a careful watch on American trends like cinnamon buns and double-drive-thrus. In this sense, the 1995 merger of Tim Hortons and Wendy's Hamburgers not only continued the long-standing continental dynamics of donut culture – which ran, in fact, back to DCA in the 1930s – but also expressed and reinforced a deeper geographic structure in Canadian economic life, which had always been precariously balanced between north–south and east–west connections.

Even as the donut shop form spread across space, it was changing. Indeed, by 1995, donut shops were quite different places than they had been twenty years before: brighter, cleaner, and offering expanded menus and new forms of service and convenience. Company motives were obviously economic, but these innovations played on notions of family, gender, and class. Donut executives and entrepreneurs imagined their ideal consumers and worked to build outlets and product lines to attract them, although their ability to both articulate and realize this vision depended on their place in the economic structure of the industry. At the end of this process of reinvention, moreover, many of the basic tensions remained. However much it seemed to Hamiltonians that Big Macs, not donuts, belonged at drive-thru windows, the fact remained that the original Tim Hortons franchise on Ottawa Street had billed itself as a 'donut drive-in.'[97] Donut shops had always walked a careful line between serving the car and being a social space, between convenience and sociability – a tension made more explicit, rather than wholly created, by the drive-thru lane. The same could be said of new designs and smoke-free outlets, which were less a violation of human rights than a new way to confront the original tension between mass market aspirations and male, blue-collar use.

Even new products signalled the triumph, rather than the decline, of the donut shop. In the early days, donut shops had aped the simple designs of coffee shops and lunch counters even while they served a more limited product line. Yet when new entrepreneurs came into the business in the 1980s with outlets offering sandwiches, soups, pies, and snacks – a product line typical of the 1950s lunch counter – none of them thought to name their new chain King Coffee Shop or Lunch Counter Delite. Indeed, it was only Hortons that became embarrassed by its original trademark – changing its corporate moniker to TDL Group, switching its signs from 'Donuts' to 'Always Fresh,' and telling anyone who would listen that 'we haven't been a donut store in a long time.'[98] But even if they might add a suffix like 'More,' or 'Fresh Food Ideas,' most entrepreneurs were thrilled to slap 'donut shop' on their signs because they knew the term signalled a particular kind of informal eatery akin to the lunch counter of the 1950s. 'Donut shop' announced a place where customers could expect to find simple meals, snacks, and coffee served quickly, but where they could also linger and observe the neighbourhood. By the 1980s, whether it served foods borrowed from yuppie bakeries, Jewish delis, or Indian restaurants, whether it bragged about 'always fresh' products or 'fresh food ideas,' whether it tried to serve women and families or stayed focused on construction workers and 'suburban wasteoids,' 'donut shop' was a kind of cultural short-hand, an announcement of a particular business form and informal social space. For donut entrepreneurs, this made for good business; for consumers, it had deeper cultural consequences.

5 Eddie Shack Was No Tim Horton: Donuts and the Folklore of Mass Culture, 1974–1999

Early in the morning of 21 February 1974, on the highway between Toronto and Buffalo, legendary defenceman Tim Horton was driving too fast. A few hours before, fresh from a hard-fought National Hockey League game, which saw the Toronto Maple Leafs defeat his Buffalo Sabres, Horton had downed a handful of painkillers and headed off into the night in his fancy sports car. After a stop in the Toronto suburb of Oakville to check on his business interests – a chain of forty Tim Horton Donut Shops – Horton pulled back onto the Queen Elizabeth Way and put the pedal down. Less than an hour later, he approached Lake Street in St Catharines, only fifteen minutes from the U.S. border. At this point, the story gets confusing. Local lore around St Catharines has it that the Ontario Provincial Police had set up a roadblock to slow him down, which Horton, it is said, swerved to avoid. According to the official version, Horton was alone on the highway that morning. No matter, since the result was the same: at high speed, the great defenceman drove off the QEW and was thrown from his car. He died minutes later.

Horton's death marked a turning point in his status as a Canadian icon. To that point, his life had had all the trappings of the classic myth of white Canadian manhood. He was born at the dawn of the Great Depression in the Northern Ontario railway town of Cochrane – a place of hard work, hard winters, and hockey rinks – and travelled south to the big city as a teenager to pursue every 'true Canadian' boy's dream of playing professional hockey. Horton patrolled NHL blue lines for twenty-two years, seventeen of them for the storied Toronto Maple Leafs. And while hockey was known as a brutal and bloody sport, and Horton was renowned for his rock-solid body checks, by all accounts Tim was a true gentleman who always kept his physical talents in perspective. Indeed, for Canadians of a certain generation, Horton was a kind of archetype of the Canadian man: humble in origins, large in talent, strong in body, and gentle in demeanour. Horton's tragic end, coming just at the close of what is widely viewed as Canadian hockey's greatest era, ought to have solidified his place in the pantheon of the Canadian man: a northern boy made good on sweat and talent, playing Canada's national pastime in its golden age.[1]

But Horton's death, instead of solidifying his status as a masculine myth, ensured for him a much different, and much quirkier, path to pop culture iconography. Today, the corporate headquarters of Tim Donut Limited oversees what is a mammoth chain by Canadian standards, comprising more than two thousand outlets nation-wide, earning almost $3 billion in gross revenues each year. There are more Tim Hortons shops than McDonald's outlets in Canada, and the chain controls almost one-quarter of the Canadian quick-service restaurant sector (the industry-updated name for fast food). Tim Hortons commands both the Canadian donut business and its cultural meaning.[2] In television commercials, in the mass media, and in donut shops themselves, the chain is celebrated as a 'national institution' and is connected to broader ideas of cultural identity, an iconic status only partially connected to memories of Tim as a Canadian hero. To donut lovers of a certain generation, Tim Horton is just a name on a sign that we pass several times every day, no more real than Ronald McDonald.

Yet the dual iconography of Tim Horton is only one part of a broader folklore of mass culture that links donut shops with existing ideas of national and local community life. This chapter analyses the emergence and shape of Canada's donut folklore, beginning with a discussion of the way it built on existing ideas of Canada. Then I review some of the broad social and cultural developments that made Canadians ready to adopt donut lore – especially the ongoing crisis of Canadian identity and the increasing saturation of the foodscape by donut shops in absence of widely shared institutions of community. Finally, I examine the 'Hortonization' of donut lore – the increasing tendency to refer to Tim Hortons, rather than generic donut shops, as Canadian or local institutions.

'Is There Anything More Canadian Than That?'

In Canada, the donut is widely believed to be the unofficial national food, and the donut shop to be a national institution.[3] Both take on deeper meanings when linked to other, more established forms of Canadiana like hockey, winter, and anti-Americanism. 'There are two things that define Canada like nothing else,' Luisa D'Amato declared in the *Kitchener-Waterloo Record*, 'hockey and donut shops.'[4] The donut/hockey nexus rests to a large degree on the dual iconography of Tim Horton, expressed nicely in a song by Toronto bar band 'go bimbo go!' which reconnects Horton's status as a masculine myth and pop icon:

Tim, Tim Horton,
More of a man than you'll ever be.
Tim, Tim Horton,
He may be gone, but his donuts, they carry on.[5]

In 1994, former Toronto Maple Leaf Eddie Shack jumped on the donut and hockey player bandwagon, lending his name to a chain of donut shops on the outskirts of Toronto. Contrasting the place of Tim Horton and Eddie Shack in the political economy of the donut and the masculine myth of hockey soon became common fare in Southern Ontario donut shops. Like Horton, Shack played for Toronto during hockey's golden age, but he would hardly make any father's list of male role models. Better known for a string of comic commercials than for any great contribution to patriotic mythmaking, Shack is a real charac-ter, much like the goofy uncle who shows up at family reunions and won't stop talking. Nor is Shack a particularly admired donut impresa-rio. His chain never totalled more than a handful of outlets. 'Tim Horton was an impressive kind of guy: short and stocky, brush cut, played for the Leafs,' summed up John Fitzsimmons of Hamilton, Ontario. 'If they'd have had an Eddie Shack Donut back then, I'd have said "I ain't going in there, the guy's a goof!" But now he's a legend. He was fun to watch, but [Eddie Shack] was no Tim Horton.'[6]

Hockey is a winter sport, and Canada is thought to be the great north-ern nation, so winter is another Canadian theme linked to donuts. Canadians eat more donuts per capita than any other nation on earth, a fact that is attributed in donut lore to our famous harsh winters. Nutri-tionists, it is claimed (although they are never named), say our seemingly insatiable craving for donuts is related to our need for fatty foods to fight off the Canadian cold.[7] While this argument is patently illogical – cold winters are no more common in Toronto than they are in, say, Cleveland – it expresses a long-standing belief that Canada's climate and geography created a distinctive identity. Historian W.L. Morton has argued that 'Canadian life ... is marked by a northern quality ...The line which marks off the frontier from the farmstead, the wilderness from the baseland, the hinterland from the metropolis, runs through every Canadian psyche.'[8] The relationship of donuts and winter can be equally lyrical: 'Winter is the perfect Canadian season,' Chad Skelton wrote in one of our national newspapers: 'Summer is too Americanized. We don't really have a Canadian way of doing it. We go to air-conditioned multiplexes to watch the latest Hollywood blockbuster, sip 7-Eleven Slurpees, play beach volleyball and eat Dairy Queen sundaes. But think of defrosting your fingers around an extra-large Tim Hortons coffee on a February morning. Now that's Canadian.'[9]

Skelton's association of seasons and consumer products with national experiences – Slurpees and summer with America, Tim Hortons and winter with Canada – is surprisingly rich in its use of national imagery. No discussion of Canadian identity strays very far from nervous references to the economic and cultural influence of the United States. Former prime minister Pierre Trudeau once said that living next to the United States 'is in some ways like sleeping with an elephant: No matter how friendly and even-tempered the beast, one is affected by every twitch and grunt.'[10] The way Canadians see and understand their southern neighbor – what might be called the Canadian 'idea of America' – is complex and multidimensional. Its negative side – anti-Americanism – has been ably studied in terms of politics, trading relationships, cultural policy, and even the products of popular culture, but it is a much more deeply rooted impulse than many of these studies convey. Yet the impulse to pull away coexists with a deep fascination with American mass culture.[11] Skelton's passage nicely encapsulates this odd duality. We consume American products, yet somehow crave a more 'genuine' Canadian mass culture experience, like a Tim Hortons coffee on a February morning.

A rambling essay scrawled on the back of three Tim Hortons napkins made the point more explicit: 'What people don't realize is that ... we ARE Americans. We buy their clothes, watch their TV, and do most things exactly the same as them ... Why we look up to "big brother" U.S. I don't know, but that can't be helped. What we can do is recognize what is ours and ours alone ... Tim Hortons, Timmy's, Horny Tims ... Seeing a Tim Hortons is just as common as seeing a Canadian flag.'[12]

The Canadian idea of America often expresses itself in the folkloric figure of the 'ignorant American.' 'People in the United States,' argued Rob Billings, whom I encountered one evening in a Coffee Time in Niagara Falls, '... they can't assimilate the difference between the United

States and Canada. I've worked with people in the United States that want to bring things into Canada, and I say *"You can't, you're crossing an international border."* They don't realize that. They just treat it as another state ... They also bring their skis up here in the summer.' One difference they do notice, he continued, puffing out his chest with ironic pride, is the donut shops: 'The U.S. people come over – I have a friend from the U.S ... and he says he's astonished, he thinks it's a joke, that [on] every corner there's at least one store.'[13]

The idea of associating the donut with crossing the border is a surprisingly common piece of folklore, especially among Canadians travelling or living in the United States.[14] 'Before we crossed the border at Fort Erie to drive south,' Phyllis Keeling wrote to me a few years ago, 'we always stopped for our last coffee and donut. As soon as we crossed the border [on the way home], we pulled into Tim Hortons.'[15] Another piece of border lore is 'the immigrant's tale': a new arrival confesses that at first, she did not understand why Canada had so many donut shops, but eventually found an understanding of the country in these odd national institutions, as with the donut patron who told CBC Radio that he thought 'Now I am a Canadian' the first time he bit into a donut.[16] Canadians living in the United States are especially likely to associate border crossings with donuts. Tales abound of Canadians abroad asking relatives to bring them a dozen Tim Horton donuts when they visit, or of expatriate Canadians associating a trip to the donut shop with returning home. Jonathan Singer, who grew up in Toronto but now lives in California, told me that whenever he returns to Canada, a donut shop is the first stop he makes, even before he goes home to drop off his luggage: 'I very much associate donut shops with Canada ... Leonard Cohen made a reference to "the holy places where the races meet" ... and I think that donut shops, in their humble and occasionally grungy way, fit the description nicely.' Singer does not eat many donuts. Rather, it is the culture of the shops that he associates with Canada, especially what he sees as its more civil political culture relative to that of the United States: 'What I do associate with Canada is the culture of acceptance, conversation, and debate ... that occurs in Canadian donut shops and very few other places. I can't think of a single U.S. equivalent.'[17]

'You Could Start Up a Band or Start Up a Drug Habit'

Another aspect of donut folklore involves claims, made by several cities, to be the 'donut capital of Canada.' Many people simply assert that the place where they live is the donut capital of Canada: I have collected references to Moncton, Port Hope, Toronto, Niagara Falls, Brantford, and many other cities. The contention is usually based on anecdotal evidence about the number of shops compared to other cities. 'Gee, I thought Niagara Falls was [the donut capital of Canada],' Peter Harvey told me in a Tim Hortons outlet near the QEW. 'It seems like there's one on every corner. Just down the street there used to be three. Like, in one little area ... you got one here, one there, one over there. If you go down Drummond Road I think there's two Tim Hortons right across from each other. They say people in Ontario like these places, but if you go to Quebec ... I think in Montreal there's only one Tim Hortons.'

Much more intriguing is a second, deeper level of the donut capital idea. Donut lovers in Hamilton and St Catharines make especially passionate and even quasi-official donut capital claims, citing statistics to prove the point, and even linking the prevalence of donut shops to a sense of local identity. 'St Catharines has the most donut shops per capita of any place in Canada,' Ben Glickman told me half-angrily in a Bakers Dozen outlet, tapping the table that separated us with his finger to emphasize each word.[18] Citing statistics about 'donut stores per capita' is the most common way to back up claims to donut capital status. The method of calculation varies, but normally involves noting that someone else has done the math. 'A friend of mine figured it out using the Yellow Pages,' one St Catharines donut store patron told me, insulating the boast from questions about the calculation process – a standard strategy with urban legends.[19] Other claims look to more weighty authorities. Many St Catharines donut aficionados insist that the city was granted this designation by an unnamed edition of the *Guinness Book of World Records*. Indeed, the former mayor, Joe McCaffery, told me as much shortly before his death, adding the other local legend that Johnny Carson had mentioned the city in these terms in a monologue. Citations of these sorts of authorities continues, unabated by their apparent inaccuracy. 'Agent N' of the self-characterized Coffee Crusaders, who wrote Internet reviews of St Catharines donut shops in the late 1990s, offered me proof of the claim in the fact that 'David Letterman once said it on his show,' although the mysterious Crusader allowed that it might be 'just an urban legend.'[20]

West up the Queen Elizabeth Way, Hamiltonians make similar claims, even granting the boast a quasi-official status. The web page of the Hamilton Public Library, under the heading 'Significant Cultural Landmarks in Hamilton,' claims that the city is the 'coffee and donut capital of Canada,' noting that the first Tim Hortons franchise was located on Ottawa Street.[21] The *Hamilton Spectator*, the city's main newspaper, sent a reporter out into local donut shops to debunk the claim that Moncton, New Brunswick, was the city most devoted to the Tim Hortons chain. Much of the resulting article, headlined 'Nice Try Moncton, We're the Tim Hortons Capital of Canada,' was an account of the dubious mathematics of per capita donut store saturation.[22]

But the specific claims are less important than the messages they carry. 'To be sure,' wrote Robert Blumstock in the *Spectator* more than a decade ago, 'we in Hamilton are never likely to have the media come in droves to discover us. We may never have anything to compare to the CN Tower or other skyscrapers and landmarks of Toronto. But there is at least one area in which we outpace our provincial capital ... We have a doughnut shop for every 5000 people while Toronto's doughnut availability is one shop for every 20000.' According to Blumstock, the simple, blue-collar nature of the city explained its devotion to donuts: 'There are our obvious attributes: a sensible, hard-working bunch who are not easily taken in by the latest food fashions.' A similar argument was advanced in St Catharines by a pair of entrepreneurs hawking 'donut capital' t-shirts: 'The doughnut title tells everyone in no uncertain terms that St Catharines citizens are honest, sober and hard-working people.'[23] This sense of ironic pride in the lack of cultural alternatives relative to other cities, and in being simple, hardworking people – what might be called 'donut populism' – underlies most of the donut capital claims I heard.

In the donut capital image, this populist impulse is turned to specific local purposes – normally, to contrast the social life of one place with that of another. 'Well, Hamilton's a simple town,' Ed Mahaj told me in an effort to explain the donut capital claim, using Toronto as a point of reference: 'I used to love playing up on it when I was doing business in Toronto. People would say "where are you from?" and I'd say, "I'm from Hamilton ... down in the east end" ... That's a rough area, and I'd play up on it ... One characteristic that people from Hamilton possess versus people from Toronto, they're much more unpretentious. People from Toronto tend to be much more pretentious – glitz and show forms a much more important part of their life.[24]

In St Catharines, Floyd Reynolds explained the claim by informing me that 'the donut's just ... about the only thing in the [city] to be devoted to.' His point of reference was not Toronto so much as an unnamed, imagined place where 'something' might actually happen. Our conversation continued on these lines:

SP: Isn't there anything else to do around here besides go to [Tim] Hortons?
FLOYD: Well, there's [Tim Hortons], or you could start up a band or start up a drug habit.
SP: Which one are you doing?
FLOYD: All three.[25]

'The Image of Their Communion'

For a widespread phenomenon, Canadian donut lore is surprisingly recent in origin. Early national references to the donut focused on its actual lineage, unapologetically recognizing its American character. As early as 1897, the donut was being used as a symbol of the way American habits were creeping into Toronto's British traditions. Beckles Willson wrote in *Saturday Night* magazine that 'Toronto ... [is] the sole British city where the inroads of ice-water and doughnuts are most manifest – at once the most English and the most American of Canadian cities.'[26] The situation had not changed by the middle of the new century, when restaurant magazines urged Canadian operators to serve donuts to attract American tourists. The tide was turning by the 1970s, however. The idea that the donut is a Canadian food seems to have emerged in southern Ontario in the late 1970s. 'Doughnuts are as integral as federal-provincial relations in the Canadian way of life,' declared the *Hamilton Spectator* in 1977, staking out a claim to one of the earliest nationalist references to the donut.[27] A few years later, donuts joined beer, back bacon, and toques as Canadian symbols in Bob and Doug MacKenzie's 'Great White North,' a popular comedy sketch on the television show *SCTV*, which originally aired in Canada but was eventually picked up by NBC in the United States. Bob and Doug's movie, *Strange Brew* (1983), featured the duo working in a Toronto brewery, eventually saving the city from Max von Sydow's evil plot to control the local populace with a concoction of hypnotic beer. They spent much of their time, however, bribing their dog with various treats, driving around Toronto in their van, and devouring dozens of Country Style donuts (which dominated the Toronto market at this time). By the late 1980s, the press was starting to claim that the donut shop had become Canada's equivalent to the English pub.[28]

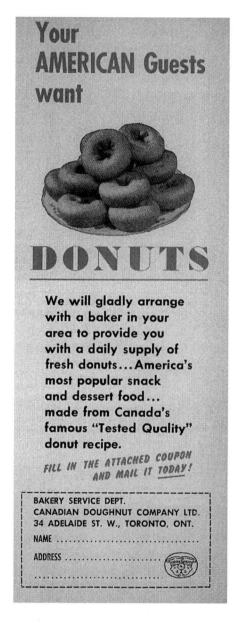

At mid-century, the donut often had American associations. (*Canadian Hotel Review and Restaurant*, 15 June 1950, 5)

The donut capital image seems to have emerged at about the same time, although associating populist meanings with the donut has a long history, especially in the United States. During the Depression, the donut took on the reputation as the 'poor man's rich food,' a cheap treat within the means of even struggling workers.[29] These democratic associations spread north of the border. In 1934, an American traveller used the donut to symbolize social levelling in Toronto, writing in the *Geographic Magazine* that 'citizens say "Sir" to policemen, yet it is a democratic place and any day at Bowle's Quick Lunch you may see knights munching a doughnut beside a taximan.'[30] Not all of these downscale images were positive. As donut shops spread through Ontario's suburbs in the 1960s, they often became elitist symbols of the lack of culinary culture outside established downtowns. Joanne Kates wrote in her *Globe and Mail* dining column that if the shopping mall were to serve as the new town common for suburban areas, it would need 'a pleasant restaurant, not a doughnut shop or a greasy spoon.'[31] By the early 1980s, pointing to donut shops (and their car culture cousins) was one way to call attention to the 'cultural wasteland' of suburban sprawl. 'For years,' Rita Daly reported in the *Toronto Star*, '[Scarborough] has borne the brunt of criticism and sarcastic jokes from people who perceive it as no-man's land – a physical and cultural wasteland "somewhere east of Toronto," comprising only gas stations, doughnut shops, and huge parking lots as far as the eye can see.' Two years later, one columnist mocked Scarborough's attempts at civic boosterism by claiming that council was contemplating a 'Doughnut Shop Hall of Fame' for Eglinton Avenue, where motorists could drive through a 'mock coconut sprinkle pastry' as they entered the borough from Toronto.[32] Perhaps donut populists saw a chance to seize the term back: at about the same time, the donut capital claim began to be used to summon pride in lack of high-brow culture. The earliest mention I have found to this appeared in *What's Up Niagara* magazine in November 1982, referring to St Catharines. In any event, the image began to proliferate in the local media in St Catharines and Hamilton after that.[33]

On the surface, both strands of donut folklore run against the origins and the fate of the commodity itself. As we saw in chapter 2, big-time donut retailers developed in Canada as branch plants or Canadian-owned versions of American mass production ideas. This process has a long history, dating back to Adolph Levitt in 1920 and the extension of his company to Canada in the 1930s. It continued in the early 1960s

By the mid-1980s, residents of cities like St Catharines and Hamilton were claiming the donut as a symbol of local identity. (*Hamilton This Month*, June 1985, p. 13. Illustrator: Lisa Hudson. Reprinted with permission of Town Media/*Hamilton* magazine)

with the arrival of American companies like Mister Donut and Dunkin' Donuts and the advent of Canadian-owned chains like Tim Hortons and Country Style (which borrowed the model of the American chains).[34] It probably reached its height when Tim Hortons merged with the American hamburger company Wendy's in 1995 – a move that did not seem to affect Tim Hortons' links to national mythology.[35] Nor did the donut shop's increasing dependence on coffee – a creature of global economic trends at a time when Canadians were more and more sensitive to globalization – put a dent in the home-grown donut rhetoric. Similarly, the blue-collar populism of the donut capital image seemed to run against the trajectory of the donut business throughout the 1980s and 1990s, which (as we saw in chapter 4) witnessed the wholesale reinvention of the donut shop – both its product line and physical form – at least partly in the hope of jettisoning its blue-collar heritage.

Nor did Canadian donut folklore explicitly recognize the regional character of Canada's donut geography. Donut shops had established a more national presence by the 1980s; even so, they remained concentrated in Ontario, as did donut folklore until the 1990s, whatever its nationalist language.[36] In many ways, this regional tension is not surprising. Like much official Canadian culture, early nationalist donut lore was simply the regional delusions of southern Ontario. 'Southern Ontario regionalism,' a group of literary critics explained, 'has been largely successful by being invisible, by resisting precise territorial definition, and by passing itself as Canadian nationalism.'[37] Donut lore remains less common in urban British Columbia, where upscale coffee shops like Starbucks are considered the bulwark of local coffee culture. In Vancouver, visitors and new arrivals notice the lack of donut shops as much as the temperate climate and scenic vistas. 'Forget flowers in January,' *Vancouver* magazine reported in May 1999. 'The real shock for in-moving Canadians is Vancouver's lack of doughnuts ... Here, muffins, scones, and cinnamon buns take top billing in bakery cases, and biscotti at coffee counters.'[38] Donut lore continues to be most deeply rooted in Ontario, and remains much less common west of Ontario and in francophone Quebec.

These tensions are probably exaggerated: American influence, global commerce, and regional culture have been part of the Canadian experience for much of this country's history. Besides, these associations of community with commodity are not statements of literal truth – the veracity of these claims is less important than the fact that the stories are being told often enough to shape or express a 'way of seeing' one's environment or imagining one's community.[39] For Benedict Anderson, almost every community (though he was writing mainly of nations) is an act of imagination. Most communities are not based on face-to-face relations: they exist because their members make a perceptual leap – they form mental connections with people they may never actually encounter. 'The members of even the smallest nation will never know most of their fellow-members, meet them, or even hear of them,' Anderson wrote in an especially powerful passage, 'yet in the minds of each lives the image of their communion.' Anderson was careful to distinguish this sort of imagination from a fiction or a hoax: 'Communities are to be distinguished, not by their falsity/genuineness, but by the style in which they are imagined.'[40] In this sense, claims about donut stores per capita or about fatty foods and Canadian winters seem less important for their relative accuracy than for the rendering of community characteristics. Much of donut folklore plays on a sense of ironic pride in marginal status, simultaneously poking fun at the unsophisticated hinterland and the pretentious metropolis. At the local level, donut capital claims use irony to 'imagine a community' that stands in opposition to a cultural centre – most often Toronto with its 'world class' pretensions. Through a broader lens, the national folklore of the donut uses an opposition in much the same way, replacing the populist irony of the donut capital with a nationalist, anti-American variant. In making these associations, donut folklore is helped along by its reference to other, more established images of nation and community.

But it is one thing to say that donut folklore is a kind of imagined community and another to explain why it has taken hold. Indeed, Anderson himself was not interested in debunking nationalism as a myth, but in explaining the timing and pervasiveness of its emergence. While emphasizing the imagined nature of communities, Anderson did not present them as free-floating ideas. He stressed throughout his book that the rise of nationalism was made possible by economic and technological developments. He discussed the way novels and newspapers, for example, 'provided the technical means for "re-presenting" the *kind* of imagined community that is a nation,' and while he was clearly interested in the cultural meaning of these two literary forms, he was careful to link their production and dissemination to more material innovations. 'Nothing perhaps more precipitated this search [for new ways of thinking],' he argued, 'than print-capitalism, which made it possible for rapidly growing numbers of people to think about themselves, and to relate to others, in profoundly new ways.'[41] Thus, for Anderson, novel ways of thinking had power because they were implanted in specific institutions, disseminated by new technologies, and consolidated in an emerging capitalist market of ideas.

Of course, the subject at hand is not the nation but the donut, yet the point remains. For half a century, Canadians had been implored by modern advertising to eat more donuts; and we had been including this lowly snack food in our festivals, breaks, and daily routines well before that. Yet donut lore did not emerge until the 1980s. What cultural work did it perform at this moment in particular? Which social developments made (some) Canadians ready to adopt an American icon as a national and local myth? I suspect that the explanation needs to account for two developments: as in the case of Anderson's nationalism, donut lore was based on both cultural dynamics and economic and institutional structures. English Canadians underwent a profound crisis of community in the 1980s, and the absence of strong cultural anchors opened space for an ironic and quirky form of imagined community; at the same time, new developments in the donut business and older ones in the mass media provided a means of disseminating donut lore.[42]

Throughout the 1980s and 1990s, many established cultural anchors seemed to be dissolving. Canada seemed to be in chronic crisis, with ongoing rounds of constitutional negotiations and conflict (1982's 'repatriation' of the Constitution without Quebec's agreement, the failures of the Meech Lake and Charlottetown Accords). No agreement seemed possible between all the provinces on a form for the Constitution. In addition, regional grievances over energy, the fiscal imbalance, social policy, and other issues, and a deeply divisive election over free trade with the United States, heightened the tense atmosphere. Even when nationalism was supposedly at its height in the late 1960s and early 1970s, Canada never had clearly agreed on national symbols or traditions. Nonetheless, in the 1980s, the lack of widely shared national values seemed endemic to the Canadian condition. One observer went so far to say that Canada was not a nation-state at all, since its federal government was not anchored to a national cultural foundation.[43] As much as it played on marginal status, donut folklore also referenced this lack of Canadian identity. In the *Toronto Star* in 1987, Chris Zelkovich described his futile search for a 'Canadian restaurant' in Toronto to show off to his American friend.[44] The pair searched the *Tourist Guide to Fine Dining* but found nothing listed under Canadian. They drove around for hours, figuring a 'brief trip around the city would produce several Canadian restaurants,' but they found nothing except ethnic food and donut shops: 'We passed Miguel's Taste of Tegucigalpa, Donut World, Moammar's Libyan Bistro, Donut Heaven, The Zen California Café, Donuts 'R Us, Pedro's Paraguayan Parlor, Donut Delite, Sasha's Siberian Trattoria and Famous Hockey Player's Donuts, but not one Canadian restaurant.' Exhausted, the pair gave up, deciding 'there are no Canadian restaurants' before heading off for 'more doughnuts.' In this sense, donut lore did more than just *reflect* the broader crisis in Canadian identity. Indeed, the crisis itself was integrated into (and became a key feature of) donut lore.[45]

Symbolic nationalism was not the only cultural anchor to be dissolving in the 1980s. Many commentators lamented the decline of the North American middle class, a development that was often connected to the passing of the mass market. Barbara Ehrenreich made the point, and its connection to consumer choice, most succinctly: 'The middle is disappearing from the retail industry ... The stores and chains that are prospering are the ones that have learned to specialize in one extreme of wealth or the other ... Whether one looks at food, clothing or furnishing, two cultures are emerging: natural fibre vs. synthetic blends, handcrafted wood cabinets vs. mass-produced maple, David's Cookies vs. Mister Donut.'[46] In Canada, the fate of the middle class attracted similar attention, both sociological and journalistic.[47] The trend was probably exaggerated, and the mass market had always been more complicated than Ehrenreich and others suggested. All that aside, the idea of fragmentation in cultural choices flowed into emerging donut lore, first by ridiculing the oversized muffin as the 'yuppie donut,' then by mocking the gourmet coffee shop and its Paris café affectations.

Indeed, donut populism was often placed in opposition to gourmet coffee houses, which spread throughout Canada in the 1980s, first by targeting indoor malls and then later by opening storefront outlets in busy, downtown, pedestrian neighbourhoods.[48] Although gourmet coffee houses aimed for volume and turnover, they marketed upscale 'atmosphere' in order to breed customer loyalty. 'Coffee houses are good places to meet friends and to take a break from the hectic pace of the city,' argued Second Cup president Alton McEwen. 'Our new design focuses on each store community and creates inviting meeting spots, reflecting each neighborhood's unique spirit and personality through the harmonious union of art, design, and music.' Describing a new outlet in an affluent area of Toronto, McEwen noted that an interior mural 'captures the essense of neighborhood ... a place where neighbors meet to chat over a fence – enjoy coffee and conversation.' The contrast of product and place was quickly picked up by donut populists. In a donut outlet in Moncton, New Brunswick – the only city outside Ontario where I heard claims of donut capital status – Eugene Leblanc provided me with a map of the social status of various coffee shops: 'It's a real social scale ... This is at the bottom, Joe Mocca's [a specialty coffee shop] is in the middle, and Starbuck's is at the top ... The bottom of the barrel is here, because ... it's a little rougher part of town. I don't mind it ... because I grew up here.' Al Stortz agreed. 'You know, all the fancy things with all that crap dumped into them,' he scoffed, jestering towards the Moss Coffee Tree across town. 'I never would go there because ... I like plain coffee ... I don't want espresso, any of that crap. My original coffee is 'Eight O'Clock Coffee' from the A&P.'[49]

Yet whatever the broader cultural context, donut folklore cannot be separated from economic and institutional questions. A single shop might produce a set of stories that weave themselves into the social life of a neighbourhood or town. These local attachments may even be communicated to a wider audience. But the folklore of mass culture is nurtured by social patterns with much greater reach, patterns that are repeated across space and time and that can be observed over multiple visits and extensive travels. The emerging structure of the donut business (the saturation of markets, the pinching of territories, the seemingly limitless possibilities for growth) provided the foundation for a popular and widespread folklore. The mass media then reinforced and disseminated that lore, both in its banal reporting of the donut's increasing commercial power and in more developed stories probing the connection between the lowly snack food and Canadian life.

Both the main threads of donut folklore – that the donut is the national food, and that certain cities are donut capitals – were, at root, simply ways to observe and acknowledge the saturation of the foodscape. What business observers saw as a saturation of markets, Canadian consumers interpreted as a cultural symbol. It was the number of donut shops in London, after all, that led the *Free Press* to wonder whether they were the Canadian version of the British pub. A few years later, the same phenomenon had management consultant Karen Castelan proclaiming that 'the doughnut is to Canada what apple pie is to America.' It was the number of shops, as well, that launched populists in St Catharines and Hamilton into claiming donut capital status. In interviews in donut shops, patrons' homespun theories about community and donuts always began with a simple observation on the ubiquity of the shops. As Peter Harvey told me: 'It seems like there's one on every corner.'[50]

Ubiquity was only the starting point. By imagining donut shops as institutions that transcended space, donut folklore played on the increasing fragmentation of social life and the lack of widely shared national symbols; it also promised to overcome them. While the division between 'yuppie' gourmet coffee houses and 'blue collar' donut shops in donut lore might appear to play on fragmentation, saying 'blue collar' was not a description of social position so much as an explanation of local cultural preferences, based on claims to mass market authenticity. While bagel connoisseurs feared the loss of authenticity when the product was transferred to mass market, donut populism imagined the mass market to be the *source*, not the enemy, of authenticity, a place where 'real' people bought simple, folksy products free of the upscale affectations of yuppies and the cultural elite. 'It's not the most expensive coffee,' noted one Hamiltonian of Tim Hortons, 'and they don't claim to pick it from the lush fields in Guatemala and carry it out on the backs of donkeys, but it's good. It's really good.'[51] In this sense, the donut capital image was only one local thread in a much larger strain of mass market populism.

The reinvention of donut shops – adding new products, brightening stores, and banning smoking, all meant to pull away from its increasingly male, blue-collar customer base – reinforced rather than undermined donut populism. Donut populists imagined that the mass market was more authentic precisely *because* it tried to serve everyone and did not target niches in an age of fragmented identity. Donut shops were, in Jonathan Singer's words, 'holy places where the races meet.' 'What I love about Tim Hortons and its ilk (not Starbucks, Second Cup or any other "cafes," mind you),' argued one observer, 'is not the donuts but the fact that it is one of the few places where all of humanity can meet.' Increasingly, the symbolic product was a coffee not a donut, but the foundation of this role as social unifier was always the donut shop's connection to the mass market and petty consumption. 'They serve coffee to the poorest of the poor and the richest of the rich and yet they treat us all as human beings,' argued the Reverend Heather Filmour, a pastor at Burlington Baptist Church. In Hamilton, the *Spectator* nicely crystallized these images into a single scene: 'Among the sit-down crowd, at one end of the counter a leather-jacketed biker and a khaki-clad tradesman share the same sports page. Farther along, two bantering youths review their weekend while a middle-age couple in casual garb discuss their plans for the day and a businessman inspects the contents of his briefcase.'[52] This theme links donut populism to the national myth of the donut. In an age of fragmented identity, regional grievances, and segmented selling, donut folklore imagines that, perhaps, donut shops can link all Canadians together, or at the very least distinguish us from Americans.

'People Don't Say "Coffee Shop" Anymore'

In 1997, Cathy Mauro, marketing director for Country Style Donuts, appeared on Toronto's local CBC radio affiliate to discuss the connection between donut shops and Canadian life. During the interview, she repeated many of the central elements of Canadian donut lore. The donut shop, she claimed, served as Canada's answer to the English pub, 'an opportunity to say hello to a friendly face, maybe to sit down at a table and talk to some other customers.' Though a Canadian institution, she continued, the connection to sociability was especially deep in particular regions: '[The donut store is a social centre] especially in Northern Ontario ... I find that if you really want to be where it's happening at ten or eleven o'clock at night, you go to a donut shop.'[53]

In many ways, Mauro's interview offered unremarkable bits of donut folklore. By this time, few of the CBC's listeners would have been surprised by any of her claims, since this sort of lore was by then common in both national and local media and in donut shops themselves. What many listeners might have found remarkable was that Mauro appeared at all. Some perhaps wondered why a marketing director for a donut chain was appearing on a public network to explain a sociological phenomenon. As it first emerged in the 1980s, donut folklore linked commodity and community, but few companies were inclined to take such conspicuous advantage of it. By 1997, however, donut lore was becoming a creature of commercial speech, and Canadians were being treated to elaborate TV commercials, purporting to be True Stories, that repackaged and rebroadcast donut lore in the name of corporate branding. This trend might have led CBC listeners to wonder at the choice of companies. In 1997, Canadians expressed donut lore in less and less generic terms: unlike Mauro, who described 'donut shops' as a national institution, more and more Canadians looked to Tim Hortons alone as the touchstone of snackfood nationalism.

Early references to the donut as national food were almost exclusively generic. While the *London Free Press* recognized the growing dominance of chains, it called the 'donut shop,' not just Tim Hortons, the

Canadian version of the British pub. In *Strange Brew*, Bob and Doug had ignored the larger Tim Hortons in favour of Toronto favourite Country Style, but only the most observant viewer (like a historian, pausing frame by frame) would have noticed, since the boxes were incidental to the story and the brand name was never explicitly identified in the dialogue. Nonetheless, the decision would have been unimaginable by the late 1990s. 'People don't say "coffee shop" anymore,' Mr Mugs franchisee Curtis Mitchell lamented in the *Hamilton Spectator*. 'They say "Hortons."' Other observers showed similar cognitive slippage, as in the *Canadian Business* story that pointed to a regular 'Tim Hortons' feature on *This Hour Has 22 Minutes* when the segment was actually shot at a Robin's Donuts in Halifax. This kind of mistake was often criticized, especially from a regional perspective. 'Your article reads as if there are no other doughnut shops in Canada except Tim Hortons – a conclusion that might be reached by someone who doesn't venture beyond the borders of the Greater Toronto Area,' one westerner complained in a letter to *Canadian Business*. 'But here on the Prairies, in Quebec and in many parts of Ontario, Tim's is far from the dominant force you make it out to be.'[54]

Just as donut lore originally grew from the form's ubiquity on the landscape, its 'Hortonization' can be partly explained by the company's increasing dominance of the industry and its ability to fill every crevice in the Canadian foodscape. As we saw in chapter 4, Hortons rose in the late 1990s to what marketing experts call a 'master brand' – a company or product, like Band-Aid or Kleenex, that defines the commodity itself. Until 1997, however, Tim Hortons did not spend much time creating or exploiting the donut shop's growing folkloric meaning. To be sure, the company had been far ahead of its competitors in advertising resources and strategies for more than a decade. In 1984, Hortons' advertising budget was $2 million (Country Style's ad budget was about $700,000 three years later), money it had been spending, since 1981, on national TV campaigns for its products. (Second-place Country Style did not resort to TV advertising until 1991 and did not include TV as a key part of its marketing strategy until 1996.)[55]

Television advertising was highly effective (Timbit sales increased 34% after one early-1980s commercial[56]), but at the time, Horton's marketing was not about to win awards for creativity or branding. According to the chain's longtime advertising manager, Ron Buist, most advertising was generated in-house until well into the 1980s, and marketing budgets continued to be relatively limited, since Ron Joyce remained suspicious of slick, agency-produced commercials and preached an 'inside out' focus on operations to build the business. Buist recalls wondering why Joyce opened scattered outlets where advertising dollars couldn't be pooled; apparently Joyce wanted the franchisees to build up business locally at first, from the ground up, believing that the most effective marketing moment was over the counter and in the community. So if many companies spent marketing dollars to sell image and identity, Tim Hortons was not one of them. Its branding efforts focused on operations, research and development, and clever but not slick product-focused ads.[57]

To a degree, the company's history gave it a special advantage in emerging donut lore. Many consumers played on the chain's early connection to hockey celebrity, which, though less relevant to younger customers and certainly no explanation for the company's dominance, did flow through many threads of donut lore. But at the time, the chain itself was hardly anxious to exploit this element of its history. Indeed, Horton had become a minor presence in the chain's public image even before his death. In the early days, the chain exploited Tim's celebrity, mainly through public appearances at grand openings and hockey references in early advertisements, but it was not a strategy that Horton himself had enjoyed very much, nor one that Ron Joyce found especially useful. Tim had shied away from the attention, often spending grand openings hidden in the back of the store. For Joyce, Horton's image deflected attention from his own focus on operations and his belief that the outlets themselves were the most effective marketing vehicle. 'The name was not important,' Joyce told Horton's biographer. 'It was operations. How do you make it work? How do you make it happen? We developed the manual, the systems, because there was nobody there to teach us.'[58]

By the 1980s, a customer looking for any sign of the great defenceman in a Tim Hortons outlet would find only a poster announcing the chain's philanthropic efforts. Tim Hortons' charitable efforts began immediately after the death of its namesake, when Ron Joyce announced the founding of the Tim Horton Children's Foundation to honour Tim's devotion to children and the underprivileged. The foundation's primary purpose at this stage was to run a summer camp for underprivileged children near Parry Sound, which opened in 1975 with two hundred children from Ontario, Nova Scotia, and New Brunswick (the three provinces where Tim Horton Donut shops were located at the time). Eventually, the foundation added other camps in Nova Scotia (1988), Alberta (1991), Quebec (1994), and Kentucky (2000).[59]

Initially, the outlets themselves were not heavily involved in funding the foundation, at least not publicly, beyond the donation box next to the cash register. In 1987, however, Atlantic franchisees decided to donate the receipts from one day's sales to help build the new camp at Tatamagouche. They continued the practice the following year, and by 1991, Camp Day in the store was a chainwide event.[60] For the public, the advent of Camp Day donations intertwined the commercial identity of the outlets much more with the philanthropic efforts of the foundation. Tim's widow, Lori Horton, actually dismissed these philanthropic efforts, asserting that the first camp had been to honour Tim and the rest to promote the chain.[61] This may be a cynical reading of the summer camps, but it is true that the company was willing to exploit its philanthropic efforts for public relations purposes. In 1991, for example, when a Burlington, Ontario, donut shop owner accused the company of killing independent shops, Ron Joyce fired off a letter to the *Hamilton Spectator* defending the company. 'We are not an uncaring corporate entity,' he argued. 'We are a chain made up of hard-working, dedicated franchisees who not only put a great deal of effort into their store operations, but also make a considerable contribution to the communities in which they operate ... Our chain created and sustains the Tim Horton Children's Foundation, which operates summer camps...for monetarily underprivileged children from communities all across Canada.'[62]

The greatest leap forward in marketing sophistication came in 1997, with the unveiling of the 'True Stories' commercials, developed by Enterprise Advertising of Toronto. These commercials – by 2001, Tim Hortons and Enterprise had aired nine of them – featured folksy tales of Tim Hortons customers doing extraordinary or quirky things to get their Tim Hortons coffee, with the tag line 'Coffee You Can Count On.' In the first commercial, set in Lunenburg, Nova Scotia, eighty-six-year-old Lillian struggles to climb a hill to visit her friends and have a coffee at her local Tim Hortons. In the second, Sammi the dog picks up coffee for his owner at a nearby drive-thru. In other commercials, cowboys ride the range near Squamish, British Columbia, before visiting a local Tim Hortons; a Canadian university student in Glasgow misses Tim Hortons as a taste of home (as did Canadian sailors serving in Kuwait); and a youth backpacking through Europe writes to his mother that he met other Canadians who recognized his Tim Hortons travel mug (nonetheless, he is ready to come home). 'Proud Fathers' begins with a flashback: Lou, a Chinese immigrant, had discouraged his son from playing and watching hockey, urging study and hard work instead. Fast-forwarding to the present, Lou's son, now a father himself, discovers that his father had secretly watched his games while drinking a Tim Hortons coffee. As Lou passes his son a coffee and cheers for his grandson, the commercial ends with the caption, 'Every Cup Tells a Story.' 'Coach,' another hockey-themed commercial, focuses on Timbits minor hockey program, selling the image of Hortons as community-minded more than a particular product. Coach 'didn't fit into the normal pattern of promoting a defined product or service,' recalled advertising manager Ron Buist. 'We had produced our first corporate commercial, promoting our company's attitude toward children and its support of community spirit.'[63]

Though different in style and content, the True Stories explored consistent thematic territory. The commercials succeeded not because they broke new creative ground but because they played so effectively on the existing staples of donut folklore and on some long-standing ideas of (English) Canada. (The ads did not run in French, Enterprise claimed, because the company was not as well established there.[64]) They were usually set, for example, in iconic Canadian *places*, features around which the Canadian geographic imagination revolves: a fishing village on the east coast, mountains in British Columbia, a curling rink in Northern Ontario, and generic locations like hockey arenas and railways. Even foreign locations, such as military duty overseas or backpacking in Europe, had a broad familiarity through iconic notions of Canadian life.[65] And the True Stories *characters* had dual qualities. They were particular (and even quirky or exotic) people who were nonetheless familiar: retired people passing time by drinking coffee, meeting fishermen, and singing with children; Chinese immigrants who were nonetheless proud hockey fathers; cowboys who needed a coffee break like everyone else. (In Lillian, the spur to identify with the character was made explicit in the line, 'perhaps you know her'). The *values and experiences* were similarly particular and generic: family relations; neighbourhoods or communities; relations in immigrant families; fun as the central experience of childhood; being away from home ... all of these were subtly merged with the fact that people made daily emotional connections to 'their' Tim Hortons. Finally, although the *posture* of the ads varied ('Sammi' and 'Surfers' were quirky and humorous, while Lillian and Proud Fathers were more sentimental, almost sappy), the scripts were united by unpretentious and straightforward language and narrative. In aggregate, the True Stories presented Tim Hortons as an everyplace institution for everyperson, and linked commercial institutions to the vital, everyday connections of community life.

The True Stories commercials could be analysed along many other thematic lines, but the fundamental point is broader: at base, the commercials performed similar cultural work to donut folklore, expressing versions of Canadiana in unpretentious terms, playing on well-established images of nation and community, and working to unite fragmented groups through simple acts of consumption. The commercials were wildly successful, doubling the chain's advertising awareness numbers in a single year and attracting wide comment and discussion in the media and on the Internet, no doubt because they flowed so perfectly from existing donut lore.[66] Lillian, for example, emerged from a story told in a Halifax focus group, with her friends (a fisherman, children, and customers in a barber shop) added when a subsequent focus group felt that the woman was too lonely. Once the series began to air, the chain was inundated with similar tales: Sammi alone produced several photographs of animals performing crazy Tim Hortons–related stunts. According to Ron Buist, once a good story was found (either from a focus group, from franchisees, or from stories in the local press), the chain needed to shape it into an effective commercial, but the advertising team was careful to make them all believable, drawing the basic narrative from real events, using actual customers as much as possible (counter staff were usually trained actors), keeping the messages familiar, and sticking with professional but unpretentious production values.[67]

Of course, the True Stories commercials did a different kind of cultural work than the richer and more organic folklore, deflecting existing meanings to the commercial purposes of the chain by carefully selecting marketable experiences and smoothing off the rough edges of the stories. Not surprisingly, this process of 'cultural selection' highlighted safe, middle-of-the-road images that played on rather than disrupted folksy Canadian values and symbols.[68] Even when characters, like a Chinese immigrant, had the potential to challenge Canadians to think about their history, the commercial deflected the narrative back into the safer ground of generational conflict (which was resolved within sixty seconds) and integration through sport and consumption. This is not surprising for a commercial, to be sure, although some companies (Benetton, for example) have tried to attract commercial attention by shocking consumers rather than reassuring them.[69] But this kind of message would have conflicted with Tim Hortons' folksy and clean-cut style. (Nor should we wait with bated breath for a True Story that starts, 'The mine is closing down,' 'Back in the strike of '99,' or 'I've been homeless for fifteen years,' however 'True' each of these stories would be.) Moreover, the broader folklore, unlike the True Stories commercials, always had the possibility of developing out of the company's control, as with the growing number of 'counter-lore' stories that cast suspicion on the corporation. The widely disseminated notion that Tim Hortons puts nicotine in its coffee (as though it wasn't addictive enough on its own) is only one example of this counter-lore, using exaggeration to call attention to corporate manipulation of taste.[70]

While the chain unveiled new True Stories at various points after 1997, much of its advertising was more banal. Hortons marshalled its awesome advertising budget to push products through media like billboards, radio, arena signage, and so on. While it focused on a consistent brand identity in all its marketing ('relaxed, caring, friendly, honest,' according to Enterprise VP Doug Poad), most of the company's advertising didn't do much to contribute new ideas to donut lore. What its $21 million ad budget *did* do by 1999 was reinforce the ubiquity of the chain. 'I tried to find a station that didn't have Hortons ads on all the time,' lamented Curtis Mitchell of Mr Mugs. 'I finally did, but the music was really bad and the customers complained.'[71]

Tim Horton Will Deliver Us

In the quarter century after Tim Horton's death, donut shops became quirky icons of local and national identity. Canadians did not invent the donut folklore so much as they added the donut to existing ways of seeing their communities: Canada as a northern country, hockey as a national sport, America as an imagined other, certain cities as blue collar, the mass market as the great leveller. Much of donut folklore played on irony and absence, poking fun at the unsophisticated hinterland and the pretentious metropolis, half-jokingly recognizing that few things united Canadians besides a coffee and donut, and that places like Hamilton and St Catharines lacked culture but made up for it with lunch-bucket charm. Many observers have noted that this sort of double-edged, ironic posture seems endemic to Canadian cultural life, driven by a belief in our status as Other. 'Canadian consciousness,' writes Andrew Wernick, 'is ... an ironic duality that borrows the clothes but not the spirit of American razzle-dazzle, and ... knows itself to be rooted in the dull daily experience of living in a peripheralized region in which nothing really happens.'[72] Perhaps, in this sense, both the donut (as a quirky snack food devoid of nutritional substance) and the donut shop (as a utilitarian commercial space with few cultivated pretensions) were perfectly suited to the ironic purposes of the Canadian popular imagination.

That consumers made these connections depended as much on developments in the donut business as it did on the cultural meaning of the commodity itself. The developing structure of the industry – the efficiency of operations, the harnessing of entrepreneurial ambition, the pinching of territories, the saturation of markets, the redefinition of the form and product line, the seemingly limitless possibility for growth – provided the foundation to build a popular and widespread folklore. Time and again, donut lore began from a simple enumeration of donut shops in the local or national foodscape, whether the result of the steady proliferation of donut shops or the dramatic growth of Tim Hortons to the McDonalds of the Donut Business. In this sense, the redefinition efforts of the major chains, which seemed to run against donut folklore, actually reinforced it, since donut shops as business forms and social spaces were able to spread much more widely, and penetrate much more deeply into the Canadian ecology of eating out, after they expanded menus, renovated interiors, and broadened their markets. More than any other company, Tim Hortons led the way in mass marketed business strategy and folkloric cultural power. The company didn't invent Canadian donut folklore, but it did exploit its growing iconic power by packaging True Stories for popular consumption. Twenty-five years after Tim Horton's death, 'his' company had far surpassed his own status as a Canadian hero.

Conclusion: Commodity and Culture in Postwar Canada

By the time I found him at Islington Avenue and Rathburn Road in Etobicoke, working away underneath the flagship store of his growing Java Joe's chain, Costas Kiriakopoulos had put his donut career firmly in the past. He had just finished opening his seventeenth gourmet coffee outlet – a freestanding location in western Toronto, just up from tony Bloor West Village. To his mind, it was nicely situated to draw in his target clientele: affluent, white-collar customers who know a good coffee when they taste one, the very opposite of the stereotypical donut store patron. 'People think it's the same,' he said of Java Joe's, 'but it's not. Your clientele is much different than a donut [shop]. I get calls from people to lease a location and they say "Oh, Country Style was here [and] Tim Hortons," and I say "That's a donut shop location, it's not for me."'

Kiriakopoulos ought to know. First on his own and then in Country Style's real estate department, he spent a baker's dozen worth of years dealing with the economics of location. But his point was about far more than just picking good real estate. 'I'm looking for a different type of people,' he said. 'I'm looking for, how could I put it, more sophisticated people in the sense [that] they know coffee. I cannot go to an area where I can't try to sell them a cappuccino or a latté or a dark blend ... [where] their answer is "just give me a coffee, that's all I want." I don't need that. I'm looking for office crowds. I'm looking for good neighbourhoods, because my stores are a bit upscale now.'

I got the impression he was talking about much more than a shift in business strategy, more than just applying the same entrepreneurial spirit to a new product. No, Kiriakopoulos seemed to be pointing to a whole new way of thinking. Though he answered my questions about Country Style and O'Donuts patiently and thoughtfully, his face really lit up when the conversation turned to Java Joe's. He became much more animated, leaning forward in his chair, pointing and gesturing to emphasize his points. He seemed to be focusing his analytic energy on solving current problems, not reliving the past.

Kiriakopoulos seemed an unlikely vehicle for understanding the history of postwar Canada. He had forged no innovative paths through the wilderness of Canadian capitalism; he had built no empires to match the usual subjects of Canadian business history; and despite his immigrant roots, he is not much of a subject for rags-to-riches myth-making. Smart, articulate, and successful, nevertheless he spent his life pursuing relatively modest entrepreneurship, plugging away at borrowed ideas, swimming in the mainstream of consumer capitalism, rising not so much to riches as to comfort. His own donut chain had grown to twenty outlets, a solid but not spectacular number, and he had borrowed its business model largely from his early training and experience with Country Style. That shop – Country Style number two in Weston – had been barely 1,200 square feet. It had cost so little that it was within the means of modest, semiskilled workers, and it sold products that cost less than a quarter. Who really cares about the history of snack food in Weston in the 1960s?

The history of the donut charts the relation among business forms, social spaces, and cultural icons – relations at the core of any understanding of postwar Canada. As a business form, donut shops began by adapting an existing mass commodity to the growing potential of car culture. Donut shops were part of the mainstream of this development: they were located along the same commercial strips as other types of drive-in commerce; they were built on lots with good access and large parking lots; and they were designed to maximize the flow of customers in and out the door. Over time, the business strategy of the chains took the donut shop even deeper into car culture. After the mid-1980s – at first reluctantly and then with increasing enthusiasm – the largest donut chains borrowed the drive-thru concept from fast-food companies like Wendy's in order to serve customers without making them leave their cars.

Donut chains were not content to open a few outlets in fringe areas like Weston. They always intended to spread out across space, to push beyond single metropolitan areas in order to exploit regional and later national markets. Though some independent shops struggled along in various parts of Canada, up until 1975, donut chains were largely confined to the urban areas between Montreal and Windsor, including the

Golden Horseshoe at the western end of Lake Ontario. Within this prospering region, donut shops exploited the development of more extensive networks of consumption. Workers and shoppers across southern Ontario were using automobiles to travel longer distances than ever before, and donut chains tapped into this new pattern. After 1975, the major companies tried to expand nationwide, although only Tim Hortons was truly successful. Hortons also redefined the market by moving out of metropolitan and urban areas to exploit small towns, which second-tier companies like Kiriakopoulos's own O'Donuts had proven viable in the 1980s.

To spread across this vast space, chains took advantage of the growing interest in franchising, an 'in between' economic form that promised to combine the efficiency of large enterprise and the utility of small entrepreneurship. Chains tapped the friendship networks, family economies, and entrepreneurial dreams of modest investors in various cities and towns, first in central Canada and later across the country. Small business dreamers were attracted to donut chains by the knowledge they provided. Once those owners understood the system, however, the franchise relationship often resulted in conflict, although franchisee discontent did not necessarily reflect fundamental resistance to the franchisor. Control was a subtle dynamic in the chains, built on brute contractual power, economic efficiency, and more subtle processes of interaction and negotiation. Even franchisees who tried to fudge revenue reports or buy unauthorized supplies were often willing to buy additional franchises when the opportunity arose. Moreover, franchisees often had advantages over independents, many of whom aspired to franchise ownership but for various reasons had to beg, borrow and steal knowledge instead.

Much of the history of the donut reinforces David Monod's point about the importance of emulation, rather than innovation, in the development of mass consumption.[1] Like Costas Kiriakopoulos, most business people involved in donut making and donut selling traded on borrowed ideas. Adolph Levitt adapted ideas from the Second Industrial Revolution; local donut wholesalers in turn bought or leased ideas from Levitt. In the 1960s, donut chains reflected the American influence on the Canadian economy, in terms of both ownership and ideas. American chains like Mister Donut opened branch plants in the Montreal–Windsor corridor as part of their own transregional growth in United States, often finding central Canada to be a more familiar business environment than certain regions of their own country. In turn, early Canadian operations borrowed some ideas from the original American chains (and later had their own problems in Quebec and the West). Franchisees then bought systems from franchisors; and independents borrowed, begged, or stole knowledge from nearby franchisees and from flour companies that wanted to sell their own versions of Levitt's original mix. Everybody borrowed designs from other informal eateries. In this process of emulating, borrowing, and adapting, ideas travelled in networks that were local, regional, national, and continental, and passed between entrepreneurs who aspired to build extensive chains and down to smaller operators who simply wanted to run one or two outlets. Though size clearly did matter – especially in the 1990s – the word 'mass' in terms such as mass marketing and mass culture was much more complicated than any simple romantic dichotomies between large and small or imposed and authentic.

A similar point can be made about donut shops as social spaces. Convenience was a powerful draw, since most of their customers were on the move, but both consumers and owners remember the shops as places of sociability, especially for working men, however brief and informal the encounters. This social space was a product of business decisions *and* consumer agency. Business strategies combined with cultural uses to link donut shops to a broader network of petty consumption at lunch counters, snack bars, and other quick service establishments that served cheap meals and cheaper sociability. Donut chains aimed for uniformity of product and appearance; even so, the social space of the donut shop often depended on neighbourhood and location. The differences were not dramatic – a few more women here, more space given over to youthful play there – but neither were differences among previous informal eateries especially wide. Like lunch counters, donut shops were a form of petty consumption, places where consumers could trade cheap purchases for time. For the price of a coffee and donut, consumers could buy a few minutes off the road, an hour out of the cold, a chance to flirt with a server, access to the local pusher, or just a few moments alone to watch the world go by. These activities were almost painfully mundane, and seem to offer intellectuals little ground on which to build either a comprehensive theory of consumer subversion or a dramatic critique of mass domination. They did, however, reflect the mundane matters of everyday life, the rendering of new institutions to the level of routine, weaved into the daily business of commuting, flirting, playing, and hanging out.

Even after some of the core features of early donut shops – especially smoking and the sit-down counter – were eliminated in the 1980s, this social atmosphere did not entirely disappear. As donut shops reinvented themselves as informal restaurants for a broad, family market (a form not totally out of line with their early aspirations), consumers came to endow them with nationalist and populist meanings. Many of these images were doubly ironic: they poked fun at both the pretentious metropolis and the unsophistocated hinterland; and they played on ironic pride in marginal status. Consumers in cities like Hamilton and St Catharines used irony to imagine a community that stood in opposition to a cultural metropolis; through a broader lens, the Canadian folklore of the donut replaced the populist irony of the donut capital with nationalist ideas. Yet however much it expressed an opposition, donut folklore evoked a more fundamental unity: a belief that in mass commodities, consumers could find authentic institutions and meanings which transcended fragmented identities and vast geographies; a belief that in trying to serve the broad middle ground of consumers, mass culture could unite diverse groups into a sort of vital centre.

The history of the donut shop as a business form, a social space, and a cultural icon demonstrates the difficulty of separating meanings and ideas from structures and institutions. At base, of course, this book is about commerce: Levitt sold machines and mixes to small entrepreneurs; donut chains sold outlets, equipment, and training to franchisees; shop owners sold products to consumers. Yet for the executives, entrepreneurs, and consumers who came together in commercial exchange, there was no neutral economic ground on which to make objective business decisions, no pure market moment free of cultural norms and assumptions. Even if they didn't always consciously express it in these terms, businesses had to imagine their consumers as much as sell them commodities. Levitt sold more than machines and materials – his business also marketed innovation in production and consumption, and required him to develop a commercial speech that reached small business owners, consumers, and housewives, convincing all these groups of the value of modern commodities. Likewise, donut chains sold a number of ideas and products – the outlets themselves, the food they sold, and the atmosphere that resulted. At each of these levels, commerce intertwined with social life and cultural meanings. Franchising was both an economic institution and a vessel for social identity, harnessing the small business dreams of modest investors, who in turn organized family economies, tapped ethnic networks, and marshalled local friendships to turn their dreams into franchise reality. The donut shop combined the design decisions of the early donut shop entrepreneurs and equipment companies with the cultural categories of consumers (informality, cheapness, gender, class), who in turn linked the donut shop form to other types of informal eateries.

The union of institutions and ideas worked both ways. Business decisions were inseparable from cultural norms and visions, but economic questions pressed against the imaginations of entrepreneurs and consumers. Structures mattered, although they arose from historical developments that were hardly neutral or natural. Even as Levitt tried to convince modest bakers to remake their production process, his company faced the real limitations of the bakery industry, which continued to be bottom heavy even as the average operator got bigger. By the 1960s, thanks to Levitt and others, both independent and chain donut shops were able to take advantage of the fact that donuts and coffee were already genuinely mass commodities that moved within well-developed economic networks. Twenty years later, in the 1980s, reinventing the donut shop was easier for big chains than for small entrepreneurs, who might see the value of a drive-through lane but could not afford the upfront expense; or who might understand the perils of video games but could not forgo the extra revenue. Economic structures, then, profoundly shaped the meaning and evolution of the donut.

Donut folklore is the most dramatic example of the union of economic structure and cultural meaning. It rose from the saturation of the foodscape – the result of conscious strategies by the major companies and the cumulative growth of smaller chains and independents – and spun into ideas of neighbourhood, city, and nation. This connection speaks to the relationship between mass culture, imagined community, and authenticity in a consumer society. The donut shop became a touchstone for imagined community not in spite of its status as a mass institution, but because of it. That it sold a mass commodity, that it became one itself, that it crossed boundaries of geography, taste, class, and gender, that it seemed to unite disparate groups of consumers, that it served 'everybody,' was precisely the source of its authenticity and folkloric power. This was especially true of Tim Hortons, which had taken pride of place in donut folklore by the 1990s as it increasingly transcended particular local and regional economies.

Costas Kiriakopoulos tolerated my questions about Country Style and O'Donuts for almost forty minutes before his attention turned abruptly back his latest, more upscale business. The phone was ringing off the hook, and Java Joe's operations manager paced in the outer office, loudly rustling through week-old phone messages to draw attention to his growing impatience. Kiriakopoulos led me out of his basement office, past a supply room where fragrant candles were stacked on long shelves, up the stairs, and through the Java Joe's outlet. It was spotlessly clean and positively homey: cherry woods provided ambiance, modest lights ensured that the seating area was neither dim nor bright, the air was fresh and clean, and the customers were, well, downright attractive. I put my coffee cup on the counter and surveyed the offerings: more candles, stuffed animals, cakes, pies, fine-looking pastries, lattés, cappuccinos, but not a donut in the bunch. 'I've never had a single donut in my stores,' he said as he led me out the door. 'Not from day one. I refuse to have any donuts.'

Notes

Abbreviations

BJ	*Bakers Journal*
CB	*Canadian Baker*
CHRR	*Canadian Hotel Review and Restaurant*
CHR	*Canadian Hotel and Restaurant*
DBS	Dominion Bureau of Statistics
DRFFC	*Directory of Restaurant and Fast Food Chains in Canada*
FP	*Financial Post*
FSH	*Foodservice and Hospitality*
GM	*Globe and Mail*
HS	*Hamilton Spectator*
LFP	*London Free Press*
OB	*Oakville Beaver*
ODJR	*Oakville Daily Journal Record*
RI	*Restaurants and Institutions*
TS	*Toronto Star*

Introduction

1 *Toronto Star* (*TS*) 20 January 1999, D1; CBC, *Metro Morning*, 22 January 1997; Steve Evenden (pseudonym), interviewed by author, Halifax, 18 July 1999. A note on spelling: the company name 'Tim Hortons' has appeared at various times as 'Tim Horton Donuts,' 'Tim Horton's Donuts,' 'Tim Horton's,' and 'Tim Hortons.' I have chosen to use 'Tim Hortons' because it reflects current usage. I have also chosen the more colloquial spelling of

'donut,' except when the older spelling ('doughnut') appears in a quotation.

2 Details of Costas Kiriakopoulos's career in the donut and coffee business are based on Costas Kiriakopoulos, interviewed by author, Etobicoke, Ontario, 19 October 2000.

3 *Bakers Journal (BJ)*, December 1999, 10.

4 Simon During, ed., *The Cultural Studies Reader* (New York: Routledge, 1993), remains a good introduction to the intellectual priorities of cultural studies. On the other side, see Thomas Frank's recent critique in *One Market under God: Extreme Capitalism, Market Populism, and the End of Democracy* (New York: Doubleday, 2000), ch. 8. Despite its limitations, Frank's critique is more satisfying than many because he tries to step back from the debate to place cultural studies in a broader intellectual context, noting how the field fits into a wider inclination to equate consumer choice with democracy – a tendency that Frank calls 'market populism.'

5 A classic discussion of this debate is Perry Anderson, *Arguments within English Marxism* (London: Verso, 1980).

6 On this point, see especially Joy Parr, *Domestic Goods: The Material, the Moral, and the Economic in the Postwar Years* (Toronto: University of Toronto Press, 1999), 8–10.

7 There are many works in this literature, but some of the classics include Susan Strasser, *Satisfaction Guaranteed: The Making of an American Mass Market* (New York: Pantheon Books, 1989); Lizabeth Cohen, *Making a New Deal: Industrial Workers in Chicago* (New York: Cambridge University Press, 1990), ch. 3; T. Jackson Lears, *Fables of Abundance: A Cultural History of Advertising in America* (New York: Basic Books, 1994); William Leach, *Land of Desire: Merchants, Money, and the Rise of a New American Culture* (New York: Vintage Books, 1993); Lawrence Glickman, *A Living Wage: American Workers and the Making of Consumer Society* (Ithaca: Cornell University Press, 1997); Michael Kammen, *American Culture, American Tastes: Social Change and the Twentieth Century* (New York: Knopf, 1999); and Gary Cross, *The All-Consuming Century: Why Commercialism Won in Modern America* (New York: Columbia University Press, 2000). Peter Stearns surveys global developments in his *Consumerism in World History: The Global Transformation of Desire* (New York: Routledge, 2001). A classic study is Sidney Mintz, *Sweetness and Power: The Place of Sugar in Modern History* (New York: Viking, 1985).

8 On eighteenth-century developments, see J.H. Plumb, *The Birth of a Consumer Society: The Commercialization of Eighteenth Century England* (London: Europa Press, 1982), and T.H. Breen, '"Baubles of Britain": The

American and Consumer Revolutions of the Eighteenth Century,' *Past and Present* 119 (1988). On general issues of periodization, see Michael Kammen, *American Taste, American Culture*; and Peter Stearns, 'Stages of Consumerism: Recent Work on the Issues of Periodization,' *Journal of Modern History* 69 (March 1997): 102–17.

9 Some definitional issues are discussed in Kammen, *American Culture*.

10 Classic studies of post–Second World War developments include Lizabeth Cohen, *A Consumer's Republic: The Politics of Mass Consumption in Postwar America* (New York: Knopf, 2003), and Thomas Frank, *The Conquest of Cool: Business Culture, Counterculture, and the Rise of Hip Consumerism* (Chicago: University of Chicago Press, 1997).

11 For the first half of the twentieth century, see in particular David Monod, *Store Wars: Shopkeepers and the Culture of Mass Marketing, 1890–1930* (Toronto: University of Toronto Press, 1996), and Jarrett Rudy, *The Freedom to Smoke: Tobacco Consumption and Identity* (Montreal and Kingston: McGill-Queen's University Press, 2005). On the post–Second World War period, see Joy Parr, *Domestic Goods*; Karen Dubinsky, *The Second Greatest Disappointment* (Toronto: Between the Lines, 1998); Doug Owram, *Born at the Right Time: A History of the Baby Boom Generation* (Toronto: University of Toronto Press, 1996), ch. 4; and Donica Belisle, 'Exploring Postwar Consumption: The Campaign to Unionize Eatons in Toronto, 1948–1952,' *Canadian Historical Review* 86, no. 4 (2005): 641–72. Michael Dawson, *Selling British Columbia: Tourism and Consumer Culture, 1890–1970* (Vancouver: UBC Press, 2004), covers the connection between tourism and consumer culture across the twentieth century, while Craig Heron surveys alcohol across four centuries in *Booze: A Distilled History* (Toronto: Between the Lines, 2003). Good surveys of some of the general issues include Donica Belisle, 'Toward a Canadian Consumer History,' *Labour/Le Travail* (Fall 2003): 181–206, and Cynthia Wright, 'Feminine Trifles of Vast Importance: Writing Gender into the History of Consumption,' in Franca Iacovetta and Mariana Valverde, eds., *Gender Conflicts: New Essays in Women's History* (Toronto: University of Toronto Press, 1992), 229–60. Though recent literature has focused more squarely on the meaning of consumption, it is important to remember that, in varying degrees, some social histories have looked at matters of consumption from the perspective of standard of living, family economy, and other issues. See, for example, Terry Copp, *The Anatomy of Poverty* (Toronto: McClelland and Stewart, 1974); Franca Iacovetta, *Such Hardworking People: Italian Immigrants in Postwar Toronto* (Toronto: University of Toronto Press, 1992); Bryan Palmer, *Working Class Experience:*

Rethinking the History of Canadian Labour, 1800–1991 (Toronto: McClelland and Stewart, 1992); Bettina Bradbury, *Working Families: Age, Gender, and Daily Survival in Industrializing Montreal* (Toronto: McClelland and Stewart, 1993); and Veronica Strong-Boag, *The New Day Recalled: Lives of Girls and Women in English Canada, 1919–1939* (Toronto: Copp Clark Pitman, 1993).

12 There is a remarkably concise discussion of some of these definitional issues in Dawson, *Selling British Columbia*, 6–7.

13 Philip Scranton, *Endless Novelty: Specialty Production and American Industrialization* (Princeton: Princeton University Press, 1997).

14 On the 'consumption ethic,' see Roland Marchand, *Advertising the American Dream: Making Way for Modernity* (Berkeley: University of California Press, 1985).

15 For an important study of another form of petty consumption, see John K. Walton, *Fish and Chips and the British Working Class* (London: Leicester University Press, 1992).

16 Many studies of mass consumption institutions – department stores in particular – emphasize their spectacular qualities. See, for example, Lears, *Fables of Abundance*; and Leach, *Land of Desire*.

17 'Economic challenge' is taken from Kenneth Norrie and Douglas Owram, *A History of the Canadian Economy* (Toronto: Harcourt Brace, 1996), 398.

18 Dawson, *Selling British Columbia*, ch. 3. See also the essays in Michael Gauvreau and Nancy Christie, eds., *Cultures of Citizenship in Postwar Canada* (Montreal and Kingston: McGill-Queen's University Press, 2003).

19 Christie and Gauvreau focus on what they call 'reconstruction culture' from 1943 to 1955 in their introduction to *Cultures of Citizenship*, 3–17. Richard Harris notes that the characteristics of present-day suburbs – homegeneity, corporate development, and so on – had emerged by the late 1950s: Harris, *Creeping Conformity: How Canada Became Suburban* (Toronto: University of Toronto Press, 2004). Magda Fahrni notes the distinctiveness of the late 1940s in the postwar narrative in *Household Politics: Montreal Families and Postwar Reconstruction* (Toronto: University of Toronto Press, 2005). Studying the United States, Lizabeth Cohen notes the importance of 1955 as a turning point in shopping-mall development and consumption patterns. Cohen, *Consumers' Republic*.

20 Interview subjects were contacted in a variety of ways. Some of the donut companies provided useful leads and information. In other cases, interviewees contacted me after the research was profiled in local newspapers. (Stories in the *Hamilton Spectator* and *St Catharines Standard* and in

Niagara Business magazine turned up especially useful contacts.) These initial interview subjects often suggested other contacts, a process that sociologists call 'snowball sampling.' Another strategy relied less on word of mouth than on tedious searching. Early on in the research, I compiled a database of potential contacts based on city directories, local newspapers, trade magazines, and government reports. The list was revised and supplemented as the research continued. Once names, addresses, and other information were noted, I simply called everybody of that name in Canada. When I found the right person, I explained my research and asked if he or she was willing to be interviewed. This 'cold call' process had limitations. Contacts were sometimes suspicious of my intentions (at first, a surprising number thought I was a telemarketer), although the vast majority agreed to be part of the research (a small number on the condition of anonymity). The cold-call procedure was especially frustrating when I was trying to contact women. The names of many women were in my database, but their names often changed after marriage or were not listed in telephone books at all – a product of the common practice of listing telephone numbers under the name of the 'man of the house.' These formal oral histories were supplemented with 'ethnographic' material. Early on in my research, I began marching into shops near my house to ask people about the connection between donuts and social life. These interviews were free-ranging, using open-ended questions about connections between donut shops and the daily patterns of interviewees. Though I encountered a considerable number of tall tales, amusing anecdotes, and urban legends, many of the conversations focused on the mundane details of everyday life: commuting, working, avoiding working, taking a break, nursing a hangover, skipping school, and meeting friends. Some of these conversations lasted only a few moments, others continued for over an hour. On a few occasions the subjects seemed interesting (and interested) enough to schedule a more formal oral history interview at a later date. This is the strategy of the folklorist or ethnologist. To give the research a more historical spin, I often simply approached the oldest people in the shop at the time. Later, I expanded the geographical reach of my donut shop visits to include every province except Alberta, Saskatchewan, and Newfoundland. Ontario remained the core of the ethnographic research, however. Though this focus has analytic justification (in Canada, donut shops originated in southern Ontario), the main reason was practical: I live in Toronto, and simply lack the resources to travel across the country interviewing donut shop patrons. (I shudder to think what a neoconservative heritage critic might have done had I requested money for such a project). Oral interviews were supplemented with correspondence (electronic and written, much of it unsolicited) from about two dozen other subjects from across North America.

21 Good introductions to this literature are Elizabeth Tonkin, *Narrating Our Pasts: The Social Construction of Oral History* (New York: Cambridge University Press, 1992), and Mary Chamberlain and Paul Thompson, eds., *Narrative and Genre* (New York: Routledge, 1998).

22 See, for example, Douglas Hunter, *Open Ice: The Tim Horton Story* (Toronto: Penguin Books, 1994); Ron Buist, *Tales from under the Rim: The Marketing of Tim Hortons* (Fredericton: Goose Lane Editions, 2003); and Ron Joyce with Robert Thompson, *Always Fresh: The Untold Story of Tim Hortons by the Man who Created a Canadian Empire* (Toronto: HarperCollins, 2006).

1 Faith, Efficiency, and the Modern Donut

1 Ernest Atalick, interviewed by author, Jordan Station, Ontario, 12 October 2000. Unless otherwise noted, subsequent quotations from Ernest Atalick are from this interview.

2 *Canadian Baker* (*CB*), May 1959, 32.

3 Ibid., 31

4 David Hounshell, *From the American System to Mass Production* (Baltimore: Johns Hopkins University Press, 1985).

5 *CB*, October 1957, 36–7; October 1960, 40.

6 *Canadian Food Industries*, March 1949, 22–5; *CB*, June 1954, 31; June 1947, 29; *Bakers Journal* (*BJ*), June 1967, 9–13.

7 On Levitt, see Sally Levitt Steinberg, *The Donut Book* (New York: Knopf, 1987), 19–39; and his obituary in *CB*, December 1953, 44–5.

8 *Toronto Globe*, 9 June 1923.

9 The question of the timing of this development is confusing. Various reports date DCA's arrival in Canada at 1934 or 1935. The company later expanded to Australia and New Zealand. *CB*, March 1947, 36.

10 *Toronto Globe*, 5 September 1936, 3; *Food in Canada*, August 1942, 10–11; *CB*, March 1947, 36.

11 *Canadian Food Industries*, November 1948, 45, 47, 49; *CB*, March 1957, 29; July 1948, 97.

12 Alfred Chandler, *The Visible Hand: The Managerial Revolution in American Business* (Cambridge, MA: Belknap Press, 1977); Susan Strasser, *Satisfaction Guaranteed: The Making of the American Mass Market* (New York: Pantheon, 1989), 3–28; Donna Gabaccia, *We Are What We Eat:*

Ethnic Food and the Making of Americans (Cambridge, MA: Harvard University Press, 1998), 36–63, 149–74; Harvey Levenstein, *Revolution at the Table: The Transformation of the American Diet* (New York: Oxford University Press, 1988), 30–43; Craig Heron, 'The Second Industrial Revolution in Canada,' in Deian R. Hopkin and Gregory S. Kealey, eds., *Class, Community, and the Labour Movement: Wales and Canada, 1850–1930* (St John's: Canadian Committee on Labour History, 1989), 48–66.

13 On Ford as 'symbol making,' see Thomas Misa, 'The Compelling Tangle of Modernity and Technology,' in Thomas Misa et al., eds., *Modernity and Technology* (Cambridge, MA: MIT Press, 2003), 11–12. On the ethos of mass production, see David Hounshell, *From the American System to Mass Production* (Baltimore: Johns Hopkins University Press, 1985), chs. 6–7. A classic study of Ford is Stephen Meyer, *The Five-Dollar Day: Labor, Management, and Social Control in the Ford Motor Company, 1908–1921* (Albany: SUNY Press, 1981).

14 Hounshell, *American System*; Richard Feltoe, *Redpath: The History of a Sugar House* (Toronto: National Heritage/Natural History, 1991); Michael Bliss, *A Canadian Millionaire: The Life and Business Times of Sir Joseph Flavelle, Bart., 1858–1939* (Toronto: Macmillan of Canada, 1978), 31–49; and A.J.E. Child, 'The Predecessor Companies of Canada Packers Limited: A Study in Entrepreneurial Achievement and Entrepreneurial Failure' (MA thesis, University of Toronto, 1960).

15 David F. Noble, *Forces of Production: A Social History of Industrial Automation* (New York: Oxford University Press, 1984), 42–79, Pam Roper, 'The Limits of Laissez-Innover: Canada's Automation Controversy, 1955–1969,' *Journal of Canadian Studies* 34, no. 3 (1999): 87–105.

16 Emile Bouvier, *The Bakery Industry in Quebec* (Sherbrooke: Economics Research Centre, University of Sherbrooke, 1969), 15–19. American developments are discussed in Sigfied Giedion, *Mechanization Takes Command: A Contribution to Anonymous History* (New York: Oxford University Press, 1948), 169–208; and in William Panschar, *Baking in America*, Volume 1, *Economic Development* (Evanston: Northwestern University Press, 1956).

17 *Toronto Globe*, 22 May 1924.

18 Charles Davies, *Bread Men: How the Westons Built an International Empire* (Toronto: Key Porter Books, 1987); Lloyd G. Reynolds, 'The Canadian Bakery Industry: A Study of an Imperfect Market,' *Quarterly Journal of Economics* 52 (August 1938): 659–78; Department of Labour, *Investigation into an Alleged Combine in the Bread-Baking Industry in Canada* (Ottawa: King's Printer, 1931), 30–46; H. Carl Goldenberg,

Breadbaking Industry in Western Canada (Combines Investigation Committee, Department of Justice, 1948); Richard Tenderenda, 'The Canadian Baking Industry,' (MA thesis, Dalhousie University, 1972), 16. On automation in the 1950s, see John Varty, 'Growing Bread: Technoscience, Environment, and Modern Wheat at the Dominion Grain Research Laboratory, Canada, 1912–1960' (PhD thesis, Queen's University, 2005), 334–6.

19 In 1931 a Department of Labour report drew a sharp distinction between modern sales practices in baking and those in other industries, condemning the application of 'aggressive sales policies' to bread. The main problem was that so much of this marketing effort was directed towards persuading consumers (through 'catchy' names, new shapes, special delivery services, and ads extolling the virtues of scientifically produced products) to switch brands: 'This is the kind of expensive competition [common] ... with such articles as motor cars, radios, washing machines, with their constantly changing models ... There is less to be concerned about when this kind of competition is brought to bear upon non-essentials. But it is not desirable that bread, as one of the most important necessaries of life, should be brought within this category. It does not require such selling efforts: the consumer does not need to be persuaded to buy bread, and should not be called upon to pay for one baker's efforts to persuade the public to buy from him rather than from a competitor.' Department of Labour, *Investigation into an Alleged Combine*, 40–1. That distinctions are to be drawn between essential and non-essential products is a classic tenet of moral economy thinking. See E.P. Thompson, 'The Moral Economy of the English Crowd in the Eighteenth Century,' *Past and Present* 50 (February 1971): 76–136. Thompson's is an extraordinarily powerful argument, although we obviously need to be careful about applying it to the twentieth century too literally.

20 Steinberg, *Donut Book*, 21.

21 *Canadian Food Industries*, November 1948, 47.

22 *New York Times*, 30 October 1952, 39.

23 Harvey Levenstein, *Paradox of Plenty: A Social History of Eating in Modern America* (New York: Oxford University Press, 1993), 75; *New York Times*, 26 September 1949, 28.

24 *Globe and Mail* (GM), 2 September 1942, 8; *GM*, 16 January 1948, 10; *CB*, April 1957, 30.

25 Bakery Research Department, Proctor and Gamble, 'Taking the "Hole" out of Doughnut Profits' (Crisco Bakery Service Series No. 2, Cincinnati, 1929); 'Dollars in Doughnuts' (1932). Thanks to Amanda Crocker for

passing on these pamphlets. On general issues of professionalizing food research, see Levenstein, *Revolution at the Table.*

26 Nina and Larry Seller, owners, Hol'n One Donuts, 1954–94, interviewed by author, Coquitlam, British Columbia, 21 August 2001. Hol N One Ontario (which had no connection to the Sellers' operation) had 652 machines operating in the province in 1964. *BJ*, October 1967, 23.

27 'Taking the Hole,' 3–4.

28 *Food in Canada*, August 1942, 10.

29 *The BYPU Cook Book: A Selection of Tested Recipes, Prepared by the ladies of the Parry Sound Baptist Church* (Parry Sound, 1899), CIHM 95320, 143–4; *The Toronto Cook Book* (Toronto, 1915) [Canadian Institute for Historical Reproduction, No. 98740].

30 Gabaccia, *We Are What We Eat*; Levenstein, *Revolution at the Table*; Strasser, *Satisfaction Guaranteed*; and Veronica Strong-Boag, *The New Day Recalled: Lives of Girls and Women in English Canada, 1919–1939* (Toronto: Copp Clark Pitman, 1993), 113–38.

31 *Toronto Daily Star*, 15 March 1920, 10.

32 The ad appeared in the *Moncton Daily Times*, 16 February 1920, 6. Thanks to Russ Johnston for the reference.

33 *Food in Canada*, August 1942, 11; Varty, 'Growing Bread.'

34 *Food in Canada*, August 1942, 11–12; 'Dollars to Doughnuts,' 48.

35 As late as 1976, for example, Margaret's Donuts of Toronto bragged of being the 'biggest producer of doughnuts in Canada and the second largest in North America,' but it distributed its donuts over a relatively small area, from Oshawa to London (about 250 kilometres). *BJ*, August 1976, 12.

36 Wayne Spencer, owner, Val's Donuts, Edmonton, 1950–70, telephone interview by author, 15 October 2001. CDC had sales representatives in all the major cities of Canada.

37 *CB*, November 1945, 22–3.

38 See, for example, *Toronto Globe*, 17 February 1933, 7.

39 *CB*, June 1949, 30.

40 Steinberg, *The Donut Book*; *CB*, October 1953, 42.

41 *CB*, October 1953, 42; September 1956, 45.

42 *CB*, June 1949, 31.

43 *CB*, June 1956, 45.

44 I borrow the term 'commercial speech' from Chris Dummitt, 'Finding a Place for Father: Selling the Barbecue in Postwar Canada,' *Journal of the Canadian Historical Association* 8 (1998), 209–33. In considering the

postwar barbecue, Dummitt uses the concept of commercial speech to broaden his lens from advertising to a wider discourse of commodities (see his n8).

45 National Council of Women of Canada, *Women of Canada: Their Life and Work* (Canadian Institute of Historical Reproductions, 11965, orig. pub. 1900?), 29.

46 *BJ*, December 1959, 9.

47 According to *Canadian Baker*, Donut Month 'brought [publicity] so forcibly to the attention of Mrs. Housewife and her family – the excitement is whipped up to such a high pitch – that its jet-force momentum is carried over for the rest of the 11 months of the year.' *CB*, October 1954, 28. For a reference to 'Mrs. Smith,' see American Society of Bakery Engineers, *Proceedings of the Ninth Annual Meeting*, 14 to 17 March 1932 (American Society of Bakery Engineers, 1932), 92.

48 See, for example, *Toronto Globe*, 28 April 1927, 15, 13 September 1933, 5; *Toronto Star (TS)* 1 March 1935, 25; 30 January 1936, 34.

49 *Toronto Globe*, 1 September 1937, 4.

50 Steinberg, *The Donut Book*, 25–7.

51 See, for example, Mike Filey, *I Remember Sunnyside* (Toronto: McClelland and Stewart, 1985); *Food in Canada*, August 1942, 13.

52 David Nye, *American Technological Sublime* (Cambridge, MA: MIT Press, 1994), and Keith Walden, *Becoming Modern in Toronto: The Industrial Exhibition and the Shaping of Late Victorian Culture* (Toronto: University of Toronto Press, 1997), ch. 3.

53 *CB*, September 1959, 24; October 1953, 43

54 *CB*, September 1941, 32.

55 *The Nourish-Meter*, Doughnut Corporation of America, 1943 (in author's possession).

56 *CB*, October 1942, 32; *Food in Canada*, August 1942, 13; *The Nourish-Meter*. Jarrett Rudy points to the importance of wartime public relations for increasing acceptance of cigarette smoking around the First World War. See his *The Freedom to Smoke: Tobacco Consumption and Identity* (Montreal and Kingston: McGill-Queen's University Press, 2005), 132–41.

57 On Coca-Cola's use of 'technical officers' to ensure Coke's distribution to GIs, and the symbolic importance of these efforts in the postwar United States, see Mark Weiner, 'Consumer Culture and Participatory Democracy,' in Carole Counihan, *Food in the USA: A Reader* (New York: Routledge, 2002), 123–42.

58 *CB*, October 1944, 20–1; July 1943, 9; January 1943, 34.

59 On 'reconstruction culture,' see the introduction to Michael Gauvreau and

Nancy Christie, eds., *Cultures of Citizenship in Postwar Canada* (Montreal and Kingston: McGill-Queen's University Press, 2003), 3–26. On Canadian attitudes on the postwar world, see Magda Fahrni, *Household Politics: Montreal Families and Postwar Reconstruction* (Toronto: University of Toronto Press, 2005), and Peter McInnis, *Harnessing Labour Confrontation: Shaping the Postwar Settlement in Canada* (Toronto: University of Toronto Press, 2002).

60 Roper, 'The Limits of Laissez-Innover.'

61 *CB*, February 1946.

62 Calculated from figures in Dominion Bureau of Statistics (DBS), *Annual Census of Manufacturers, Bakeries, 1962* (June 1965), table 6B. Inflation figures from DBS, Prices Division, *Prices and Price Indexes, December 1962* (February 1963), table 8. Donut sales increased faster than those of most other bakery products except buns.

63 *CB*, June 1947, 29.

64 *CB*, October, 1958, 22, 42; October 1960, 30–1, 49.

65 *BJ*, October 1967, 18.

66 *CB*, October 1960, 31; *BJ*, October 1967, 18; Jim Charade, manager, Vachon donut plant, interviewed by author, Mississauga, Ontario, 9 May 1998.

67 *BJ*, August 1974, 18; August 1976, 6.

68 Kenneth Sleeman, former manager, Glaz-O-Nut, telephone interview by author, 22 August 2001. Sleeman is the son of one of the early owners of the company. On the importance of gluten in the rhetoric of mechanized baking, see Varty, 'Growing Bread,' 140–2.

69 *CB*, February 1953, 38.

70 *New York Times*, 26 September 1949, 28.

71 Aloyzia Atalick interview; *BJ*, April 1960, 22.

72 The classic study of this type of industrial development examines the nineteenth century. See Raphael Samuel, 'The Workshop of the World,' *History Workshop Journal* 3 (Spring 1977): 6–72. For a similar view of baking in Canada in the nineteenth century, see Ian McKay, 'Capital and Labour in the Halifax Baking and Confectionary Industry During the Last Half of the Nineteenth Century,' *Labour/Le Travailleur* 3 (1978): 63–108.

73 DBS, *Bakeries*, Cat. 32-203, table 4A. On the variety of products produced, see DBS, *Manufacturers of Bakery Products in Canada*, 1960, 1964.

74 DBS, *Bakeries*, Cat. 32-203, table 4A; *CB*, May 1959, 31, October 1960, 31. In 1959 the DBS changed its method of counting and recording bakery size, so comparisons between the 1950s and 1960s are difficult to make.

75 *BJ*, October 1967, 23.

76 There are two especially illuminating articles on the compromises in actual donut plants in *CB*, October 1953, 35–41.

77 One justifiably classic statement of this dynamic is James Scott, *Seeing Like a State* (New Haven: Yale University Press, 1999).

78 By 1976, for example, Margaret's was producing 25,000 donuts daily. *BJ*, August 1976, 12.

79 David Monod, *Store Wars: Shopkeepers and the Culture of Mass Marketing, 1890–1939* (Toronto: University of Toronto Press, 1996).

80 Sleeman interview; Brazier interview.

2 'Our New Palace of Donut Pleasure'

1 *Oakville Daily Journal Record* (*ODJR*), 15 January 1966, 5.

2 Michael Schudson, 'Advertising as Capitalist Realism,' in *Advertising: The Uneasy Persuasion* (New York: Basic Books, 1984), 215.

3 Mike Filey, *I Remember Sunnyside: The Rise and Fall of a Magical Era* (Toronto: Dundurn Press, 1996); Lynn Korbyn, co-owner, Sally's Donuts, early 1960s, interviewed by author, Hamilton, Ontario, 21 February 2002.

4 On the origins of the companies, see John Jakle and Keith Sculle, *Fast Food: Roadside Restaurants in the Automobile Age* (Baltimore: Johns Hopkins University Press, 1999), 200; Robert Rosenberg with Madelon Bedell, *Profits from Franchising* (New York: McGraw Hill, 1969), 27–31; Robert Metz, *Franchising: How to Select a Business of Your Own* (New York: Hawthorn Books, 1969), 123–30; *Canadian Hotel and Restaurant* (*CHR*), 15 May 1968, 44; and *Boston Sunday Globe*, 23 April 2000, 6–7 (thanks to Marc Abrahams for this reference).

5 On Charade and Horton, see Douglas Hunter, *Open Ice: The Tim Horton Story* (Toronto: Viking Press, 1994), 306–48. Information on Country Style's origins is from Kevin Watson, interviewed by author, 22 October 1999. (Watson is the son of one of the early directors of the company, and worked in various positions in the Country Style headquarters until the late 1990s.)

6 F.H. Leacy, *Historical Statistics of Canada*, 2nd ed. (Ottawa: Statistics Canada, 1983), series T147-194.

7 In 1953, Ontario had the highest penetration of automobiles, averaging 0.9 cars per family. In 1971, British Columbia led the provinces with 1.6 cars per family (at the time, the Ontario figure was 1.44). The national figures were as follows: 0.72 autos per family in 1953, 1.21 in 1966, 1.37 in 1971. See Dominion Bureau of Statistics (DBS), *The Motor Vehicle*, Cat. 53-203, table 3. Note that in 1955, Ontario, Alberta, and British Colum-

bia provided markets for automobiles larger than indicated by their populations. Not surprisingly, automobile ownership was skewed by income.

8 G.T. Bloomfield, 'No Parking Here to Corner: London Reshaped by the Automobile, 1911–1961,' *Urban History Review* 17, no. 2 (1989): 150; Stephen Davies, 'Reckless Walking Must Be Discouraged: The Automobile Revolution and the Shaping of Modern Urban Canada' *Urban History Review* 17, no. 2 (1989), 123–38. On the stagnation in car ownership, see Royal Commission on Canada's Economic Prospects, *The Canadian Automotive Industry* (September 1956), 24, table XI. Canada had 9.9 persons per car in 1929 and 10.4 in 1945. In Ontario, the figures were 7.0 and 7.2.

9 In coining the term 'drive-in society,' Kenneth Jackson discusses the interstate highway, the garage, the motel, the drive-in theatre, the gasoline service station, the shopping centre, and other developments. Jackson, *Crabgrass Frontier: The Suburbanization of the United States* (New York: Oxford University Press, 1985), 246–71. For a similar (if briefer) Canadian view, see Graham Fraser, 'The Car as Architect,' *City Magazine* 2, no. 5 (1976): 44–51.

10 General issues of road building are discussed in Donald F. Davies, 'Dependent Motorization: Canada and the Automobile to the 1930s,' *Journal of Canadian Studies* 21, no. 3 (1986): 106–32; Larry McNally, 'Roads, Streets, and Highways,' in Norman Bell, ed., *Building Canada: A History of Public Works* (Toronto: University of Toronto Press, 1988), 31–58; Yves Brussière, 'L'automobile et l'expansion des banlieues: le cas de Montréal, 1901–2001,' *Urban History Review* 18, no. 2 (1989): 159–65; David Monaghan, 'Canada's "New Main Street": The Trans-Canada Highway as Idea and Reality, 1912–1956' (MA thesis, University of Ottawa, 1997).

11 *Financial Post (FP)*, 16 October 1954, 17; 24 March 1962, 67. For a general discussion of industrial decentralization across North America before 1950, see Richard Walker and Robert D. Lewis, 'Beyond the Crabgrass Frontier: Industry and the Spread of North American Cities, 1850–1950,' *Journal of Historical Geography* 27, no. 1 (2001): 3–19. In 1968, Paul Thomas surveyed 1,529 workers at factories in a Toronto suburb and discovered a combination of extensive commuting by automobile and continued reliance on public transit by workers from older neighbourhoods in west Toronto – a fact that qualifies the image of the car-commuting worker. See Thomas, 'Rexdale: A Case Study of Suburban Industry' (MA thesis, University of Waterloo, 1968), 133–7.

12 *Hamilton Spectator (HS)*, 19 August 1961, in 'Streets in Hamilton' Scrapbook, vol. 4, 1960–1969, 69, Special Collections, Hamilton Public Library.

13 Atwater quotation from *FP*, 5 November 1955, 30. Despite their status as emblematic of postwar commercial development, shopping malls were still few in number into the mid to late 1950s. Metro Toronto had 29 plazas by 1955, although many of these were quite small by later standards, often only one row of shops. Ten years later the number had increased to 174. Mall development slowed down within metropolitan Toronto in the early 1970s; even so, the total number of plazas had grown to 271 by 1975. In other communities, shopping malls developed quite late into the postwar period. Gerald Bloomfield noted that even in 1961, London, Ontario, only had three shopping centres, comprising 150,000 square feet of retail space. Metropolitan Toronto Planning Department, Research Division, *The Toronto Region Strip Retail Areas and Shopping Centres*, 1976; Bloomfield, 'No Parking Here to Corner,' 155. The point about the lethargic development of malls can be extended to other staples of postwar Canada. Indeed, many of the stereotypes of 'postwar' development – large, mass-produced subdivisions, shopping malls, chain restaurants like McDonalds, families with televisions, and so on – can actually be dated more precisely to the years after 1955. See also Lizabeth Cohen, *A Consumers' Republic: The Politics of Mass Consumption in Postwar America* (New York: Knopf, 2003), 5.

14 For an example of the evolution of auto-oriented strips, which often grew haphazardly to serve growing local populations that lacked sufficient commercial choices, see Adams Farrow Associates, *Yonge Street, Town of Richmond Hill, a Report* (Richmond Hill Planning Board, 1959), available in the Urban Affairs Branch, Toronto Public Library. On malls, note that from 1951 to 1966, the City of Toronto's share of Metropolitan area's retail sales decreased from 81.6 to 48.4 per cent. *Toronto's Retail Strips* (City of Toronto Planning Board, April 1976), 4, note 4. One study of retailing in seventeen markets in the Quebec City–Windsor corridor calculated that between 1951 and 1961, merchants in fringe areas enjoyed a 136 per cent increase in total dollar volume compared to 36 per cent for central city merchants, though average sales per suburban outlet still trailed those per downtown retailers in all markets except Toronto. Thayer Taylor, 'Seven Million Consumers All in a Row,' from *Sales Management*, 10 November 1963, reprinted in Isaiah Litvack and Bruce Mallen, eds., *Marketing: Canada* (Toronto: McGraw Hill, 1962), 45. On the general development of shopping malls, see Gareth Shar, 'Shopping Centre Developments in Toronto,' in John A. Dawson and J. Dennis Lord, eds., *Shopping Centre Development: Policies and Prospects* (New York: Nichols Publishing, 1985), 105–25; James W. Simmons, *Toronto's Changing Retail Complex: A Study in Growth and Blight* (Chicago: University of Chicago,

Department of Geography, Research Paper No. 104, 1966); City of
Toronto Planning Board, *Toronto's Retail Strips: A Discussion Paper on
the Viability and Future of Strip Retailing in the City* (April 1976); Metro-
politan Toronto Planning Board, *Shopping Centres and Strip Retail Areas,
Metropolitan Planning Area* (Metro Toronto Planning Board, Research
Division, April 1970); and Robert Koblyck, 'The Ottawa Street Shopping
Area and the Greater Hamilton Shopping Centre' (BA thesis, McMaster
University, 1960).

15 Rosenberg, *Profits from Franchising*, 149.
16 *Might's Toronto Directory* (Toronto: Might's Directories Limited), 1963.
17 *Vernon's London City Directory* (Hamilton: Vernon Directories), 1965.
   Gerald Bloomfield, 'Lodging at the Interchange in London, Ontario,'
   Canadian Geographer 40, no. 2 (1996): 173–80 discusses the development
   of Wellington Street.
18 Robert Pando, 'A Description and Analysis of Urban Land Use Expansion
   in Waterloo's Urban Fringe' (MA thesis, University of Waterloo, 1969).
19 Allan Asmussen, cofounder of Donut Queen (Kitchener-Waterloo), 1968,
   interviewed by author, Waterloo, 10 September 2001; Calvin LeDrew,
   owner, Donut Queen, Sydney, Nova Scotia, 1964–1970, telephone interview by author, 8 August 2001; *HS*, 17 April 1977; Ron Joyce with Robert
   Thompson, *Always Fresh: The Untold Story of Tim Hortons by the Man
   Who Created a Canadian Empire* (Toronto: HarperCollins, 2006), 149.
20 On the Pen Centre, see John Jackson, *St Catharines: Canada's Canal City*
   (St Catharines: St Catharines Standard Ltd., 1992), 54
21 Nina and Larry Seller, interviewed by author, Coquitlam, British Columbia, 21 August 2001; various clippings, Seller Family Scrapbook, in possession of Nina Seller; *Vancouver City Directory* (Vancouver: BC Directories),
   1960, 1965, 1970, 1975; Vancouver Telephone Directories, 1960–75. On
   the timing of mall-building in metropolitan Vancouver, see Louis Redstone,
   New Dimensions in Shopping Centres and Stores (New York: McGraw
   Hill, 1973), 191–3.
22 Woodward's was a chain of department stores. Nina and Larry Seller interview. In Edmonton, Eugene Pechet followed a similar shopping-mall strategy with his three Dolly Donuts outlets, the first of which opened in 1970.
   Eugene Pechet, telephone interview by author, 8 September 2001.
23 *Population Statistics for Ontario, 1969* (Economic Analysis Branch, Economic and Statistical Services Division, Ontario Department of Treasury
   and Economics, October 1969), 11. The seven CMAs were Toronto,
   Hamilton, Kitchener-Waterloo, London, Windsor, Ottawa, and Sudbury
   (all of which had at least one chain donut shop by 1970). On the Tim

Hortons in Dundas, see *Wentworth Marketplace*, 31 October 1973, 3. On the relationship between Hamilton and Dundas, see Irene Myers, 'Dundas: An Urban Study' (BA thesis, McMaster University, 1954), 38–41; and Michael Czyz, 'West Hamilton: A Study in Urban Geography,' (BA thesis, McMaster University, 1959), 48–9.

24 Outlet three was at Dundas and Islington in a western suburb of Toronto, while outlet four was on Danforth Avenue near Victoria Park Avenue in the east end of the city. James Lemon, *Toronto since 1918: An Illustrated History* (Toronto: Lorimer, 1985); F.R. Berchem, *Opportunity Road: Yonge Street, 1860 to 1939* (Toronto: Natural Heritage / Natural History, 1996); Lyn Foster, 'Islington Village: Towards a Streetscape Plan' (School of Landscape Architecture, University of Guelph, 1982); F.D. Cruikshank, *A History of Weston* (Weston: Weston Historical Society, reprint, 1983); Weston Historical Society, *Memories of Weston: A Collection of Essays* (Weston: Weston Historical Society, 1981); Seneca College Community Research and Training Unit, *Weston Town Centre: A Preliminary Study of the Weston Business Improvement Area* (North York, 1979).

25 John Weaver, *Hamilton: An Illustrated History* (Toronto: James Lorimer, 1982); John Weaver, 'From Land Assembly to Social Maturity: The Suburban Life of Westdale (Hamilton), Ontario, 1911–1951,' *Histoire sociale/ Social History* 11 (1978): 411–40; Angela Monaco, 'A Historical Report: Ottawa Street North' (unpublished paper, 1986). On Concession Street, see *HS*, 3 January 1986, A3; John Johansen, *Concession Street in Context: A Chronological History of the Concession Street District, Hamilton, Ontario* (Hamilton: Concession Street Business Improvement Association, 1994); and Hamilton Mountain Heritage Society, *Mountain Memories: A Pictorial History of Hamilton Mountain* (Hamilton: Hamilton Mountain Heritage Society, 2000).

26 *Might's Toronto Directory*, 1935; Monaco, 'Ottawa Street,' 21; Koblyk, 'Greater Hamilton.'

27 Hunter, *Open Ice*, 338. John Weaver reports that the population of Hamilton Mountain increased almost tenfold in the quarter-century after the war, from around 10,000 to almost 100,000. The Kenilworth access was widened to four lanes in 1958, one of several improvements in transportation corridors up the mountain. In 1960, 75,000 cars travelled mountain access roads daily, a figure that had reached 130,000 by 1972. Weaver, *Hamilton: An Illustrated History*, 175.

28 Kiriakopoulos interview. On commuting patterns to the industrial area near Toronto's airport (located in one of the city's western suburbs), see Thomas, 'Rexdale,' 137.

29 Tim Hortons had six outlets in Hamilton in 1970. Some years after Charade's first donut shop closed, Hortons re-entered Toronto's drive-in culture by taking over the locations of Donut Fair, a small chain that failed in 1970. Donut Fair was developed as a spin-off of Friar Tuck Food Shops, founded in Scarborough in September 1968 to sell hamburgers, hot dogs, and roast beef sandwiches from buildings with a '12th century theme.' *CHR*, 15 August 1968, 53; 15 April 1969, 54.

30 Population figures from *Financial Post Report on Markets*, 1965–75. In his account of building Tim Hortons, Joyce noted that there was never a conscious plan to develop smaller cities, but that he was nonetheless drawn into the strategy by its many advantages, notably less competition and the ability to develop the local market without a big advertising expenditure: *Always Fresh*, 64.

31 On Niagara Street, see *Vernon's City of Welland and Town of Port Colborne Directory* (Hamilton, ON, 1962–70); Welland Planning Office, *City of Welland Existing Land Use Map* (1969).

32 *Niagara Falls Review*, 22 February 1973, 10; Jackson, *St Catharines: Canada's Canal City*, 54; *FP*, 17 November 1962, 20; 23 March 1963, 26.

33 John Fitzsimmons, interviewed by author, Hamilton, 25 January 1998.

34 Mister Donut, *Highlights from a Market Analysis of Mister Donut Stores* (Fall 1966), 2, from private collection.

35 Chester Liebs, *Main Street to Miracle Mile: American Roadside Architecture* (Boston: Little Brown, 1985), 39.

36 In the early days, Tim Hortons signs spun around.

37 No specific measurements were provided for Dunkin' Donuts' visibility. Rosenberg, *Profts from Franchising*, 137. By comparison, Red Barn Hamburgers required an outlet to be visible from five hundred feet from both directions. *RI*, May 1965, 31. The Kipling Plaza outlet and the Jane and Wilson outlet both still exist, as do the plazas, although the former is now a Dunkin' Donuts and the latter is a Vietnamese restaurant. That an old Mister Donut would be transformed into an ethnic restaurant is symbolic of the social changes occurring in Toronto's suburbs.

38 Hi-Ho Drive-Ins around Windsor and White Spot Restaurants in Vancouver would be two examples of these local chains. For a discussion of roadside commerce in Canada, see Steve Penfold, 'Selling by the Carload: The Early Years of Fast Food in Canada,' in Madga Fahrni and Robert Rutherdale, eds., *Creating Postwar Canada: Community, Diversity and Dissent* (Vancouver: UBC Press, forthcoming).

39 *TS*, 30 April 1965, 10.

40 *CHRR*, 15 August 1961, 36–40; 15 May 1964, 42–7; 15 May 1966,

38–44; *CHR*, 15 May 1968, 44–51; 15 March 1970, 43–9; 15 March 1971, 20–3.

41 *CHR*, 15 March 1970, 47–9.

42 The exact figures, expressing the ratio of outlets to population, were as follows: in Hamilton, hamburgers 1:30,250, chicken 1:44,000, and donuts 1:80,670; in London, burgers 1:17,538, chicken 1:45,600, and donuts 1:76,000. *CHR*, 15 March 1971, 23.

43 The magazine found one donut shop operating in each of Regina and Saskatoon but not in any other western cities. This may suggest that the figures are slightly inaccurate, since four Hol'N One Donut Houses were operating in greater Vancouver at the time. *CHR*, 15 March 1971, 23.

44 These enumerations are based on my database of donut shop locations, compiled from community newspapers, city directories, telephone books, and interviews.

45 The phrase 'solid market' is from *CHR*, 15 March 1970, 44.

46 *Scarborough Mirror*, 17 January 1973, 7; *Might's Metropolitan Windsor City Directory* (Toronto: Might's Directories); *Might's Oakville Directory* (Toronto: Might's Directories).

47 Albert Debaeremaker, telephone interview by author, 18 March 2000.

48 Stephen Ududec, Ideal Donut, interviewed by author, Winnipeg, 19 October 2001; Doug Nichol, 'Ideal Donut: The Hole Story,' in Kris D. Munt, ed., *Adventures in Small Entrepreneurship in Manitoba* (Winnipeg: Red River Community College, 1985), 93–100. On automobile commerce in Niagara Falls, see Karen Dubinsky, *The Second Greatest Disappointment: Honeymooning and Tourism at Niagara Falls* (Toronto: Between the Lines, 1999), 128–30, 177–97.

49 Mike Dawson's excellent study of tourism in British Columbia, which emphasizes the power of cultural producers, is one recent example. Michael Dawson, *Selling British Columbia: Tourism and Consumer Culture* (Vancouver: University of British Columbia Press, 2004), especially 13.

50 Al Stortz, interviewed by author, Welland, Ontario, 17 April 1998; Debaeremaker interview.

51 On general issues of road planning in Metropolitan Toronto, see Timothy Colton, *Big Daddy: Frederick G. Gardiner and the Building of Metropolitan Toronto* (Toronto: University of Toronto Press, 1980); Christopher Leo, *The Politics of Urban Development: Canadian Expressway Disputes* (Toronto: Institute of Public Administration of Canada, 1977).

52 In the mid-1960s, Damas and Smith undertook traffic surveys and planning studies for several Ontario municipalities, including Sarnia, Cornwall, Oakville, Burlington, Brantford, Pembroke, Timmins, Georgetown,

Renfrew, Port Colborne, Galt, Preston, and Smiths Falls. Margison and Associates was another influential firm, producing new traffic plans for Kingston, Brantford, and several other communities.

53 Liebs, *Main Street to Miracle Mile.*

54 I discuss some issues of anti-drive-in sentiments in Steve Penfold, 'Are We to Go Literally to the Hot Dogs? Drive-ins, Parking Lots, and the Critique of Progress in Toronto's Suburbs, 1965–1975,' *Urban History Review* 33, no. 1 (2004): 8–23.

55 Scarboro Official Plan Review, *Commercial Policy Study*, October 1976, prepared by James F. MacLaren Ltd. for the Scarboro Planning Board), 2–9, 4–17.

56 *CHRR*, 15 December, 1964, 8, citing a Bank of Montreal survey. The switch to coffee consumption was noticed at the end of the war. In 1946, *Food in Canada* reported that coffee consumption had increased about one-third from the prewar to the postwar period, although tea drinking still far surpassed coffee consumption. Annual coffee consumption was estimated at about 200 cups per person, compared to 800 cups for tea. *Food in Canada*, October 1946, 22; November 1946, 9–10.

57 *CHRR*, 15 November 1965, 68; *RI*, February 1959, 11. The coffee break was much less common in Quebec than other provinces.

58 *CHRR*, 15 November 1956, 68. The Pan American Coffee Bureau, an organization of major coffee producers, apparently coined the term 'coffee break' in the early 1950s as a marketing effort. See Mark Pendergrast, *Uncommon Grounds: The History of Coffee and How It Transformed Our World* (New York: Basic Books, 1999), 53–4. The practice of providing mid-morning and/or mid-afternoon breaks seems to predate the coining of the phrase, however. These breaks were becoming standard (first in offices) before the Second World War.

59 Pan-American Coffee Bureau, *Coffee Drinking in Canada* (New York, 1970), 50, table 35. Coffee drinking became more important the farther west you travelled: tea remained the dominant drink in the Maritimes, while coffee was slightly ahead in Ontario and dominant in British Columbia. Note also that statistics for consumption of coffee and tea are sometimes confusing and difficult to compare across time, since each report seems to pick a different measure of consumption (percentage of population that drinks coffee or tea, per capita consumption, number of cups per day) and often does not provide details on how the information was gathered.

60 Edith Crabb, letter to author, dated 20 October 1998; Seller interview. In 1960, 32 per cent of workers used outside sources to get coffee for their

coffee breaks. *RI*, July 1960, 11. The overall trend over the 1960s was towards getting coffee supplied in the workplace. *Foodservice and Hospitality*, 9 October 1967, 16.

61 Jim Charade told Tim Horton's biographer that tea was the most popular drink at his first donut outlet in Scarborough. Hunter, *Open Ice*, 339. Accurate statistics on this point do not survive, but few donut shop owners remembered tea being a prominent part of their sales. This is not surprising, since even at the peak of its popularity, tea was not a popular drink in restaurants and snack bars. Tea drinkers tended to be particular about the way their cup was brewed, so rather than suffer the indignity of sipping a cup slapped together by a rushed waitress, most switched to the more reliable cup of coffee when eating out.

62 *Scarborough Mirror*, 23 April 1969, 48. For efforts to standardize coffee at Tim Hortons in the early days, see Joyce, *Always Fresh*, 115–7.

63 The literature on the historical development of coffee is vast, but see William Roseberry et al., eds., *Coffee, Society, and Power in Latin America* (Baltimore: Johns Hopkins University Press, 1995), especially the introduction by Roseberry and the essay by Michael Jiménez; W. Clarence-Smith and S. Topik, eds., *The Global Coffee Economy in Africa, Asia, and Latin America, 1500–1989* (Cambridge: Cambridge University Press, 2003); and John Talbot, 'Where Does Your Coffee Dollar Go? The Division of Income and Surplus along the Coffee Commodity Chain,' *Comparative Studies in International Development* 32, no. 1 (1997). On 'forgetfulness' in modern consumption, see William Cronin, *Nature's Metropolis: Chicago and the Great West* (New York: Norton, 1991), 256; and Warren Belasco, 'Food Matters: Perspectives on an Emerging Field,' in Warren Belasco and Philip Scranton, eds., *Food Nations: Selling Taste in Consumer Societies* (New York: Routledge, 2002), 8–9.

64 See chapter 1.

65 On the increasing use of options within a standard format, see Joy Parr, *Domestic Goods* (Toronto: University of Toronto Press, 1999); James Flink, *The Automobile Age* (Cambridge, MA: MIT Press, 1998), ch. 12; and Gary Cross, *An All-Consuming Century: Why Commercialism Won in Modern America* (New York: Columbia University Press, 2000), 88–103.

66 Tim Lambert, interviewed by author, St Catharines, 19 May 1998.

67 Lalonde interview; Brian Wallace, letter to author, dated 24 October 1997.

68 See Roland Marchand, *Advertising the American Dream: Making Way for Modernity* (Berkeley: University of California Press, 1985); David Gartman, *Auto Opium: A Social History of American Automobile Design*

(New York: Routledge, 1994); Regina Braszczyk, *Imagining Consumers: Design and Innovation from Wedgewood to Corning* (Baltimore: Johns Hopkins University Press, 2000); and Parr, *Domestic Goods*.

69 Parr, *Domestic Goods*.

70 To be precise, donuts were different from appliances or cars, since the idea (outside of the donut/fancy distinction) was *not* to use variety to segment the product line into different price levels. In a broader way, however, both spoke to a consumer culture committed to choice through superficial variety.

71 On take-out, see *CHRR*, 15 September 1955, 23–4; *RI*, July 1959, 28–9, 36; *FSH*, 16 January 1967, 16. 'Give Ma a Treat' is from a Tasty Drive-in advertisement, *Times and Guide* (Weston, Ontario), 23 June 1960, 8.

72 In the late 1970s, Americans spent 35 per cent of their food dollar on eating out. Canadians still hadn't reached that figure in the early 1990s. Changes in patterns of eating out are frustratingly elusive, as survey strategies have shifted over time (both in terms of who and what was asked), making direct comparisons difficult. Existing statistics do appear to indicate that industry observers were correct in identifying an increase throughout the 1960s and 1970s. In 1953, for urban families in the middle-income range, 8.7 per cent of the weekly total food dollar was spent eating out (if other Canadians had been factored in, it is likely the figure would have been lower). DBS, *Urban Food Expenditure, 1953*, Cat. 62-511, 11. In 1969 the average Canadian (in this survey, including a broader geographic and income spectrum) spent about 17 per cent of his or her food dollar away from home. DBS, *Family Food Expenditure in Canada, 1969*, Cat. 62-531, table 2. By 1982, the average Canadian reported spending 25.3 per cent of his or her food dollar at restaurants. DBS, *Family Food Expenditure in Canada, 1986*, Cat. 62-531, table 1. Note that food 'eaten out,' 'food away from home,' and food eaten 'at restaurants' are not exactly the same thing, so these figures are offered as suggestive rather than conclusive. At all points, moreover, the figures varied by income, region/province, urban/rural, and other factors.

73 Note that Jakle and Sculle, in their comprehensive history of fast food, treat the donut as a breakfast food. Jakle and Sculle, *Fast Food*, 197–200.

74 Joyce cited in *ODJR*, 8 May 1971, 8; 'Mister Donut Market Analysis,' Fall 1966, 10, from private collection.

75 Mister Donut, *Advertising and Promotions Manual*, 1967, from private collection.

76 Jenny Bryce, Tim Hortons server, early 1970s, interviewed by author, Selkirk, Ontario, 9 January 1998.

77 North York Public Library, North York History Collection, Jesse Dean, 'Streetwork Report: Don Mills Youth Scene' (1971), 18.

78 Rosenberg, *Profits*, 149; *FP*, 21 May 1966, 17. (Danziger was Mister Donut's Director of Franchising.)

79 Recent work has cautioned against overgeneralizing about prosperity, which was not shared equally by all regions, races, classes, genders, and so on. 'Not everyone,' historian Robert Rutherdale sums up, 'was born at the right time.' Robert Rutherdale, 'Framing Fatherhood in Transition: Domesticity, Consumerism, and Resistance Narratives,' paper presented to the annual meeting of the Canadian Historical Association, Quebec City, 2000. See also Alvin Finkel, *Our Lives: Canada after 1945* (Toronto: James Lorimer, 1997), ch. 1; and Bryan Palmer, *Working Class Experience: Rethinking the History of Canadian Labour, 1800–1991* (Toronto: McClelland and Stewart, 1992), 305–7.

80 Morgan Reid, cited in *FP*, 21 February 1953. On the connection between the mass market and family life, see Elaine Tyler May, *Homeward Bound: American Families in the Cold War Era* (New York: Basic Books, 1988), 162–82; and Harvey Levenstein, *Paradox of Plenty: A Social History of Eating in Modern America* (New York: Oxford University Press, 1993), 101–18.

81 On the postwar middle class, see Andrew Hurley *Diners, Bowling Alleys, and Trailer Parks: Chasing the American Dream in Postwar Consumer Culture* (New York: Basic Books, 2001); Cohen, *Consumers Republic*; and S.D. Clark, *The Suburban Society* (Toronto: University of Toronto Press, 1966).

82 This point seemed clear to many thinkers even in the 1950s. For a discussion see Cohen, *Consumer's Republic*; Ronald Edsforth, 'Affluence, Anti-Communism, and the Transformation of Industrial Unionism among Automobile Workers, 1933–1973,' in Ronald Edsforth and Larry Bennett, eds., *Popular Culture and Political Change in Modern America* (Albany: SUNY Press, 1991), 101–25; and Shelly Nickles, 'More Is Better: Mass Consumption, Gender, and Class Identity in Postwar America,' *American Quarterly* 54, no. 4 (2002): 581–622

83 Upper-income brackets consumed only 47% more donuts than lower-income brackets. *CB* August 1959, 11; Mister Donut, *Market Analysis*, 8.

84 This occupational profile is based on a sample of four streets in the market area of four different donut shops for 1967 (Mister Donut in Kitchener, Mister Donut on Dundas Street East in London, Country Style Donut at

Progress and Kennedy, and Country Style on Lawrence Avenue in Scarborough), using city directories for each city.

85 *Metropolitan Toronto – Planning Facts* (Prepared by the Research Department, Social Planning Council of Metropolitan Toronto, September 1966); DBS, Census of Canada, 1961, Series 95-530, *Population and Housing Characteristics by Census Tracts – Toronto, 1961*; DBS, Census of Canada, 1961, Series 95-541, *Migration, Fertility and Income by Census Tracts, 1961*. On fast food chains advertising to children in this period, see Kathleen Toerpe, 'Small Fry, Big Spender: McDonald's and the Rise of Children's Consumer Culture, 1955–1985' (PhD thesis, Loyola University of Chicago, 1994).

86 *FP*, 23 March 1966. The following discussion of the diversity within the mass market is indebted to Liz Cohen, *Consumers' Republic*, 292–344.

87 *CB*, February 1965, 34.

88 *FP*, 8 April 1967, 5.

89 *Toronto Telegram*, 21 July 1970, 18; *ODJR*, 8 May 1971, p. 8.

90 Charade interview; Lori Broadfoot, server, Ideal Donuts, early 1970s, interviewed by author, Winnipeg, 19 October 2001; Lalonde interview.

91 Diners had typically been male spaces. See Andrew Hurley, 'The Transformation of the American Diner,' 1,286–8.

92 Sandy Willard, interviewed by author, Binbrook, Ontario, 21 February 2002; anonymous former Tim Hortons franchisee, interviewed by author, 11 August 2001; Kiriakopoulos interview; Ed Mahaj, interviewed by author, Oakville, Ontario, 6 January 1998. In fact, women's smoking had achieved a certain respectability by this time, although it was not without ambiguities. See Jarrett Rudy, *The Freedom to Smoke: Tobacco Consumption and Identity* (Montreal and Kingston: McGill-Queen's University Press, 2005), 148–70.

93 Broadfoot interview; Al Stortz, interview.

94 Jenny Bryce interview. Note: For a short time in the early 1970s, Tim Hortons outlets served ice cream cones. On the broader pattern of server–customer relations and its connection to restaurants as social spaces, see Dorothy Sue Cobble, *Dishing It Out: Waitresses and Their Unions in the Twentieth Century* (Chicago: University of Illinois Press, 1991), ch. 2; Marcus Klee, 'Between the Scylla and Charybdis of Anarchy and Despotism: The State, Capital, and the Working Class in the Great Depression, Toronto, 1929–1940' (PhD thesis, Queen's University, 1998), ch. 8; and Hurley, 'Transformation of the Diner.'

95 Certainly the work was dangerous, especially travelling to and from late-night shifts. In 1965, one Mister Donut server was murdered on her way to a night shift in suburban Toronto. Her husband lamented that he normally drove her right to the outlet, but that he had to work a night shift that day.

96 Tom Busnarda, interviewed by author, Welland, 15 January 1998; Allan Asmussen interview.

97 Rita Browne, interviewed by author, Dunnville, Ontario, 9 January 1998.

98 *CHRR*, 15 November 1945, 30.

99 Ontario Store Fixtures had a 'package plan,' which it installed in restaurants across the country. *CHRR*, 15 June 1962, 44. See *CHRR*, 15 January 1965, 2–23, for discussion of the various types of counters and stools.

100 Joyce, *Always Fresh*, 49–50, 107–8.

101 Andrew Hurley discusses this point in his *Diners, Bowling Alleys, and Trailer Parks*. See also Clark, *The Suburban Society*.

102 Hurley, *Diners, Bowling Alleys, and Trailer Parks*, 21–105. See also his 'From Hash House to Family Restaurant: The Transformation of the American Diner,' *Journal of American History* 83 (March 1997): 1282–308.

103 American restaurant categories did not always transfer well to the Canadian experience. When Controlled Foods (a restaurant company that operated several different types of eateries, including several A&W drive-ins) decided to copy the 'California coffee shop' (the industry designation for informal full-service restaurants like Denny's) for the Canadian market under the name 'Fuller's Coffee Shops,' the company's market research revealed 'that to the Canadian public, the terminology meant small cafés with donuts and two kinds of pie.' Company executives decided to change the name to 'Fuller's Restaurant.' *Foodservice and Hospitality* (FSH), April 1971, 78. In Canada, the diner's role as an informal neighbourhood eatery was filled by different versions of lunch counters, coffee shops, snack bars, and restaurants, which served simple menus of soups, sandwiches, and light meals to customers at a few tables and a counter with stools. In 1957, Canadian restaurant expert E.J. Spence equated 'what is called ... "the dairy lunch" in the US' with what Canadians called 'the coffee shop.' In both cases, according to Spence, 'the menu is carefully restricted to items which have a short preparation time or can be held in finished form successfully. Properly equipped for maximum efficiency and with the right type of menu, they can provide the fastest food which is available.' *CHRR*, 15 February 1957, 23. Note also that unlike 'diner,'

which seems to have had a downscale meaning, terms like lunch counter and coffee shop seemed to describe food service establishments that ranged from nice to dingy. On diners, a random survey of thirty city directories across Canada from the 1930 to 1960 revealed fewer than ten examples of 'diners,' but several lunch counters and coffee shops. Typical ratios were Windsor 1932 (total of 112 restaurants, 21 of which were lunch counters, 36 cafes, 0 diners); London 1955 (151 total restaurants, 16 snack bars, 11 coffee shops, 20 lunch counters, 0 diners); and Brantford 1960 (47 total restaurants, 12 lunch counters, 9 coffee shops, 0 diners). No doubt, a more thorough examination of informal eateries would reveal many regional, local, and neighbourhood variations.

104 *Fountains in Canada*, 15 May 1959, 12, 14.

105 *Manual of Operating Procedures, Mister Donut*, circa 1967 from private collection.

106 Ron Buist reports that the early customer base of Tim Hortons was 55 per cent men and 45 per cent women. Buist, *Tales from under the Rim* (Fredericton: Goose Lane, 2003), 203.

107 Mister Donut, *Highlights from a Market Analysis*, 4; Chris Pappas, interviewed by author, Etobicoke, Ontario, 7 December 2000.

108 Richard Harris, *Creeping Conformity: How Canada Became Suburban* (Toronto: University of Toronto Press, 2005).

109 See chapter 4.

110 *Oakville Beaver (OB)*, 2 July 1970; *ODJR*, 30 June 1970. Peter Simpson is a pseudonym. His actual name is publicly available in media accounts of his arrest, but as microfilm copies of a forty-year-old local newspaper are less easily available than a book published in 2008, and since there is no analytic value in using his real name, I have changed it to avoid dredging up old embarrassments.

111 Dean, 'Don Mills Youth Scene', 10; *ODJR*, 29 December 1970, 4; 7 January 1971, 4; 15 May 1971, 4.

112 On the history of youth and leisure, see Tamara Myers, *Caught: Montreal's Modern Girls and the Law* (Toronto: University of Toronto Press, 2006); Michael Gauvreau, 'The Protracted Birth of the Canadian Teenager: Work, Citizenship, and the Canadian Youth Commission, 1943–1955,' in Gauvreau and Christie, eds., *Cultures of Citizenship in Postwar Canada* (Montreal and Kingston: McGill-Queen's University Press, 2003), 201–38; Shirley Tillotson, *The Public at Play: Gender and the Politics of Recreation in Post-War Ontario* (Toronto: University of Toronto Press, 2000); Mary Louise Adams, *The Touble with Normal: Postwar Youth and the Making of Heterosexuality* (Toronto: University of

Toronto Press, 1997); and Doug Owram, *Born at the Right Time: A History of the Baby Boom Generation in Canada* (Toronto: University of Toronto Press, 1996).

113 Jesse Dean, 'Don Mills Youth Scene' (North York, 1970), 11. On St Catharines, see Halaiko interview.

114 *Mister Donut Market Analysis*; Pappas interview. On the timing of the baby boom, see Owram, *Born at the Right Time*, 4–5. On youth as consumers more generally, see *FP*, 21 May 1966, 13; Serge Gouin, Bernard Portis, and Brian Campbell, *The Teenage Market in Canada: A Study of High School Students in London, Ontario, and Chicoutimi, Quebec* (School of Business Administration, University of Western Ontario, 1967); and B.A. Ratcliffe, 'A Survey of the Drive-In Restaurant Industry in Vancouver with Guidelines for Streamlining an Installation' (BComm essay, University of British Columbia, 1968).

115 *Scarborough Mirror*, 26 February 1969, 12. See also *Bramlea Guardian*, 24 May 1967, M11. Police occasionally expressed frustration at having to act as 'bouncers' for plaza owners. See, for example, *ODJR*, 25 March 1971.

116 *TS*, 7 July 1970, 10.

117 Oakville Town Council, *Minutes*, 6 July 1970, Item 29. *ODJR*, 2 July 1970, 1.

118 Town of Oakville, Bylaw 1970–98, 'A Bylaw to Prohibit Loitering and Nuisances on Public Highways,' passed 7 July 1970.

119 *TS*, 8 July 1970, 13.

120 Kenneth Cmeil, 'The Politics of Civility,' in David Farber, ed., *The Sixties: From Memory to History* (Chapel Hill: University of North Carolina Press, 1994), 263–90. The complaints of Brock Street residents are enumerated in *OB*, 2 July 1970, 1.

121 *ODJR*, 30 June 1970, 1; *OB*, 9 July 1970, 11; *ODJR*, 2 July 1970, 4.

122 *OB*, 29 October 1970, A28. On the power of civil rights language in Canada, see Owram, *Born at the Right Time*, 166–7.

123 Dean, 'Don Mills Youth Scene.' One strong supporter of Dean's involvement with local youth was Alderman Dennis Timbrell, a former high school teacher who was a Progressive Conservative by inclination. *Don Mills Mirror*, 9 September 1970, 7. Some municipalities also established youth squads that were meant to reach out to kids rather than just arrest them. In Scarborough, the unit was dubbed 'the plaza patrol.'

124 *TS*, 8 July 1970; *ODJR*, 15 September 1970, 3; 16 October 1970, 1; 20 October 1970, 1; 23 October 1970, 4; 10 November 1970, 1; Oakville Town Council, *Minutes*, 19 October 1970, 16 November 1970. Councillor Harry Barrett and Deputy Reeve William Gillies joined Mannell in voting for repeal. Gillies was the former secretary of the Oakville Labour Council.

125 *OB*, 22 October 1970, 1; *ODJR*, 9 July 1970, 4. Even the server at the Tim Hortons outlet disagreed with her boss's no hippies policy, telling a reporter, 'at least the hippies are well behaved and clean up after themselves.' More research should be done on hair and other style questions in the 1960s, especially where adults defended youth. Even in conservative Oakville, anti-hippie measures (such as school bans or police harassment) hardly met with universal adult approval. While generational politics powerfully shaped ideas of appearance and comportment, family loyalties, a liberal belief in the right to individual self-expression, or a conviction that flamboyant fashion was a harmless phase might lead adults to defend rather than condemn long-haired youth. For two such cases, where long-haired youths received unqualified public support from parents, including a mother who admitted disapproving of her son's long hair, see *ODJR*, 12 September 1969, 4; 17 October 1969, 1; 21 October 1969. For a nuanced discussion of hair debates in America, see Gael Graham, 'Flaunting the Freak Flag: *Karr v. Schmidt* and the Great Hair Debate in American High Schools, 1965–75,' *Journal of American History* 91, no. 2 (2004): 522–43.

126 *ODJR*, 20 October 1970 1; *OB*, 22 October 1970, A8.

127 *OB*, 18 July 1970, 1.

128 *ODJR*, 2 July 1970, 1.

129 *OJR*, 11 July 1970, 1; 31 May 1971, 4.

130 Ambault interview; Haliako interview; Pappas interview.

131 *ODJR*, 14 July 1970, 1.

132 The standard discussion of how business saw economic potential in the counterculture is Thomas Frank, *The Conquest of Cool: Business Culture, Counterculture, and the Rise of Hip Consumerism* (Chicago: University of Chicago Press, 1997).

133 *ODJR*, 14 July 1970, 1.

3   'He Must Give Up Certain Things'

1 William Stockwell, franchisee, Country Style Donuts, 1969–74, interviewed by author, London, 25 September 2000.

2 Ibid.

3 John Lorinc, *Opportunity Knocks: The Truth about Canada's Franchising Industry* (Scarborough: Prentice Hall, 1995), is a good introduction to recent issues in Canadian franchising.

4 Thomas Dicke, *Franchising in America: The Development of a Business Method* (Chapel Hill: University of North Carolina Press, 1992); Stan Luxemberg, *Roadside Empires: How the Chains Franchised America* (New

224 Notes to pages 99–100

York: Viking, 1985), 2–47; Tom Pendergrast, *For God, Country, and Coca-Cola* (New York: Basic Books, 2000), 69–81; Harry Kursh, *The Franchise Boom* (New York: Prentice Hall, 1969); Robert Metz, *Franchising: How to Select a Business of Your Own* (New York: Hawthorn Books, 1969). On Canadian developments, see *Canadian Business*, May 1960, 131; *Canadian Hotel Review and Restaurant (CHRR)*, 15 August 1963, 50; 15 February 1964, 33; *Financial Post (FP)*, 4 April 1964, S8; 21 May 1966, 17; July 1974, F13.

5 *Canadian Business*, May 1960, 131.

6 My thinking on this question is heavily indebted to David Monod's examination of the 'folklore of retailing' (Monod, *Store Wars* [Toronto: University of Toronto Press, 1996], 54–99), and to the discussion of the 'markets of the mind' in Christopher Armstrong and H.V. Nelles, *Monopoly's Moment* (Philadelphia: Temple University Press, 1986), 322–3. 'There are markets in men's minds,' they write of earlier struggles with economic change, 'images of institutions and norms, which determine what is fitting, what is just, and acceptable in transactions.'

7 Advisory Committee on Human Investment in Entrepreneurial and Venture Enterprises, *Recommendations on Ways and Means of Encouraging the Initiation, Survival, and Growth of Small Business in the Province of Ontario*, December 1972, 1–2. This impulse spanned the twentieth century. Early in the century, civic populists feared that the loss of small business would mean 'our ruin as a free people.' Armstrong and Nelles, *Monopoly's Moment*, 146. H.H. Stevens covered similar ground a quarter-century later, calling independent retailers 'the finest expression of democratic life to be found anywhere' as he championed their interests through his Select Committee on Price Spreads and Mass Buying. J.R.H. Wilbur, 'H.H. Stevens and the Reconstruction Party,' in Ramsay Cook et al., eds., *Politics of Discontent* (Toronto: University of Toronto Press, 1967), 55.

8 David Bellamy, 'The Small Business Loans Act.'; House of Commons, *Debates*, 21 November 1960, 57; 28 November 1960, 262, 263, 260; 21 November 1960, 58.

9 Canadian Chain Store Association, 'Submission to the Royal Commission on Dominion-Provincial Relations,' March 1938, 2.

10 Galbraith argued that in the postwar world, big business, big government, and big labour would balance one another out, combining to provide social security broadly conceived – job or career stability, white-collar opportunities, generous benefits, and decent wages. Galbraith's ideas (and

other glorifications of big business) are discussed in Jonathan Bean, *Beyond the Broker State: Federal Policies toward Small Business, 1936–1961* (Chapel Hill: University of North Carolina Press, 1996), 117–20. See also the chapter 'Economic Security' in Galbraith, *The Affluent Society* (New York: Mentor Books, 1958), 84–100. From the perspective of male workers, there is an evocative reconstruction of the romantic myth of corporate security in Susan Faludi, *Stiffed: The Betrayal of the American Man* (New York: William Morrow, 1999), 3–101.

11 Allan Asmussen, cofounder of Donut Queen (Kitchener-Waterloo), 1968, interviewed by author, Waterloo, 10 September 2001.

12 House of Commons, *Debates*, 28 November 1960, 267. See also Monod, *Store Wars*, 149–94; *FP*, 16 January 1954, 28; 28 January 1956, 7; 16 November 1957, 11; 23 June 1962, 26; 13 October 1962, 53; *Canadian Hotel and Restaurant* (*CHR*), May 1965, 37; *Industrial Canada*, October 1962, 26–9; August 1963, 22–5; *Canadian Chartered Accountant*, January 1962, 132–7.

13 *Canadian Business*, October 1948, 26–7.

14 *Report of the Minister's Committee on Franchising* (Department of Financial and Commercial Affairs, July 1971), 39–44.

15 *Jirna Ltd. v. Mister Donut of Canada Ltd.* (1973), 13 DLR (3d) 656. See also Steven Finley, 'Antitrust Aspects of Franchising in the United States and Canada' (Master of Law thesis, Institute of Comparative and Foreign Law, McGill University, 1974); J. George Vesely, 'Franchising as a Form of Business Organization – Some Legal Problems,' *Canadian Business Law Journal* 2 (1977), 34–67; Steven Iczkovitz, 'A Canadian Perspective on Franchising,' *Chitty's Law Journal* 21, no. 3 (1973): 73–93.

16 Lynda Lalonde, Tim Hortons franchisee, 1969–93, telephone interview by author, 30 January 1999. A note of method: The remainder of this chapter examines the 'franchise experience' in the donut industry, based in part on interviews with about twenty franchisees who entered the business between 1960 and 1980 and half a dozen independent operators, supplemented by material from local newspapers, the business press, and other sources. Interviews covered questions about how franchisees heard about the business; how they decided to enter the donut business; how much research they did on the industry; how they raised the money; issues of training, hiring employees, and the use of family members to run the shop; their ongoing relations with the company; how and why they left the business; and general impressions of the industry. I also asked questions about customers, outlet locations, and community life, but these issues are discussed

in other chapters. My interview style is informal rather than scientific, so interviews did not necessarily follow this exact order every time. Some interviewees preferred to remain anonymous.

17 This literature is now so vast, with so many specialized journals, conferences, and influences, that scholars now routinely refer to 'entrepreneurial studies' as a discipline. For a sampling of definitional efforts, most of which offer more volume than clarity, see Pierre-Andre Julien, *The State of the Art in Small Business Entrepreneurship* (Brookfield, VT: Ashgate Publishing, 1998), 117–49; Wee-Liang Tan, 'Entrepreneurism: It Is Time for a Clearer Definition,' *Journal of Small Business and Entrepreneurship* 13, no. 1 (1996): 5–8; Ivan Bull and Gary Willard, 'Towards a Theory of Entrepreneurship,' in Ivan Bull, Howard Thomas, and Gary Willard, eds., *Entrepreneurship: Perspectives on Theory-Building* (New York: Pergamon, 1995), 1–16; Paul Burns and Jim Dewhurst, eds., *Small Business and Entrepreneurship* (London: Macmillan Education, 1989); William Gartner, '"Who Is an Entrepreneur?" Is the Wrong Question,' *American Journal of Small Business* 12, no. 4 (1988): 11–32; James Carland, Frank Hoy, and Jo Ann Carland, '"Who Is an Entrepreneur?" Is a Question Worth Asking,' *Journal of Small Business* 12, no. 4 (1988): 33–40; and James Abnor, 'The Spirit of Entrepreneurship,' *Journal of Small Business Management* (January 1988): 1–4.

18 Sam Shneer, Mister Donut franchisee, 1962–82, interviewed by author, North York, 22 October 2000.

19 George Etzel, interviewed by author, 3 March 2002.

20 Gary O'Neil of Tim Hortons is probably the most successful of this latter type of franchisee. He left his job in a Hamilton steel plant to buy the chain's first Maritime franchise in 1974 and eventually opened more than thirty outlets around New Brunswick. Larry Keen bought into Tim Hortons in 1969 and grew his investment to ten outlets with various partners in two provinces, although he eventually became more active in the Burger King chain, which he joined in 1977. Through his company, the Larry Keen Group, he currently operates twenty-seven Burger King outlets in eastern Ontario and western Quebec. Until the late 1970s, single-outlet operators were the most common. In 1967, only 15 per cent of Mister Donut franchisees owned more than one outlet. Ten years later, the figure was 25 per cent. That same year, Tim Hortons had eighty-three outlets and seventy-five franchisees. Ron Buist, *Tales from under the Rim* (Fredericton: Goose Lane, 2003), 76. Multiple outlet operators like Keen and O'Neil became more common in the late 1970s and early 1980s, as chains acceler-

ated their growth partly by building on existing franchisees. O'Neil, for example, opened his first outlet in 1974 and his second in 1978.

21 I say more about franchisees starting their own chains in Chapter Four.

22 Chris Pappas, Country Style Franchisee, 1964–80s; owner, Old Mill Donuts, early 1980s, interviewed by author, Etobicoke, 7 December 2000.

23 Dave Ambeault, interviewed by author, Markham, Ontario, 8 March 2002.

24 Ron Hewitt, interviewed by author, Brantford, Ontario, 10 August 2001. On the issue of sorting through myths, memory, and experience in oral history, see Elizabeth Tonkin, *Narrating Our Pasts: The Social Construction of Oral History* (New York: Cambridge University Press, 1992), and Mary Chamberlain and Paul Thompson, eds., *Narrative and Genre* (New York: Routledge, 1998).

25 Lawrence Lovell-Troy portrayed Greek owners of pizza shops in Connecticut in the 1970s as 'individual businessmen, attempting on their own to reverse the trend of declining profit margins and fighting the rationally-organized competition from the Pizza Huts, the Howard Johnsons, and the McDonalds of America.' See his 'Kinship Structure and Economic Organization among Ethnic Groups: Greek Immigrants in the Pizza Business' (PhD thesis, University of Connecticut, 1979), 240.

26 *Canadian Baker* (CB), January 1963, 14. Etkin's King Donut was not related to the King Donut in Oshawa at the time, or to the King Donut in St Catharines in the 1970s and 1980s. Etkin later became a franchisor himself, cofounding the Mr Transmission chain of auto repair shops. See his obituary in the *Toronto Star* (*TS*), 6 November 1980, A3.

27 Eugene Pechet, owner, Dolly Donuts, Edmonton, 1970–75, interviewed by author, 8 September 2001.

28 Russell K. Knight, 'The Independence of the Franchise Entrepreneur,' *Journal of Small Business Management* (April 1984): 52–69; Lorinc, *Opportunity Knocks*, 71–93.

29 Deborah Asmussen, co-owner, Donut Queen, Waterloo, 1968–94, interviewed by author, Waterloo, 10 September 2001. Appearing at club meetings was a standard public relations technique for Mister Donut. In the early 1980s, a group of British sociologists found a similar resonance between the outlook of franchisees and independents in different areas of the service sector. John Stanworth, James Curran, and Jensine Hough, 'The Franchised Small Enterprise: Formal and Operational Dimensions of Independence,' in James Curran, John Stanworth, and David Watkins, eds., *The Survival of the Small Firm,* Volume 1 (Brookfield, VT: Gower Publishing, 1986), 246.

30 On the complexities of 'independence' in small business, see Monod, *Store Wars*.

31 Calvin LeDrew, owner, Donut Queen, Sydney, Nova Scotia, 1964–70, telephone interview by author, 8 August 2001.

32 A number of franchisees ended up selling real estate after leaving the donut business.

33 LeDrew interview. On Levitt, see chapter 1.

34 Stephen Ududec, Ideal Donut, interviewed by author, Winnipeg, 19 October 2001; Doug Nichol, 'Ideal Donut: The Hole Story,' in Kris D. Munt, ed., *Adventures in Small Entrepreneurship in Manitoba* (Winnipeg: Red River Community College, 1985), 93–100.

35 Unfortunately, no one bothered to perform systematic studies of franchisees in the early days of the industry, so my evidence is largely anecdotal.

36 On the entry of corporate executives and middle managers into franchising in the late 1980s, see *Hamilton Spectator* (*HS*), 25 February 1995, C16; Dave Slatter, Mr Mugs Franchisee, 1990–present, interviewed by author, Brantford, 10 August 2001; Lorinc, *Opportunity Knocks*, 79–83. On early difficulties securing loans, see Ron Joyce, *Always Fresh* (Toronto: Harper-Collins, 2006), 58. Lorinc also discusses the formation of special franchise divisions within the major banks in the late 1970s. See Lorinc, *Opportunity Knocks*, 95–8. In the 1960s, however, even the leaders in franchising in the United States – companies like Burger King and McDonalds – had difficulty convincing banks that loans to franchisees were good investments. John Love, *McDonalds: Behind the Arches* (New York: Bantam Books, 1995), 162–70. The figures for costs of franchises in the 1960s are taken from *CHRR*, 15 August 1961, 38; 15 May 1964, 44–5; 15 May 1966, 43; 15 May 1968, 49.

37 Pappas interview; Douglas Hunter, *Open Ice: The Tim Horton Story* (Toronto: Penguin Books, 1994), 338; Stockwell interview.

38 Anonymous former franchisee, interviewed by author, 11 August 2001.

39 Though Canada had been a destination for Greek immigrants since the nineteenth century, the rate of immigration rose dramatically after the Second World War. On the general development of the Greek community in Canada, see Peter Chimbos, *The Canadian Odyssey: The Greek Experience in Canada* (Toronto: McClelland and Stewart, 1980).

40 *Might's Toronto Directory*, 1964–74. Similarly, Mr Submarine executive Bernard Levinson noted that many of his chain's franchisees were of Greek origin. *Financial Post Magazine*, April 1977, 43.

41 *Mister Donut Phone Directory (Franchisees and Suppliers)*, published by Mid-Atlantic Store Owners Advisory Council, 1977 (in possession of Sam Dimakis). These figures can be read the other way: the farther you get from Toronto, the less Greek (indeed, the less immigrant-based) the business became: outside of Toronto, names like Majerle, Livesey, Collett, Jolley, and Wilson were common, and only two of the sixteen non-GTA outlets were Greek owned. The situation is similar for Country Style, which grew outside of the GTA by drawing in franchisees with Anglo names like Stockwell, Wallace, and Watson.

Based on the biographies of early franchisees that I have compiled (based on interviews, local newspapers, directories, and other sources), Tim Hortons apparently relied much less on immigrant communities than the other chains. This probably reflected the fact that it had so few stores in Toronto, where Mister Donut and Country Style relied most heavily on Greek franchisees. The one exception actually proves the rule: Gus Panagakis took over a Tim Hortons outlet in St Catharines in 1971. He came to the chain through a Toronto connection, however, having served as a baker in the chain's North York outlet. He later told a *St Catharines Standard* reporter that when he agreed to take over the Lincoln Mall outlet, he had never heard of St Catharines. *Standard*, 21 February 2004.

42 Greek immigrants had established a beachhead in the restaurant business early in the century, and study after study in the postwar period enumerates continued Greek participation in the industry: of 1,066 Greek small businesses across Canada in 1966, 680 (about 64 per cent) were restaurants; in 1969, 44 per cent of Greek small business owners in Thunder Bay were restaurateurs; two years later a study in London, Ontario, found that restaurants comprised 71 per cent of the small-businesses owned by Greek immigrants. Chimbos, *Canadian Odyssey*, 52; See also Peter Chimbos and Carol Agocs, 'Kin and Hometown Networks as Support Systems for the Immigration and Settlement of Greek Canadians,' *Canadian Ethnic Studies* 15, no. 2 (1983): 51–2; Judith A. Nagata, 'Adaptation and Integration of Greek Working Class Immigrants in the City of Toronto, Canada: A Situational Approach,' *International Migration Review* 4, no. 1 (1969): 44–69. For a parallel example of Greek concentration in one segment of food service, see Lawrence A. Lovell-Troy, 'Ethnic Occupational Structures: Greeks in the Pizza Business,' *Ethnicity* 8, no. 1 (1981): 82–95. See also Dennis Clark, 'Ethnic Enterprise and Urban Development,' *Ethnicity* 5, no. 2 (1978): 108–18.

43 Gus Anastakis (pseudonym), interviewed by author, 8 March 2000.

Lawrence Lovell-Troy found a similar process of chain recruitment among Greek pizza shop owners in Connecticut. See his 'Kinship Structure and Economic Organization,' 37–76, 242–51.

44 By comparison, there were about 8,000 people from the Prairie provinces; about 21,000 from England, 11,000 from Scotland, 13,000 from Italy, 6,000 from Poland, and 5,000 from Germany. The total population of the city was 270,000. Dominion Bureau of Statistics (DBS), Census of Canada, 1961, Cat. 92–547, *Population: Place of Birth*, tables 49 and 52. Relatively little work has been done on internal migration in Canada. Commenting on the importance of the theme, one DBS study put it accurately but bureaucratically: 'Interesting and important as the external migration streams may be, they are dwarfed in volume by the migration streams flowing within Canada.' Leroy Stone, *Migration in Canada: Some Regional Aspects* (Ottawa: DBS, 1969), 26. One notable exception to the paucity of postwar studies of internal migration is Karen Dearlove, '(Im)Migration and Community Building: Newfoundlanders in Cambridge, Ontario,' paper presented to the Annual Meeting of the Canadian Historical Association, York University, May 2006.

45 Joyce, *Always Fresh*, 8–25, 59–60, 72.

46 Ambeault interview; Thomas Majerle, Mister Donut franchisee, 1966–80, telephone interview by author, 15 December 2000; Joyce, *Always Fresh*, 73–4.

47 Tracing the relationship between family and business is murky analytic ground. Some historians have stressed the importance of family relations in earlier forms of franchising and small business, trying to supplement the many studies of mass consumption that have focused on large, male-dominated corporations. Unfortunately, these efforts have not blunted the power of the image of the 'mom and pop shop' in either the popular or the academic mind. The phrase obscures much more than it illuminates, especially since it is more often a romantic lament than an analytic description. Certainly, a family-owned business might allow women a greater role in management than a corporate operation, but given the somewhat chequered history of the family as an institution, the connection was not automatic. Historians have done some studies of women and small business, but more gender-sensitive work could be done on 'entrepreneurial masculinity' as a source of identity that shut women out of even small business operations (or at least tried to). For discussions of gender themes in business, see Kathy Peiss, '"Vital Industry" and Women's Ventures: Conceptualizing Gender in Twentieth Century Business History,' *Business History Review* 72 (Summer 1998): 219–41, and Susan Strasser, *Satisfaction Guar-*

anteed: The Making of the American Mass Market (New York: Pantheon Books, 1989), ch. 3.

48 Sylvia Cultrera, Country Style Franchisee, beginning 1975, telephone interview by author, 4 March 2000; Anita and Judy Halaiko, Mister Donut franchisees, 1967–75, interviewed by author, Welland, 19 March 2002.

49 Harold and Rose Bonaparte, Mister Donut franchisees, 1963–83, interviewed by author, North York, 1 November 2000.

50 Ambeault interview; Sam Shneer interview.

51 Mister Donut Promotional material, *Franchise Guide* (Princeton, NJ, 1969), 248.

52 Otto Seegers, President, Seegers Fabulous Foods, 1964–71, interviewed by author, North York, 9 November 2001.

53 Seegers interview.

54 David Hounshell, *From American System to Mass Production* (Baltimore: Johns Hopkins University Press, 1985); Daniel Nelson, *Frederick Taylor and the Rise of Scientific Management* (Madison: University of Wisconsin Press, 1980).

55 On fast food labour processes, see Ester Reiter, *Making Fast Food: Out of the Frying Pan and into the Fryer* (Montreal and Kingston, McGill-Queen's University Press, 1996). On McDonald's, see John Love, *Behind the Arches* (New York: Bantam Books, 1986). Harold Shneer of Red Barn bragged that 'we take the most popular foods [and] put their preparation and serving on an assembly line basis.' *CHRR*, 15 February 1964, 33.

56 Buist, *Tales from under the Rim*, 62. See chapter 1.

57 Otto Seegers's Bakers Donutshop manual listed strength as one requirement of a baker: 'He must be able to stand on his feet long hours, and be strong enough to lift 100 pound bags.' 'Manual: The Bakers Donutshop,' (in Otto Seegers's possession), 24. One early Tim Hortons baker reported that a female baker was employed at his outlet in the late 1960s. Harold Fox, baker, Tim Hortons, 1968–79, interviewed by author, 22 January 1998.

58 Both McDonald's and Red Barn used exclusively male counter staff, figuring that female servers would attract rowdy teenage boys, which would scare off the family trade. Some hamburger chains, and many more independents, did use female servers.

59 Letter to author from Della Smith, Tim Hortons worker, mid-1970s, letter dated 26 October 1997.

60 On the labour process of serving, see Dorothy Sue Cobble, *Dishing It Out: Waitresses and Their Unions in the Twentieth Century* (Urbana: University of Illinois Press, 1991).

61 *Manual of Operating Procedures, Mister Donut*, circa 1967 (*MOP-MD*), section 4: Sales and Customer Service, p. 4.

62 These were only two of many rules relating to appearance; others concerned make-up, deodorant, washing, and so on. *MOP-MD*, section 1: Personnel, pp. 11, 14–5, 51–2.

63 'No Tipping' signs are in plain view in photographs of Tim Hortons and Mister Donut outlets in this period. On tipping across the sitdown counter, see Joan DeNew, Tim Hortons server, early 1970s, interviewed by author, Hamilton, 18 November 1997; Interview, Jenny Bryce.

64 *Manual of Operating Procedures: Mister Donut*, section 1: Personnel, p. 49, private collection.

65 Harold Fox interview; Joyce, *Always Fresh*, 41. Joyce notes that to assist his early efforts to systemize baking practices, he turned to Jo Lowe, the outlet's mix supplier: ibid., 40.

66 On the notion of the semiskilled worker, see especially Craig Heron and Robert Storey, 'Work and Struggle in the Canadian Steel Industry, 1900–1950,' in Heron and Storey, *On the Job: Confronting the Labour Process in Canada* (Montreal and Kingston: McGill-Queen's University Press, 1986), 218.

67 Steve Ferguson, interviewed by author, Surrey, British Columbia, 15 August 1999.

68 Speaking of semiskilled workers in the steel industry, Heron and Storey argued that they were 'not as indispensable as the old craftsman,' but employers still relied on their 'regularity, stability and experience.' Heron and Storey, 'Work and Struggle,' 218.

69 Judy Halaiko interview.

70 On Tim Hortons, see Joyce, *Always Fresh*, 41. Peter Mertons of Country Style sat on a committee regarding training in community colleges. See *Bakers Journal (BJ)*, December 1975, 6. On professionalizing training for fast food service, see Reiter, *Making Fast Food*, 78–9. On training women to be bakers, see Al Watson's comments in *BJ*, August–September 1980, 20. On paying bakers under the table, see Ron Ansett interview. Bakers were paid between $65 and $85 a week in the mid–1960s.

71 'Project "Emancipation through Automation,"' Report to Mister Donut Franchisees, 5 March 1968, from Private Collection (hereafter cited as 'Emancipation').

72 'Emancipation,' 1–2, 10.

73 Sam Shneer interview; Majerle interview.

74 'Emancipation,' 22

75 Pappas interview; Bonaparte interview; Lalonde interview.

76 Tom Brazier, Margaret's Donuts, interviewed 19 November 1997; 'Margaret's Frozen Donut Shells,' company promotional material, circa 1977 (courtesy of Tom Brazier); *BJ*, February 1979, 16–17. Margaret's

Donuts was a wholesale operation started in the late 1940s, and had grown to one of Canada's largest donut producers by the 1970s. See chapter 1.

77 In 2000, Tim Hortons and a large European baking company announced joint plans to build a bakery products plant in southwestern Ontario, where they would produced par-baked products for distribution to Hortons outlets across Canada. Tim Hortons Press Release, 6 March 2001, archived on the company's website, http://www.timhortons.com.

78 *Manual of Operating Procedures: Mister Donut*, section 1, 27, 44–8, private collection.

79 Ibid., sections 1, 2, 9, 10, 11; Manual: The Bakers Donutshop.

80 Costas Kiriakopoulos, interviewed by author, Etobicoke, Ontario, 19 October 2000.

81 *CB*, September 1966, 11; Pechet interview; Asmussen interview.

82 Sam Shneer interview.

83 Dimakis interview; Pappas interview; Majerle interview.

84 Dunkin Donuts promotional material, *Franchise Guide* (Princeton, NJ, 1969), 143.

85 By the mid-1970s, DCA was training Country Style franchisees to bake. Cultrera interview.

86 Pappas interview; Kiriakopoulos interview; anonymous former Tim Hortons franchisee, interviewed by author, 9 August 2001.

87 Joyce, *Always Fresh*, 105.

88 *Hamilton Spectator* (HS), 16 March 1977, 81; *Foodservice and Hospitality* (FSH), June 1977, 6. For more on Donut University, which provided four weeks of training in its early days, see Joyce, *Always Fresh*, 104–5.

89 Shneer interview.

90 Tom Alderman's article on franchising in *Canadian Magazine*, 18 April 1970, is a good general discussion of early oversight by franchisors.

91 Bonaparte interview.

92 Many franchisees preferred not to talk about this question, others denied the practice was common, and a few were willing to discuss it in general terms. In any case, I agreed not to mention names when describing these practices.

93 Tim Hortons opened its first warehouse in 1971.

94 I agreed not to mention names when describing these practices.

95 There is a sample Mister Donut contract in Select Committee on Small Business, 'The Impact of Franchising on Small Business,' hearings before the Subcommittee on Urban and Rural Economic Development of the Select Committee on Small Business, United States Senate, 20–22, 27 January 1970, 242–8. See also 'Sample Contract: Dunkin' Donuts Inc.,'

in Robert Rosenberg with Madelon Bedell, *Profits from Franchising* (New York: McGraw Hill, 1969), appendix B.

96 For a discussion of the introduction of technology to monitor operations in a different sector of franchising, see Patricia MacDermott, 'From Franchising to Microtechnology: An Analysis of a Corporate Strategy' (PhD dissertation, University of Toronto, 1982).

97 Many people told me this in formal interviews and in informal, off-the-record conversations.

98 Joyce, *Always Fresh*, 74.

99 One of Wallace's stranger ideas was 'importing' 160-ounce jugs of spring water from Middlesex County and selling them in his donut shop – an idea he borrowed from a similar operation in Florida. London consumers were not overcome by the idea. *London Free Press (LFP)*, 23 September 1967, 27.

100 On this dispute, see *LFP*, 9 November 1974; 20 November 1974, 20 February 1981, in London Public Library, Subject File: Country Style Donuts. For another case where franchisees resisted termination through the courts, with some success, see *Tim Donut v. Boudreault*, 6 B.L.R. (12 February 1979). In this case, Tim Hortons was chastised by the court for overly aggressive termination, even though Boudreault was in serious arrears for rent and supplies. The court called the chain's behaviour 'improper and high-handed.' 'It is difficult to understand,' the court wrote in ruling in favour of the bulk of Boudreaut's claim, 'how the plaintiff could, despite this ineptly drawn contract, so rashly consider that it had the right to trespass on these premises in the circumstances, as it did, seize and take the goods, physically lock out the defendant, and deal with the goods and chattels and the premises henceforth as its own property, without an accounting to the defendant ... The plaintiff's conduct, purporting to be an exercise of rights under this agreement, was an arrogant disregard of the defendant's rights. This conduct, in some measure, was consistent with Mr. Fitchett's [the Tim Hortons Vice President] attitude while testifying. I was left with the impression that this trial was an imposition on the plaintiff.'

101 Bonaparte interview.

102 Larry Keen, Tim Hortons Franchisee, 1969–present, telephone interview by author, 28 September 2000.

103 Archives of Ontario, RG 31-56, Records of the Grange Committee, Box 4, File 4.15, Questionaires, 1970–1.

104 Majerle Interview.

105 *Jirna v. Mister Donut*; Buist, *Tales*, 47; Joyce, *Always Fresh*, 61.

106 Pappas interview.

107 I have borrowed this phrase from Michael Bliss, *A Living Profit: Studies in the Social History of Canadian Business, 1883–1911* (Toronto: McClelland and Stewart, 1974).

4   Expansion and Transformation

1 *Marketing*, 1 March 1976, 4; 10 May 1976, 9; 3 January 1977, 2; 26 September 1977, 4.

2 *Bakers Journal (BJ)*, August 1976, 6.

3 On fast food developments in the 1970s, see Penfold, 'Selling by the Carload,' in Magda Fahrni and Robert Rutherdale, eds., *Creating Postwar Canada: Community Diversity and Dissent* (Vancouver: UBC Press, forthcoming).

4 *Toronto Telegram*, 7 July 1970, 36; *Jirna Ltd. v. Mister Donut of Canada Ltd.* (1973), 13 DLR (3d) 656. See also Steven Finley, 'Antitrust Aspects of Franchising in the United States and Canada,' (Master of law thesis, Institute of Comparative and Foreign Law, McGill University, 1974); J. George Vesely, 'Franchising as a Form of Business Organization – Some Legal Problems,' *Canadian Business Law Journal* 2 (1977): 34–67; and Steven Iczkovitz, 'A Canadian Perspective on Franchising,' *Chitty's Law Journal* 21, no. 3 (March 1973): 73–93.

5 Tim Hortons grew by twelve outlets in 1976, but planned for twenty-five the following year. Figures on revenues from *Hamilton Spectator (HS)*, 16 March 1977, 81; *Foodservice and Hospitality (FSH)*, October 1977, 30. On the deal with Mercantile, see Ron Joyce, *Always Fresh* (Toronto: HarperCollins, 2006), 97–8.

6 Lori Horton claimed that she was under the influence of drugs and alcohol when she accepted one million dollars and a company car for her half-share of the company in 1975. According to Horton, she was not responsible at the time and was taken advantage of by both Joyce and her own lawyer. The lawsuit was settled in favour of Joyce. The most succinct summary of the case is in the *Toronto Star (TS)*, 19 December 1992, A1. Joyce reviews his side in *Always Fresh*, 165–78.

7 *HS*, 16 March 1977, 81; *FTC*, 21 January 1985, 7.

8 *Toronto Telegram*, 20 August 1970, 36. The regional structure of the donut business at this time was typical of the broader fast-food business, where relatively few companies had established a real national presence.

9 *Directory of Restaurant and Fast Food Chains in Canada (DRFFC)*, 1985–90.

10 Ron Ansett, regional director for Canada, Mister Donut, 1981–89, interviewed by author.

11 *Marketing*, 25 September, 1972, 2; 2 June 1980, 2; *DRFFC*, 1993.

12 Ron Buist, *Tales from under the Rim* (Fredericton: Goose Lane, 2003);
Halifax Chronicle-Herald, 15 August 1995, B1.

13 *Financial Post* (*FP*), 8 October 1983, S2; A. Victoria Bloomfield, 'Tim
Hortons: The Growth of a Canadian Coffee and Doughnuts Chain,'
Journal of Cultural Geography 14 (Spring–Summer 1994): 6; Buist, *Tales*,
57, 76.

14 See chapter 2.

15 Joyce, *Always Fresh*, 117. Tim Hortons also found that donuts made up a
higher percentage of store sales in the west. Buist, *Tales*, 58.

16 Joyce, *Always Fresh*, 137–8.

17 This phenomenon is plainly visible in the 1995 map of Dunkin Donuts
outlets in John Jakle and Keith Sculle, *Fast Food: Roadside Restaurants in
the Automobile Age* (Baltimore: Johns Hopkins University Press, 1999), 95.

18 Joyce, *Always Fresh*, 99, 138.

19 Ibid., 141–2; John Lorinc, *Opportunity Knocks* (Scarborough: Prentice-
Hall, 1995), 147–8; Kiriakopoulos interview.

20 Lance Jacklin, vice president, Donut Diner, interviewed by author, St
Catharines, 20 May 1998; *Business Monday Magazine* (*London Free
Press*), 2 July 1990, On Grandma Lee's, see *BJ*, February–March 1982,
26–7.

21 Carla Garagozzo, interviewed by author, London, ON, 12 March 2002.

22 One exception was Holey Donuts, which collapsed amid allegations of
fraud in 1989. *TS*, 27 March 1989, A1, A8; 5 January 1990, A2; *BJ*,
October 1985, 18, August–September 1989, 14.

23 *Winnipeg Free Press*, 17 June 1980, 17.

24 *Vancouver City Directory*; *Winnipeg City Directory*; *Winnipeg Free Press*,
17 June 1980, 17. Robins eventually scattered outlets across the country,
but remained concentrated in the West.

25 Kiriakopoulos interview; Lorinc, *Opportunity Knocks*; *DRFFC*, 1990,
1992, 1994; Jacklin interview; *St Catharines Standard*, 4 January 1993,
B1; *BJ*, August–September 1996, 21.

26 *TS*, 19 July 1979, 3.

27 *Temiskaming Speaker*, 17 November 1982, 2; *London Business Monthly
Magazine*, 1 July 1991, 33.

28 *Kitchener-Waterloo Record*, 15 July 1986, in Kitchener Public Library,
Subject Files: Restaurants.

29 Owen Sound Directory; *BJ*, August–September 1987, 6.

30 *Financial Times of Canada (FTC)*, 22 January 1985, 6; *Winnipeg City Directory; Edmonton City Directory; Saskatoon City Directory; Regina City Directory.*

31 Tim Hortons opened its first outlet in Quebec in 1977, but its second did not come until 1983, leaving the market to Dunkin Donuts (which had few outlets outside Quebec). Hortons went west in 1978, but still had only five outlets (four in B.C., one in Edmonton) in 1983. Buist, *Tales*, 57.

32 There is a succinct summary of these developments in Kenneth Norrie, Doug Owram, and J.C. Herbert Emery, *A History of the Canadian Economy*, 3rd ed. (Toronto: Thomson Nelson, 2002). The phrase 'economic challenge' appears on page 364. On the social consequences of the crisis, see Steven High, *Industrial Sunset: The Making of North America's Rust Belt, 1969–1984* (Toronto: University of Toronto Press, 2003).

33 On the cultural politics of gasoline in the 1970s, see David Nye, *Consuming Energy: A Social History of American Energies* (Cambridge, MA: MIT Press, 1998), 217–48; David Anderson, 'Levittown Is Burning! The 1979 Levittown, Pennsylvania, Gas Line Riot and the Decline of the Blue-Collar American Dream,' *Labor: Studies in Working Class History of the Americas* 2, no. 3 (2005): 47–65.

34 On the Brazil frost, see John Talbot, *Grounds for Agreement: The Political Economy of the Coffee Commodity Chain* (Baltimore: Rowman and Littlefield, 2004), 68–71. Asmussen quoted in *Kitchener-Waterloo Record*, 31 July 1975, 1.

35 *Winnipeg Free Press*, 17 June 1980, 17; *TS*, 19 July 1979, 3; *Globe and Mail (GM)*, 8 June 1984, R2; Joyce, *Always Fresh*, 211; Dave Slatter, Mr Mugs franchisee, Brantford, Ontario, interviewed by author, 10 August 2001. The early 1980s crisis caused problems, but they seem to have come at the debt-servicing end of the business rather than at the sales and consumption level. The deal between Tim Hortons and the Mercantile Bank had set an interest rate of 'prime plus one percent,' so when interest rates spiked to over 20 per cent, debt servicing became a major problem. While the crisis subsided, the company laid off staff and reverted to leasing rather than buying land. Joyce, *Always Fresh*, 145–6.

36 *Windsor City Directory*, 1976–96.

37 *GM*, 8 June 1984, R2.

38 *HS*, 25 July 1995, A1; *Kitchener-Waterloo Record*, 22 January 1997, F1.

39 *St Catharines City Directories.*

40 Burke, cited in *St Catharines Standard*, 18 March 1989, 17.

41 See David Monod, *Store Wars* (Toronto: University of Toronto Press, 1996), 54–98, 286–339.

42 *HS*, 5 February 1992, T1; *St Catharines Standard*, 10 April 1999, A10.

43 Hewitt interview. In his exposé of the franchise industry, journalist John
    Lorinc related the story of Tom Wadden, a former sales manager interested
    in getting into the donut business near his home in Tottenham, a small
    town perched on the fringe of Toronto's booming suburban belt. In 1992,
    Wadden tried to interest Country Style and Tim Hortons in coming to the
    area, but neither company thought the town was large enough to support
    an outlet. Wadden eventually bought a Mister C's franchise, only to have
    Tim Hortons open a shop down the street in early 1995. Apparently,
    remarked Lorinc, 'Tottenham was a good spot for a donut store after all.'
    Lorinc, *Opportunity Knocks*, 168.

44 Garagozzo interview; 'Afton Subsidiary Purchases the Assets of Donut
    Delite Café,' press release, 25 June 1996, archived at http://www.afton-
    food.com/press/donutpress; 'Afton Food Group Ltd. Announces the Acqui-
    sition of Robin's Foods Inc.,' press release, 1 March 2000, Canada
    Newswire: http://www.newswire.ca/releases/March2000/01/c8945.html.

45 *HS*, 11 July 2001, C1; *TS*, 23 March 2002, F1.

46 *HS*, 22 July 2000, A3.

47 Joyce, *Always Fresh*, 78.

48 *Canadian Business*, September 1983, 36.

49 *FSH*, April 1988, 28.

50 At the time, a coffee and donut sold for 90 cents and a muffin and coffee
    for $1.20.

51 Donna Gabaccia, *We Are What We Eat: Ethnic Food and the Making of
    Americans* (Cambridge, MA: Harvard University Press, 1998), 2–10.

52 *CHRR*, 15 February 1961, 18–20; *BJ*, August 1968, 20; October 1968,
    23–5; *TS*, 4 July 1967, 22. See also *TS*, 20 October 1953, 16.

53 *BJ*, August–September 1987, 28; August–September 1988, 26.

54 *FP*, 16 October 1996, 6; *FSH*, June 1996, 14; November 1996, 34;
    December 1996, 29–32; September 1997, 18.

55 *FTC*, 22 April 1991, A11; *FSH*, March 1996, 12; December 1996, 31.
    Bagels turned out to be an enormous operations problem. One Kitchener
    columnist complained that 'as I wait in line for my morning coffee at
    Tim's, the line now moves slower as one server after another abandons the
    counter for the bagel toaster.' *Kitchener-Waterloo Record*, 8 August 1996,
    D5. Ron Joyce admitted the product was a problem: 'The bagel has been
    one of our biggest challenges because you have to toast it. It is a time-con-
    suming process. We are trying to do everything we can to speed up service.
    But we don't know what the answer is yet.' Quoted in *Kitchener-Waterloo
    Record*, 22 January 1997, F1.

56 *Halifax Daily News*, 12 October 1990, in Halifax Public Library, Subject File: Bakers and Bakeries.

57 *FP* 16 October 1996, 6; *HS*, 30 August 2001, A10; *Georgia Straight*, 14 August 1999, 25. Borrowing popular concepts from other chains did not ensure success. When cinnamon buns became a fad in 1987, donut shops scrambled to add the product, but it never reached the expected heights, and donut chains scaled back. Pizza was similarly unsuccessful. 'We spend a lot of time and money telling people how good our coffee and doughnuts are and then expect them to come in for pizza,' commented Rick Curren of Mister Donut of Canada. *BJ*, August–September 1983, 17; May 1986, 23; January–February, 1987, 86; November 1987, 16; December 1988, 12.

58 The decline was especially dramatic in Ontario, from 7.6 donuts in 1975 to 3.1 in 1984. Maritimers continued to be enthusiastic donut eaters, falling from 6.1 in 1975 to 5.7 in 1984. Figures from *BJ*, October 1985, 38–40. Mertons, quoted in *FTC*, 2–8 March 1992, 10. Responding to early concerns about health, Country Style experimented unsuccessfully with a 'whole wheat donut' in the late 1970s. *BJ*, October 1988, 22. On rise of concerns about health, see Levenstein, *Paradox of Plenty: A Social History of Eating in Modern America* (New York: Oxford University Press, 1993), 237–55; Warren Belasco, *Appetite for Change: How the Counterculture Took on the Food Industry* (Ithaca: Cornell Paperbacks, 1993), 218–28.

59 *BJ*, September 1990, 22; August–September 1983, 16.

60 The addition of new products can be followed in the donut industry review each September in the *Bakers Journal*, 1980–9. At Tim Hortons, the Break Away concept was shelved after operational problems. 'It was supposed to fill a hole that we needed to be in better and bigger real estate,' Ron Joyce commented. 'I think we put too much effort into that philosophy rather than the actual operation.' Nine Break Aways were opened in different cities across eastern Canada, but only four were still operating in 1985, and the idea was shelved. Sandwiches did not return to the chain's menu until 1993. *FTC*, 20 January 1985, 7.

61 *Wendy's Financial Report*, 1998. *HS*, 10 August 1995; *FSH*, July 1998, 46. In 1999, Country Style announced plans to twin with A&W Hamburgers.

62 *HS*, 6 March 1992, A14.

63 *LFP*, 27 November 1975, 8; *FSH*, February 1976, 29. Non-smoking sections were not common. In 1985, though 66% of the population did not smoke, only 17% of restaurants in the Waterloo region, for example, provided non-smoking seating. *Kitchener Waterloo Record*, 17 January 1985, D1, D3, in Subject File: Restaurants, Kitchener Public Library.

64 Some were new outlets, but the process of converting an existing Tim

Hortons to non-smoking was expensive and convoluted. Fixtures were given a thorough scrub-down, vents were purged, filters replaced, and so on, all to ensure a completely non-smoking environment. *HS*, 28 March 1983, 18 January 1985, in Hamilton Public Library, Special Collections, Subject File: Tim Donut Limited; *St Catharines Standard*, 21 October 1993, B1; *LFP*, 15 February 1994, D10. Non-smoking outlets did save money in ventilation and maintenance costs, however. A smoking outlet required an initial outlay of $2,500 for smoke-eating fans as well as ongoing maintenance costs related to smoke residue of about $500 a year. *HS*, 18 January 1985, in Hamilton Public Library, Special Collections, Subject File: Tim Donut Limited.

65 By 1994, 70 of Tim Hortons 750 outlets were non-smoking. The figure had increased to 200 of 1,197 by 1996. *London Free Press (LFP)*, 15 February 1994, D10; *FSH*, July 1996, 36; 'It's New Years Resolution Time: Tim Hortons Quits Smoking!' press release, archived on Tim Hortons Web page: http://www.timhortons.com.

66 Cathy Mauro, Director of Marketing, Country Style Donuts, interviewed by author, 22 October 1999 (Mauro has since left the company); Lorinc, *Opportunity Knocks*, 153.

67 David Estok, 'Timbit Nation,' *Report on Business Magazine* (December 2002), 79; Buist, *Tales*, 117. In 1983, Country Style estimated that 72 per cent of its customer base were men. *BJ*, August–September. 1983, 16.

68 Christine Lambert, letter to author, dated 4 May 1998; Mauro interview.

69 Harvey Cardwell, president of Robin's, quoted in Lorinc, *Opportunity Knocks*, 153; *Marketing*, 28 September 1992, 5.

70 *BJ*, August–September 1987, 30; *HS*, 18 January 1985, in Hamilton Public Library, Special Collections, Subject File: Tim Donut Limited.

71 *HS*, 6 March 1992, A14. By comparison, Coffee Time's 1992 gross revenue was $15.9 million and Coffee Way's was $5.225 million. Maclean Hunter Publishing, *DRFFC*, 1994.

72 *FP*, 9 February 1990, 11, reporting on a study conducted by U of T business professor Jerry White, who was provided with aggregate sales tax totals from about 260,000 businesses in Ontario.

73 *TS*, 21 January 1982, A6.

74 *TS*, 6 January 1982, A13.

75 *HS*, 18 January 1985, 12 June 1992, in Hamilton Public Library, Special Collections, Subject File: Tim Donut Limited. Hortons had twenty outlets in Hamilton in 1985.

76 *Atlantic Progress*, September 1997, 12. See also *St Catharines Standard*, 22 September 1998, B3.

77 Jakle and Sculle, *Fast Food*, 60–2; *CHR*, November 1975, 46; Borough of Etobicoke, *Restaurant Study, 1980,* Borough of Etobicoke Planning Department, 1 April 1980, 37–8 (Etobicoke was at the time a suburb of Toronto). In one 1973 Statistics Canada study, only 7.6 per cent of franchised food service outlets reported offering a 'car order pick up wicket,' the category closest to what we would now call a drive-thru window. Statistics Canada, *Franchising in Canada's Food Service Industry* (Ottawa: Statistics Canada, 1973), table 4. McDonald's did not open its first drive-thru window (in Oklahoma City, Oklahoma) until 1975. The chain later adopted the window as a chain-wide strategy. By 1995, 90 per cent of McDonald's freestanding units in the United States had drive-thru windows. See Love, *Behind the Arches*, 390–1. Among the large chains, Wendy's Hamburgers pioneered drive-thru lanes in 1970. The idea was a standard part of a Wendy's restaurant by the time the chain arrived in Canada in 1975. See D. Daryl Wyckoff and W. Earl Sasser, *The Chain Restaurant Industry* (Lexington: Lexington Books, 1978), 100.

78 Jim Fitzpatrick, telephone interview by author, 15 March 2000.

79 The idea was less than successful, most notably because of the difficulty of establishing market territories. Kevin Watson, executive vice president, Country Style Donuts, interviewed by author, 22 October 1999 (Watson has since left the company); *Marketing*, 14 July 1986, 2.

80 *HS*, 19 February 1998, A3; Ansett interview.

81 In 1980 an Etobicoke planning department report recommended that the city require space to stack at least ten cars. Borough of Etobicoke, *Restaurant Study, 1980*, 16–7, 37–9.

82 New lots were more promising: by 1988, most of Mister Donut's twelve drive-thrus had not been added to existing Ontario stores; rather, they were built into new outlets in the Maritimes and Quebec, where property costs were lower and buildings could be properly sited on the lot as they were initially constructed. *BJ*, August–September, 1988, 31; Ansett interview.

83 I have borrowed the term 'up-size' from recent fast food strategies. The term does not seem to have been common in the donut business in the 1980s, although the practice it describes goes back to the advent of the donut shop.

84 *HS*, 19 February 1998, A3; *BJ*, August–September, 1987, 24. More recently, Ron Joyce argued that drive-thrus made Tim Hortons too dependent on coffee, especially when diversification was the company mission. Joyce, *Always Fresh*, 184–5.

85 *BJ*, August–September, 1987, 24. Even in 1990, the chain had only two drive-thru lanes. *BJ*, August–September, 1990, 22.

86 *BJ*, August–September 1989, 22.

87 *BJ*, August–September, 1988.

88 *BJ*, December 1999, 10; *FSH*, October 1999, 36.

89 By 2001, Tim Hortons had 916 drive-thru lanes (out of about 2,000 outlets). *National Post*, 24 March 2001, A6. See also *Report on Business* (December 2002), 79–84. In 1999, Country Style had drive-thrus at one-third of its outlets. *FSH*, October 1999, 36.

90 Patti Jameson, vice president, Corporate Communications, Tim Hortons, interviewed by author, 15 September 1999 (Jameson has since left the company); *HS*, 3 February 1994, in Hamilton Public Library, Special Collections, Subject File: Tim Donut Limited. The chain also had seven single-lane drive-thru-only outlets. *BJ*, August–September 1997, 24. Double drive-thrus emerged in American fast food in the mid-1980s. Jakle and Scule, *Fast Food*, 60–2. Ron Joyce notes he spotted them first in Florida. Joyce, *Always Fresh*, 112–13, 185.

91 Hewitt interview; *HS*, 22 July 2000, A3.

92 Jameson interview; Mauro interview. In 1987, Ron Ansett told the *Bakers' Journal* that a 'majority' of drive-thru customers were women. *BJ*, August–September, 1987, 28.

93 *HS*, 3 February 1994, in Hamilton Public Library, Special Collections, Subject File: Tim Donut Limited.

94 This customer also organized a demonstration outside the shop, although the turnout – fifteen – was disappointing. *HS*, 18 March 1995; 27 March 1995 in Hamilton Public Library, Special Collections, Subject File: Tim Donut Limited. On Prince Edward Island, sales at Tim Hortons outlets dropped so dramatically that the company actually reversed the non-smoking policy, taking out a full-page ad in the *Charlottetown Guardian* apologizing for the move and absolving the local franchisee of responsibility. But smokers' complaints rarely had this effect. Joyce, *Always Fresh*, 183.

95 Colin Regan (pseudonym), interviewed by author, Surrey, British Columbia, 26 August 1998; Al Stortz, interviewed by author, Welland, Ontario, 17 April 1998.

96 Both chains opened outlets in Florida in the early 1980s (partly targeting so-called 'snow birds' – Canadians living or vacationing in the southern United States). Hortons moved into western New York in 1992. None of these efforts represented a comprehensive strategy of targeting the American market, which came only after Tim Hortons merged with Wendy's in 1995.

97 See the Tim Hortons ad in *HS*, 4 May 1964.

98 Patti Jameson, vice president of corporate communications, quoted in *Toronto Sun*, 23 February 1997, 54.

5   Eddie Shack Was No Tim Horton

1 On Tim Horton's life, see Douglas Hunter, *Open Ice: The Tim Horton Story* (Toronto: Penguin Books, 1994), and Lori Horton and Tim Griggs, *In Loving Memory: A Tribute to Tim Horton* (Toronto: ECW Press, 1997). Roy MacGregor, *The Home Team: Fathers, Sons, and Hockey* (Toronto: Penguin Books, 1995) explores the theme of father–son relations through sports. The masculine and nationalist themes of hockey in Canada are critically analysed in Richard Gruneau and David Whitson, *Hockey Night in Canada: Sport, Identities, and Cultural Politics* (Toronto: Garamond Press, 1993). See also Paul Rutherford, *When Television Was Young: Primetime Canada, 1952–1967* (Toronto: University of Toronto Press, 1990), 241–55. David Whitson nicely explores some of the issues of identity raised by the marketing of hockey and the globalization of the NHL. See his 'Hockey and Canadian Identities: From Frozen Rivers to Revenue Streams,' in David Taras and Beverly Rasporich, eds., *A Passion for Identity*, 3rd ed. (Toronto: ITP Nelson, 1997).
2 According to the *Bakers Journal*, there were 5,689 donut shops in Canada at the end of 1999. This figure represented about 10 per cent of the nation's commercial restaurants. *BJ*, December 1999, 10.
3 Many countries have iconic national foods (although most cuisines are, in fact, regional). There is a healthy amount of scholarship on this kind of 'food nationalism,' but a good place to start is Warren Belasco and Philip Scranton, eds., *Food Nations: Selling Taste in Consumer Societies* (New York: Routledge, 2001).
4 *Kitchener-Waterloo Record*, 22 February 1992, B1. In discussing 'donut folklore,' I rely heavily on 'field trips' to donut shops to interview customers.
5 Quoted in *Saturday Night*, September 1999, 72.
6 John Fitzsimmons, interviewed by author, Hamilton, 25 January 1998. On Eddie Shack, see Ross Brewitt, *Clear the Track: The Eddie Shack Story* (Toronto: Stoddart, 1997).
7 See, for example, *Toronto Star* (*TS*), 21 August 1995, B3.
8 Cited in Northrop Frye, 'National Consciousness in Canadian Culture,' in *Divisions on a Ground: Essays on Canadian Culture* (Toronto: House of Anansi, 1982). The northern vision of Canada has a long history, especially in nationalist thought. It is often linked to various forms of antimod-

ernism, although its form, articulation, and political possibilities can shift wildly depending on the era, the medium of communication, and so on. On the origins of the northern vision in Canada, see Daniel Francis, *National Dreams: Myth, Memory, and Canadian History* (Vancouver: Arsenal Pulp Press, 1997); and Carl Berger, 'The True North Strong and Free,' in Peter Russell, ed., *Nationalism in Canada* (Toronto: McGraw Hill, 1966).

9 *Globe and Mail* (*GM*), 19 November 1996, A18.

10 This was part of an address given to the National Press Club in Washington in March 1969. See *GM*, 16 October 1999, A10.

11 For a survey of the long history of anti-Americanism, see J.L. Granatstein, *Yankee Go Home: Canadians and Anti-Americanism* (Toronto: Harper-Collins, 1996). The various essays in David Flaherty and Frank Manning, eds., *The Beaver Bites Back? American Popular Culture in Canada* (Montreal and Kingston: McGill-Queen's University Press, 1993), are remarkable for the way they leave aside sloganeering nationalism and convey the multiplicity and ambiguity of Canadian reactions to American culture. I have been particularly influenced by the introduction by Frank Manning and the essays by Andrew Wernick and Paul Rutherford.

12 'A Slice of Canadiana,' by Kirsten of Brantford, Ontario, at http://www.tvo.org/eh/users/Je96ep.

13 Rob Billings (pseudonym), interviewed by author, Niagara Falls, 14 August 1999.

14 For a discussion of ideas of border crossings, see Patrick McGreevy, *The Wall of Mirrors: Nationalism and Perceptions of the Border at Niagara Falls* (Orono: Borderlands, 1991); and Roger Gibbons, *Canada as a Borderland Society* (Orono: Borderlands Project, 1989).

15 Letter to author, dated 15 November 1997.

16 *Metro Morning*, CBC Radio, 22 January 1997. See also 'An Englishman Falls in Love,' the story of a culture-shocked English visitor who 'decided to move to Canada [based] solely on the fact that it's the place you find Tim Hortons coffeeshops,' online at http://www.jungleweb.net/vangaurd/coffeeshop.

17 Matthew Truch, letter to author, 28 October 1999; Jonathan Singer, interviewed by author, Toronto, 27 December 1999.

18 Ben Glickman (pseudonym), interviewed by author, St Catharines, 25 April 1998.

19 On urban legends, see Jan Brunvand, *The Vanishing Hitchhiker: American Urban Legends and Their Meaning* (New York: Norton, 1981).

20 Joe McCaffrey, interviewed by author, 12 November 1997; Agent N, letter to author, dated 17 October 1999.

21 Hamiltonians reacted poorly when reminded that the original Tim Horton
   Donut was actually opened by Jim Charade on Lawrence Avenue in Scarborough, a suburb of Toronto. Charade later opened his first franchised
   location (and fourth outlet) on Ottawa Street in Hamilton. Eventually, I
   stopped bringing it up.

22 See Mark Higgins, 'Forget B.C. or Brazil: For Real Coffee, Try Moncton,'
   GM, 18 May 1994; Paul Benedetti, 'Nice Try Moncton, We're the Tim
   Hortons Capital of Canada,' *HS*, 24 May 1994. Moncton is one of the few
   cities outside southern Ontario that makes any claim to donut capital
   status. The claim is always brand specific – citing Tim Hortons per
   capita – never more generally donut stores. In the parking lot of the
   Mountain Road Tim Hortons, one Canadian sailor shook his head
   dismissively and told me that 'there used to be a Mister Donut down the
   street, but it went out of business fast ... This is a Tim's town.'

23 Robert Blumstock, 'Doughnut Lovers Give Hamilton Its Unique Flavor,'
   HS, 10 August 1988, in Hamilton Public Library, Special Collections,
   Subject File: Tim Donut Limited; Rob McConnell, quoted in 'Duo Cele-
   brates Donuts,' *St Catharines Standard*, 14 May 1994, in Local History
   Room, St Catharines Public Library, Subject File: Donuts.

24 Ed Mahaj, interviewed by author, Oakville, 6 January 1998.

25 Floyd Reynolds (pseudonym), interviewed by author, St Catharines,
   24 May 1998. See also Michael Collins, 'What Have They Got That We
   Don't?' *What's Up Niagara*, July 1988, 10.

26 *Saturday Night*, 8 May 1897. Thanks to David Kimmel for this reference.

27 *HS*, 6 March 1977, 81. Precisely dating the emergence of oral folklore is
   obviously difficult, since only written records survive.

28 See, for example, *London Free Press (LFP)*, 16 May 1987, p. 10.

29 Levitt Steinberg, *The Donut Book* (New York: Knopf, 1987), 10.

30 Cited in 'Historic Toronto – A Look at the History of the Corporation of
   the City of Toronto' (City of Toronto, n.d.). Thanks to Charlene Kish for
   this reference.

31 *GM*, 14 July 1975, 11.

32 *TS*, 23 February 1982, EAST2; *TS*, 24 April 1984, EAST4. The author of
   the article, Jim Byers, was actually half-mocking his native North York in
   this column as well.

33 *What's Up Niagara*, November 1982, 57; *Hamilton This Month*, June
   1985, 13.

34 See chapter 1.

35 The sale to Wendy's was big news in Canada, with many press reports
   calling Tim Hortons 'a national institution.' See *TS*, 9 August 1995, B1,

B3; 21 August 1995, B3, *GM*, 4 July 1995, B10; 15 March 1995, B21;
9 August, 1995, B1, B4.

36 The earliest non-Ontario donut folklore reference I have found appeared
(ironically) in the *Globe and Mail* in 1994, referring to Moncton as the
Tim Hortons capital of Canada. *GM*, 18 May 1994.

37 Christian Riegal, Herb Wyile, et al., *A Sense of Place: Re-Evaluating
Regionalism in Canadian and American Writing* (Edmonton: University of
Alberta Press, 1998), 11.

38 *Vancouver*, May 1999, 14.

39 John Berger, *Ways of Seeing* (London: Verso, 1972).

40 Benedict Anderson, *Imagined Communities: Reflections on the Origin and
Spread of Nationalism* (London: Verso, 1991), 6.

41 Ibid., 22, 36.

42 Catherine Carstairs also points to the importance of the crisis of Canadian
identity in her excellent study of the nationalist marketing message of
Roots clothing. See her 'Roots Nationalism: Branding English Canadian
Cool in the 1980s and 1990s,' *Histoire sociale/Social History* 39, no. 77
(May 2006): 235–55. Unlike Roots nationalism, however, donut lore was
not the result of a conscious strategy of branding. Roots took pains to
position itself within Canadian iconography; it was largely consumers and
the media who did this for donuts and donut shops, at least until the late
1990s. See below.

43 Robert Collins, *Culture, Communication and National Identity: The Case
of Canadian Television* (Toronto: University of Toronto Press, 1990).

44 In the decades after the Second World War, tourist officials and hospitality
journalists urged Canadian restaurateurs to invent a distinctive 'Canadian
cuisine,' mainly so that it could be sold to visiting Americans, who were
thought to be hungry for such expressions of local culture. Typically, sug-
gestions included dishes like back bacon, butter tarts (which American
travellers apparently considered 'a typical national treat'), Nova Scotia
salmon, and New Brunswick lobster. *CHRR*, July 1963, 26, 51–4. See also
CHRR, 15 May 1947, 70; 15 April 1948, 62. Not surprisingly, most of
these 'national' dishes, insofar as they were associated with Canada at all,
were actually regional in character. Sidney Mintz points out that most
cuisines are regional rather than national. See Mintz, *Tasting Food, Tasting
Power: Excursions into Eating, Culture, and the Past* (Boston: Beacon
Press, 1996). See also the various essays in Warren Belasco and Philip
Scranton, eds., *Food Nations: Selling Taste in Consumer Societies* (New
York: Routledge Press, 2002).

45 *TS*, 13 October 1987, N5. Though I see no empirical way to prove it, the

integration of the Canadian crisis into donut lore by consumers themselves may suggest a deeper and more organic meaning than other forms of consumerist nationalism (e.g., Roots).

46 *Time*, 3 November 1986.

47 See especially 'The Rise and Fall of the Middle Class,' a two-part *Ideas* program on CBC Radio, 14 and 28 June 1993.

48 *Report on Business Magazine*, January 1987, 52–3; *FP*, 7 May 1983, 22; 28 August 1991, 39; *GM*, 4 October 1995, B12; *FSH*, September 1996, 73–8.

49 McEwen, cited in Martin Pegler, *Cafés and Coffee Shops* (New York: McGraw Hill, 1995), 34; Eugene LeBlanc, interviewed by author, Moncton, New Brunswick, 17 July 1999; Stortz interview.

50 *LFP*, 16 May 1987, 10; 9 September, 1992, C1; Peter Harvey interview.

51 *HS*, 13 April 2000, A8.

52 Rain Barrel Web page, http://www.geocities.com/SoHo/Den/6460/ 1999oct06; *HS*, 4 July 1994, in Hamilton Public Library, Special Collections, Subject File: Tim Donut Limited; *HS*, 14 August 1992, C5.

53 CBC, *Metro Morning*, 15 February 1997.

54 *HS*, 22 July 2001, A3; *Canadian Business*, 21 August 2000, 40; 18 September 2000, 12.

55 Buist, *Tales from under the Rim* (Fredericton: Goose Lane, 2003), 121–15; Cathy Mauro, Director of Marketing, Country Style Donuts, interviewed by author, 22 October 1999 (Mauro has since left the company).

56 Buist, *Tales*, 127–8.

57 Ibid., 113–38. Naomi Klein, *No Logo: Taking Aim at Brand Bullies* (Toronto: Vintage, 2000) is a now classic look at the use of pumped-up marketing budgets to sell style and identity.

58 Douglas Hunter, *Open Ice* (Toronto: Penguin, 1994), 343, 375. On the shops themselves as the main marketing vehicle for the chain in the early days, see Joyce, *Always Fresh* (Toronto: HarperCollins, 2006), 49, 107–10.

59 Joyce gives his account of the development of the camps in *Always Fresh*, 119–35.

60 The basic narrative can be followed in *Tim's Times*, Spring 1999; Spring 2000.

61 Hunter, *Open Ice*, 530. It should be noted that Lori Horton had a long history of conflict with Joyce, and sued him in 1987. She also sued the company over the use of Tim's image in the shops. She lost, but the company took them down to respect her wishes. *HS*, 6 May 1995, in Hamilton Public Library, Special Collections, Subject File: Tim Donut Limited.

62 *HS*, 17 February 1992, A6.

63 The commercial summaries are based on my own notes. The Buist quotation is from Buist, *Tales*, 163. Though Coach featured children, one major difference between Tim Hortons and McDonald's advertising in this period is the fact that Tim Hortons aimed its marketing efforts almost exclusively at adults. There were only a few exceptions, including sponsorship of local children's sports (under the name Timbit) and some product giveaways like the 'Find Timbit' collectible cup in 1991. *HS*, 30 August 1991, in Hamilton Public Library, Special Collections, Subject File: Tim Donut Limited.

64 *Marketing*, 27 January 1997, 4.

65 On the east coast small town as iconic, see Ian McKay, *The Quest of the Folk: Antimodernism and Cultural Selection in Twentieth Century Nova Scotia* (Montreal and Kingston: McGill-Queen's University Press, 1994). On icons of the west, see Michael Dawson, *Selling British Columbia: Tourism and Consumer Culture, 1890–1970* (Vancouver: UBC Press, 2004).

66 *Marketing*, 16 February 1998, 1.

67 Buist, *Tales*, 147, 156; *Marketing*, 27 January 1997, 4.

68 The now classic study of the process of 'cultural selection' in Canada is McKay, *Quest of the Folk*.

69 Psai Falk, 'The Benetton-Tosami Effect: Testing the Limits of Conventional Advertising,' in Mica Nava et al., eds., *Buy This Book: Studies in Advertising and Consumption* (London: Routledge, 1997), 64–83.

70 The company made a point of explicitly denying the charge. See http://www.timhortons.com.

71 *Marketing*, 20–7 December 1999, 17; *HS* 22 July 2000, A3.

72 Andrew Wernick, 'American Popular Culture in Canada: Trends and Reflections,' in *The Beaver Bites Back?* 297. On Canadian identity and irony, see also Linda Hutcheon, *Splitting Images: Contemporary Canadian Ironies* (Toronto: Oxford University Press, 1991).

Conclusion

1 David Monod, *Store Wars: Shopkeepers and the Culture of Mass Marketing, 1890–1939* (Toronto: University of Toronto Press, 1996).

Index

39–49, 111–18; and maternal
labour, 29–31, 35–7; meaning of,
11–12, 29–31, 35–7, 39, 76–80,
166–72, 182–8, 190–6; as national
icon, 166–9, 172, 177, 180–1,
182–8; as populist icon, 169–72,
174, 177, 180–2, 182–8; and
regional variations of taste, 35,
82–3; scientific research on, 23–7,
38; use of mix to make, 23–5, 76,
114–15, 193. *See also* Canadian
Doughnut Company; Doughnut
Corporation of America
'donut capital of Canada,' cities
claiming to be, 169–72, 174, 177,
180–1
Donut Café, 139
Donut Castle, 6, 141
Donut Delight (Saskatchewan), 143
Donut Delite (Ontario), 6, 139, 147,
147, 156
Donut Diner, 6, 139, 140
Donut Hole, 80, 90, 91, 93
Donut Queen (Kitchener–Waterloo,
Ontario), 141, 159. *See also*
Asmussen, Deborah and Allan
Donut Queen (Saint John, New
Brunswick), 157
Donut Queen (Sydney, Nova Scotia).
See LeDrew, Calvin
donut shops: baking in, 111–18; and
consumer culture, 76–80; cost of
franchise, 97–8, 106; design of, 64,
79–80, 84–5, 87–8, 122, 153–8,
176; early development, 53–69;
early market, 78, 80–90, 83–5,
87–90, 90–96; early revenues, 128;
explosion of new franchisors in
1970s and 1980s, 138–41; growth
in bad economic times, 145; inde-
pendently-owned, 54, 103–6,
119–20, 131, 140–1, 143, 146–7,
148, 156–7, 185, 191–3; as male
institution, 83–5, 88, 154–8;
meaning of, 11–12, 76–80,
166–72, 182–8, 190–6; and
'middle market', 80–90, 179–80;
as national icons, 166–9, 172, 177,
180–1, 182–8, 194; origins in
Canada, 52–4; as populist icons,
169–72, 174, 177, 180–2, 182–8,
194; regional nature of, 143,
146–8, 176–7; share of donut business, 130–1; sitdown counter,
84–5, 87–8, 96, 155–6, 193–4;
smoking in, 84–5, 154–5, 157,
193–4; as working-class institution, 83–4, 88, 154–8; and youth,
90–96, 156–7; and women, 154–6,
161; workers at, 114–17. *See also*
Canadian Style Donuts; Country
Style Donuts; Coffee Time; Cross
Country Donuts; Dolly Donut;
Donut Café; Donut Castle; Donut
Delight; Donut Delite; Donut
Diner; Donut Hole; Donut Queen;
Donut World; Downyflake Donuts;
Dunkin' Donuts; Global Donuts;
Hol'n One Donut Co. Ltd.; Ideal
Donut; King Donut; Mister C's
Donuts & More; Mister Donut;
Mr Mugs; Nuffy's Donuts;
O'Donuts; Robin's Donuts; Swiss
Pantry Donuts; Tim Hortons; Your
Donuts
Donut World, 6
Doughnut Corporation of America
(DCA), 48–9, 76, 163; effect on
smaller bakers, 42, 48–9; expan-
sion to Canada, 21; founding of,